LANGUAGE, TEACHING, AND PEDAGOGY FOR REFUGEE EDUCATION

INNOVATIONS IN HIGHER EDUCATION TEACHING AND LEARNING

Series Editor: Patrick Blessinger

Recent Volumes:

INNOVATIONS IN HIGHER EDUCATION TEACHING
AND LEARNING   VOLUME 15

LANGUAGE, TEACHING, AND PEDAGOGY FOR REFUGEE EDUCATION

EDITED BY

ENAKSHI SENGUPTA
The American University of Kurdistan, Iraq

PATRICK BLESSINGER
St. John's University, USA
International HETL Association, USA

Created in partnership with the
International Higher Education Teaching and
Learning Association

https://www.hetl.org/

United Kingdom – North America – Japan
India – Malaysia – China

Emerald Publishing Limited
Howard House, Wagon Lane, Bingley BD16 1WA, UK

First edition 2019

British Library Cataloguing in Publication Data
A catalogue record for this book is available from the British Library

ISBN: 978-1-78714-800-0 (Print)
ISBN: 978-1-78714-799-7 (Online)
ISBN: 978-1-78743-938-2 (Epub)

ISSN: 2055-3641 (Series)

ISOQAR certified
Management System,
awarded to Emerald
for adherence to
Environmental
standard
ISO 14001:2004.

Certificate Number 1985
ISO 14001

INVESTOR IN PEOPLE

CONTENTS

PART II
TECHNOLOGY AND HIGHER EDUCATION

LIST OF CONTRIBUTORS

Carine Allaf	Qatar Foundation International, Washington, USA
David Banes	David Banes Access and Inclusion Services, Milton Keynes, UK
Patrick Blessinger	St. John's University and International HETL Association, New York, USA
Marika Gereke	Institute of Political Science, Goethe University, Frankfurt, Germany
Haydeé Ramírez Lozada	Pontifical Catholic University of Ecuador, Esmeraldas, Ecuador
Wadzanai F. Mkwananzi	University of the Free State, Bloemfontein, South Africa
Subin Nijhawan	Department of English and American Studies (IEAS), Goethe University, Frankfurt, Germany
Kathy O'Hare	University College Cork, Cork, Ireland
Donald Reddick	Kwantlen Polytechnic University, British Columbia, Canada
Chrystina Russell	Global Education Movement (GEM), Southern New Hampshire University, Manchester, USA
Elizabeth Rutten-Turner	Saint Alphonsus Center for Global Health and Healing, Idaho, USA
Lisa Sadler	Langley School District, British Columbia, Canada
Maggie Mitchell Salem	Qatar Foundation International, Washington, USA
Heather Smyser	Independent Researcher, Texas, USA
Matt Thomas	University of Central Missouri, Missouri, USA
Enakshi Sengupta	The American University of Kurdistan, Kurdistan Regional Province, Iraq

Damian Spiteri	The Malta College of Arts, Science and Technology (MCAST), Paola, Malta
Shai Reshef	University of the People, California, USA
Nina Weaver	Global Education Movement (GEM), Southern New Hampshire University, Manchester, USA
Merridy Wilson-Strydom	University of the Free State, Bloemfontein, South Africa
Katherine Landau Wright	Boise State University, Idaho, USA
Yuankun Yao	University of Central Missouri, Missouri, USA

PART I

SEEKING HIGHER EDUCATION

INTRODUCTION TO LANGUAGE, TEACHING, AND PEDAGOGY FOR REFUGEE EDUCATION

Enakshi Sengupta and Patrick Blessinger

ABSTRACT

Research conducted on refugees and their learning abilities has generally been myopic in nature, highlighting only the challenges and barriers faced, and less focus has been given to the enormous work and achievements accomplished both by non-profit bodies, educational institutions, and refugees themselves. Research has been conducted in the past where learning has been studied from a psychological perspective, as opposed to drawing on the learner theory. Refugees and asylum seekers have been lumped together as a homogenous group, and studies of single language groups have made conclusions that may not apply to others. This chapter, which serves as the introductory chapter to the book, speaks about the inflow of refugees and the growing need of education for an entire generation displaced from their home countries. The chapter highlights educational access, policies, and the importance of language learning. The last section of this chapter is dedicated to present an overview of the chapters in this book which speaks about some exemplary work done by individuals and institutions from Africa to Germany.

Keywords: Migrants; trafficking; multilateralism; students; language requirement; young learners

INTRODUCTION

Displacement tracking matrix flow monitoring data have shown in recent days that an estimated 30,971 migrants and refugees have arrived in Europe between January and April 2018, using different sea and land routes. Although this

Language, Teaching and Pedagogy for Refugee Education
Innovations in Higher Education Teaching and Learning, Volume 15, 3–15
Copyright © 2019 by Emerald Publishing Limited
All rights of reproduction in any form reserved
ISSN: 2055-3641/doi:10.1108/S2055-364120180000015003

represents a 39% decrease when compared to the 50,400 registered in the same period in 2017, the picture still looks very grim. More than half of the migrants and refugees registered this year arrived in Greece (14,352). Italian authorities reported that 9,467 migrants and refugees who attempted to cross the Central Mediterranean in unsafe dinghy boats were rescued and brought to Sicily and coastal areas in the South of Italy. Another 6,690 individuals arrived in Spain through the Western Mediterranean route. The remaining 462 migrants and refugees were registered in Bulgaria and Cyprus. Most of the refugees are using smuggled routes and availing the help of human traffickers from Libya (International Organization for Migration [IOM], 2018)

Burdened with the number of existing refugees who arrived in 2017, Europe has been overwhelmed with the flow of migrants again this year and a row has deepened among countries to share the burden of the inflow of refugees. We have witnessed in the recent past the growth of far-right political parties that have refused to house the refugees. Italy has canceled a meeting with France amid a growing diplomatic row over a refugee ship that Rome refused to accept. French President Emmanuel Macron severely criticized the Italian government's refusal, calling them insensitive and irresponsible for having denied entry to the rescue ship containing a number of hapless people seeking refuge. Austrian Chancellor Sebastian Kurz, known for his anti-immigrant sentiments, agreed on the need to curb uncontrolled migration and crack down on people trafficking. Italy did not take President Macron's criticism well and has now challenged France to take in the refugees it promised under a European Union (EU) agreement and has counter accused France of turning back 10,000 migrants at Italy's northern border. Italian far-right Interior Minister Matteo Salvini said that France had committed to accepting 9,816 refugees under a 2015 scheme, but it had accepted only 640 in three years (*The Australian*, June 14, 2018).

German Chancellor Angela Merkel is facing crisis at home and among her neighboring countries due to her policy to accept refugees in Germany. Addressing her parliament, she mentioned that the migration crisis could become the "make-or-break one for the EU." She urged the politicians to manage it and she implores that the people in Africa will still believe that people in Europe and especially Germany are guided by values and believe in multilateralism and not unilateralism. The rest of the world she said will be looking up to the European nations for help and not stop believing in them and in the system of values that has made Europe so strong in the past (Meredith, June 28, 2018, CNBC). While countries are battling out as to who will shoulder the burden of the refugees how and where does it leave those who have walked on foot for days, swam across nation not knowing whether they will survive, fleeing persecution and impending death in their home country.

THE CURRENT SCENARIO

The current wave of displacement is having a choking effect on nations. More than 65 million people around the world have been forced to flee their homes.

Although more than 40 million have sought shelter within their own countries and are now referred as internally displaced people or IDPs, more than 22 million others are seeking new lives as refugees, in neighboring countries or have traveled far, crossing nations and rough terrain to seek refuge in European nations. Although half of all displaced people currently come from just three countries (Syria, Afghanistan, and Somalia), the responsibility for this growing crisis is, nonetheless, a global one, requiring nations and organizations, including educational institutions at all levels, to work together to address the growing problem. The refugee crisis will not go away on its own. The problem will presumably continue to worsen if not addressed in a globally collaborative way (Blessinger & Sengupta, 2017).

The IDPs are more likely to seek protection in cities and among the host communities, rather than in refugee camps. Housing the refugees or the IDPs in the cities or the outskirts has significant consequences for the local authorities who are responsible for meeting their protection and assistance needs. The integration of refugees and IDPs is a task that can be confusing and complex. It is a dynamic and multifaceted process, which requires constructive efforts by all willing parties, including a state of mind on the part of the refugees that will help them to adapt and accept the host society without having to sacrifice their own cultural identity. On the other hand, it also needs a readiness on the part of host communities and public institutions to welcome refugees without prejudice and meet the needs of a diverse population (Sengupta & Blessinger, 2018). The displaced require access to social services in the medium-to-long term. Short-term emergency measures of housing, food, and medical care are not a sustainable means to provide education, skills training, psychosocial support, or health care. In the long term, these refugees will have to be given the right to earn a sustainable livelihood and have to be provided with security without the threat of eviction or impending deportation. These facilities have to be accomplished within an urban context, where there may already be pressure on labor and housing markets as well as social services. Scarcity of resources and fear of losing their jobs to the freshly arrived refugees lead to tension between established residents and new arrivals. Welcoming refugees who arrive spontaneously, or increasing the number of refugee resettlement slots, are political decisions for national leaders, which at times are made without taking into consideration the sentiments of those who are residing in those towns. Balancing the moral duty and responding to a humanitarian catastrophe with the needs and wishes of existing constituents is complex, and increasingly so at a time of rising ethnic nationalism in Europe and other parts of the world.

Popular attitudes toward refugees are also problematized by the views possessed by politicians and media. For every positive narrative, we hear horrific accounts of cases of xenophobia and violence against refugees, often generated by misinformation and lack of cultural understanding. Such unfortunate incidents can be avoided by the outreach potential and communication skills of local authorities where refugees are hosted and by raising awareness of why refugees need safety, security, and compassion to help host communities prepare for new arrivals (Brand & Earle, 2018).

The situation is not confined to Europe or the Middle East alone. Southeast Asia has seen a similar story with the rise of Rohingya refugees fleeing persecution in Myanmar. Risking death by sea or on foot, nearly 700,000 Muslim minorities have fled the destruction of their homes and persecution in the northern Rakhine province of Myanmar (Burma) for neighboring Bangladesh since August 2017 (BBC News, 2018).

Housed in make-shift tents and with the advent of monsoon, the Rohingya refugee camps of Cox's Bazar face the risk of water-borne disease among the inhabitants of the congested bases. So far, health authorities have found 873 Rohingya patients suffering from acute watery diarrhea, doubling the number every week. Authorities in Bangladesh are working around the clock to undertake urgent steps to face the emergencies: 169 medical centers equipped with doctors and medical staff are providing treatment to the Rohingyas and even that is not enough to combat such a medical crisis (Sumon, 2018).

Similar stories are repeated in the other half of the world where thousands of Ukrainians, who have fled war in their own country and are now living in make-shift homes and even hotels as refugees on the borders of Eastern Europe. Their destiny remains overlooked and unknown as their plight remains to be highlighted by politicians and the media. Western parts of Ukraine have become home to several thousand refugees, who have fled the armed conflict in Donbas (Cincurova, 2015).

EDUCATIONAL ACCESS

Faced with a choice between complete dependence, isolation, humiliation, indignity, and a bleak future, the refugee population is struggling to meet their basic needs. In their struggle, the need for education is losing its priority and this may result in one of the biggest disasters in human civilization, resulting in an entire generation who are barely literate. As refugee children get older, the problem of accommodating them in schools in host countries becomes bigger. Only 23% of refugee adolescents are enrolled in secondary school, compared to 84% globally. The picture is even worse in low-income countries, which host 28% of the world's refugees. The number in secondary education is disturbingly low in these countries, amounting to only 9% as offering education to refugee students is not their immediate priority (United Nations High Commissioner for Refugees [UNHCR], 2016). The plight of refugee girls remains all the more disadvantaged with very few of them enrolling in primary schools. The number dwindles in secondary schools with fewer than seven refugee girls for every 10 refugee boys (UNHCR, 2016).

In order to find a working solution to the problem, politicians, diplomats, officials, and activists from around the world have gathered from time to time, trying to create a path for addressing the plight of the ever-increasing number of refugees. The outcome of their discussion resulted in the New York Declaration for Refugees and Migrants, which was signed by 193 countries. This declaration gave special emphasis to education as a critical element of the international response. Apart from that, the ambition of Sustainable Development Goal 4 is to deliver high quality education for all people around the world and promote lifelong and life-wide learning. Signatories to the New York Declaration for Refugees and Migrants (2016) declared, "access to quality education, including for host communities, gives fundamental protection to children and youth in displacement contexts, particularly in situations of conflict and crisis."

Despite the overwhelming support of these declarations and all good intentions expressed in several drafts and plans, refugees to date remain in the real danger of being left behind in terms of their education.

LANGUAGE LEARNING

Language learning is crucial to refugee children; mainly, the language of the host country. Hence, most of the time, language becomes central to such policies, with a "language requirement" often making the learning of the host language a central element in entry to receive education. Learning the language of the host country is necessary for integration with the host community and other fellow students. Learning a language that was hitherto unheard of can be a very daunting and challenging exercise unless accompanied with some positive learning experience and gaining slow confidence in their effort.

Language learning is a combination of teachers' efforts, curriculum, and social activity. It cannot be achieved in isolation and needs the company, support, and stimulation of everyone involved. This will help to overcome the multiple challenges faced both by the educationist and the receivers. Undoubtedly, the classroom plays a part in this, but learning does not end within the walls of the classroom. Vanegas (1998) draws on both these areas to propose task-based language learning; more realistic and autonomous activities within the classroom. Allwright (1998) talks about the possibilities of practitioner-led research ("exploratory practice") in addressing reasons for not learning. Learning of language takes place informally through engagement with others in the local community. Case studies have been showcased in this book to best understand what contributes to the success of these young learners by encouraging them to reflect on their experiences and share their experience with their classmates and teachers. While such projects are being conducted with the refugee and immigrant students,

> unexpected alliances were formed, which transcending the boundaries of culture, nationality, class and religion ... students and teachers have multiple, shifting identities and allegiances, which are national, local, gender based and religious and some of these are more salient than others at different times

and they all contribute toward learning opportunity for these students (Bryer, Winstanley, & Cooke, 2014, p. 31).

Kleinmann (1982), who worked in the United States in 1980s with Vietnamese learners, highlighted refugee-specific barriers and challenges, highlighting "survival, prevocational and occupation related language goals." He also stressed on several external factors which affect learning: "Nesting Patterns" and "Transition Anxiety" (Schuman cited in Kleinmann, 1982). Zahirovic (2001) in his work with Bosnian refugees suggested low acquisition of English is not only due to difficult learning conditions, but also a reaction to exile. Blake's research (2003) while commenting on learning abilities of women also suggested that training provision for refugee women is underpinned by ideologies that actually pose a barrier to learning.

Language has been seen as a quick step toward gaining employment in the host countries. Bloch's research suggested language as a barrier to work, and Employability Forum and Refugee Council research look at English as a second or foreign language [ESOL] as a part of a pathway of progression into employment (Employability Forum, 2003; Shiferaw & Hagos, 2002).

In this book, case studies are highlighted where universities are striving to create a borderless world of education, a community for the people, built around a democratic, meritocratic model that encourages the very best for every student, without considering whether the students have traversed hundreds of miles on foot to become a keen learner. These universities and access points have opened the gates to higher education for every eligible person, regardless of their origin, their differences in religion or race, and their status as a citizen or a refugee, only to create a better world and a better future for everyone.

CHAPTER OVERVIEWS

Damian Spiteri in his chapter, "Asylum-seeking Students' Experience of Higher Education in the UK," focuses on the perceptions of young men in the United Kingdom who come from an asylum-seeking background. It explores the choices they have in the context of both (i) taking up and (ii) remaining in further/higher education; particularly, in the light of the growing limitations to people seeking asylum in the United Kingdom that have characterized British immigration policy since the 1990s. Care has been taken to relate to their personal narratives and thereby the rich variety of social backgrounds, family structures, ethnic groups, racial identities, belief systems, and religions, each has come from. The chapter shows the insecurities they face as their future is uncertain and how they contribute to enriching the cultural mosaic of universities. It does this by unpacking notions of student identity and refugee identity and shows how the lives of students are influenced by their individual life plans. Their desire to reach these life plans meant that their narratives were located within the context of broader cultural narratives than had their university studies only would have been focused upon, or had they to be seen mainly as "asylum seekers." This chapter also shows the centrality of work in the life of young men. The interviewees explained effectively how they were reframing their self-identity by aiming to graduate in an area of studies that offers them a likely promise of employment, rather than being awarded sympathy for being asylum-seekers or refugees.

David Banes, Carine Allaf, and Maggie Mitchell Salem examine the issues, the needs to be addressed in delivering a twenty-first century digital approach to education for refugees and displaced people through their chapter, "Refugees, Education, and Disability: Addressing the Educational Needs of Arabic-speaking Refugees with Learning Challenges." The chapter reviews published estimates of the numbers of those refugees with a disability or other special needs and recommends a proactive and anticipatory approach based upon a universal design, and a universal design for learning principles across the educational delivery chain. The delivery chain is defined as the process by which a solution is designed and delivered to learners and seeks to integrate the need for an accessible platform, featuring both hardware and software, accessible content capable of being presented in a range of formats and meeting clear standards, and, where teachers or educational facilitators are involved in the final step of delivery that they should have the skills and knowledge to address individual needs in teaching and learning. The chapter further suggests that the application of such principles has significant benefits to the wider refugee and host population that is engaging in learning. By adopting a social model of disability, the concept of situational disability is introduced. Situational disability describes situations where standard designs of technology and content cannot be accessed as due to the setting the user is in, whether that be briefly or longer term. For displaced people and refugees, the impact of displacement with inconsistent access to education and resources establishes a fluid setting in which many find devices and content inaccessible for periods of time. The importance of engaging with learners with a disability in designing a solution to ensure that all learners have the opportunity to participate and achieve their aspirations.

In the chapter "Conceptualizing Higher Education Aspirations Formation among Marginalized Migrant Youth in Johannesburg, South Africa," authors Wadzanai F. Mkwananzi and Merridy Wilson-Strydom have conducted studies on youth aspirations which have been growing significantly in recent years. However, there has been little written on sub-Saharan Africa; particularly, on marginalized migrants and their ambitions for school progression. Drawing on a qualitative case study on the lives and educational aspirations of marginalized migrant youth in Johannesburg, South Africa, this chapter outlines how experiences of marginalization shape these young people's educational aspirations. Using the capabilities approach to analyze the data, the chapter argues for four types of aspirations, namely resigned, powerful, persistent, and frustrated aspirations. This conceptualization of aspirations provides a different way of thinking about aspirations formation in contexts of marginalization, disadvantage, and vulnerability as experienced by migrant youth in the study, as well as others living in similar environments. In doing so, the chapter also highlights the importance of understanding the intersection of individual agency and structural conversion factors and recommends that addressing marginalization requires removing barriers that limit opportunities for these youth.

"Occupation-Based Didactic Model for English Language Teaching to Refugees to Improve Their Sustainability and Social Integration" written by Haydeé Ramírez Lozada highlighted the guidelines of the United Nations, and the objectives directed to end poverty and inequalities, promoting, pacific and inclusive societies, which protect man generically and all his rights. She added that to achieve this, education is a vital dimension. As the official document states among its objectives: there is an emergency to promote and guarantee the right of refugees to have access to work and other forms of sustainable ways of living. With the purpose to contribute to this main aim, a linking project, which consisted of teaching English to a community of refugees in the province, was carried out by the Pontifical Catholic University of Ecuador in Esmeraldas, in collaboration with the UNHCR, and students from the Applied Linguistics School, from 2015 to 2017. The population of refugees that participated in the project was divided into two groups: enterprising refugees, who lived and worked in Esmeraldas, and those who were going to be resettled in another country, which generally was an English-speaking one, such as the United States of America, New Zealand, or Canada. Those refugees were of different ages and levels of English, and in some cases, they were illiterate even in their mother tongue: Spanish. With the empirical, analytical, and hermeneutic methods, a diagnosis of the teaching-learning process was made, which revealed the necessity to teach English to refugees based on their communicative needs according to their jobs. This chapter presents an occupations-based didactic model for English language teaching to refugees which was designed based on those needs, with its components, principles, and regularities. This theoretical contribution permitted the proposal of a methodology for English language teaching. The results revealed the development of meaningful learning, motivation, and communicative competence in English connected to the refugees' occupations.

Heather Smyser in her chapter, "Adaptation of Conventional Technologies with Refugee Language Learners: An Overview of Possibilities," wrote on research on computer-assisted language learning and mobile-assisted language learning, which generally studies collegiate language learners. Even research on the acquisition of literacy through digital media (e.g., Chen, 2010, and to a certain extent, Bloch, 2007) privileges academic and digital literacies (Bawden, 2001). However, it is unclear how well these findings apply to refugee learners, who sometimes have experienced interrupted schooling and had little exposure to technologies found in the resettlement context. Little research concentrates on the use of technology to aid language acquisition among this population. Instead, it generally focuses on the social integration aspect of technology (e.g., Caidi & Allard, 2005) or the use of mobile technology, both pre- and post-resettlement (e.g., Leung, 2011). By better understanding the digital literacies refugees already possess, we are better able to bridge this digital divide (Thorne & Reinhardt, 2008; Warschauer, 2002) and can move toward to researching how to capitalize on the technological skills refugees already possess to facilitate language learning. To address this, this chapter reviews available literature on how refugees worldwide use multiple forms of technology, their levels of access to such technology, and considerations for pre- and post-resettlement technological options. It identifies best practices for employing technology to facilitate language acquisition in light of the multifaceted constraints that refugees face. It concludes by outlining the suitability of different technologies as a means of facilitating language development within a myriad of contexts and gives recommendations for future research on using technology to facilitate language learning at all proficiency levels.

"How Social Media Can Play a Role in an Educational Context, in an Informal Refugee Camp in Europe" by Kathy O' Hare speaks about refugees who are currently in transit in Europe and have little or no access to media platforms and internet connections. Mainstream media often represents refugees in a pejorative manner by using suggestive and powerful language that contributes toward negative stereotyping. www.jungalaradio.com is a community-led digital radio station situated in the Calais Refugee Camp. The authors trained refugees over a 12-month period to create and disseminate their own digital content.

They used Twitter, Facebook, Soundcloud, and YouTube to distribute digital content. The theoretical frameworks that support the project include: issues of citizenship (Rygiel, 2011), the state of exception (Agamben, 1998), acts of deterrence, direct control, and dissuasion (Carling & Hernández-Carreterob, 2011). The premise of this research is that given the opportunity and access to a digital and social space, a core team of participants can grow and develop their digital and communication skills that will enable them to create their own digital content. Participatory action research was used as a methodology for this project. Participants faced many barriers when attempting to develop digital and communication skills. The learning itself became a form of activism for participants and researchers. The French government uses a politics of control to disrupt and prevent social development in the camp and prevent the community from becoming a resource. Agamben's state of exception theory (1998), acts of direct control, deterrence, and dissuasion (Carling & Hernández-Carreterob, 2011), and France's state of emergency influenced project operations, participants' creativity, and learning outcomes.

Donald Reddick and Lisa Sadler in "Postsecondary Education and the Full Integration of Government-assisted Refugees in Canada: A Direction for Program Innovation" highlighted about Canada and its immigration policies. Canada's immigration goals are multifaceted and ambitious, reflecting both a desire to attract those who can contribute economically and culturally, and to offer attracting immigrants who will contribute to their economy while at the same time offering protection to the displaced and the persecuted refugees. Alongside these goals is a pledge that at the same time, Canada has lofty goals to ensure that newcomers will receive the services and supports they need to fully integrate into Canada's cultural and economic landscape. This chapter argues that post-secondary institutions who works in partnership with the community schools can facilitate economic and cultural integration among newcomers and vulnerable refugee groups. However, our previous research revealed that refugee youth face many barriers in accessing the Canadian post-secondary education. The authors hypothesize that efforts to increase access to post-secondary education – and thereby facilitate the accomplishment of immigration goals – would be most effective when specific age groups within the refugee demographic are targeted; in particular, if they target younger children who have spent more time in the Canadian education system, while simultaneously building their ethnic cultural capital. This approach requires a shift in settlement practice which can meet initial and urgent settlement needs and develops economic and cultural capacity in the long run for refugees arriving in Canada. Refugee children can benefit from the Canadian education system over a period of year. The authors have envisioned a program that on one hand helps refugees to gain benefits from post-secondary education and on the other hand builds academic sufficiency by offering programs and pathways that is more inclusive in nature and caters to the challenges faced by this vulnerable group.

"Literacy Instruction without Borders: Ideas for Developing Best Practices for Reading Programs in Refugee Settings" has been written by Matt Thomas, Yuankun Yao, Katherine Landau Wright, and Elizabeth Rutten-Turner.

The authors write about the current time of considerable refugee crises, and the future being uncertain if we consider how and when things may improve. World leaders, such as those working through the United Nations, are trying to proactively plan to meet the needs of refugees, both now and into the future, to make the best of these difficult realities, especially for those going through them. So, how can we manage this refugee reality well, in a way that proactively seeks to meet the special needs of those in refugee settings? It will likely involve moving past meeting needs focused solely on safety and security, reaching instead toward the higher levels of personal development as well, especially education, and, specifically to this chapter, literacy development. The authors contend that in order to support refugee education, generally, we need to identify best practices for supporting reading programs in refugee settings. The chapter addresses this aspect of education related to the refugee crises. More specifically, this chapter discusses the basic design and assessment of literacy education programming in refugee settings that parallels designs for traditional school-wide literacy programs, which we have in place in more stable regions of the world. The authors attempt to converge the fields of literacy education with refugee studies to make recommendations for supporting refugees' literacy education with the goal of preserving their native language and literacy while preparing them for the future.

Chrystina Russell and Nina Weaver in their chapter, "Reaching Refugees: Southern New Hampshire University's Project-based Degree Model for Refugee Higher Education," draw on experiences of developing a refugee higher education model to argue there are three core components that must be present for the successful delivery of higher education degrees to refugee and displaced populations: (1) an inherently flexible mode of degree delivery and assessment; (2) resource-intensive blended learning with on-the-ground access to academic support; and (3) provision of innovative interventions and resources to address context-specific needs. In exploring these features, the authors focus on a case study from Rwanda, where Southern New Hampshire University (SNHU) partners with Kepler, a local Non-Governmental Organisation (NGO), to deliver US-accredited Associate and Bachelor's degrees to refugee and local host populations. Operating in five countries, SNHU's refugee higher education programs are made possible by an innovative degree developed by SNHU called "College for America," which combines a project-based degree associated with mastery-based assessment. Evidence from this model proves that it is possible for a full degree program to be successful in reaching refugee learners and achieving positive learning and employment goals. This chapter argues that the key to SNHU's success in reaching refugee learners is its novel degree pathway built on an online learning model, in combination with a blended learning delivery model that offers robust academic and non-academic support on-the-ground. The chapter offers an overview of the program model and evidence from the pilot program to build an argument for developing more effective and inclusive models for refugee education. The chapter also explores the implications around higher education as a solution and alternative to displacement, as well as discusses the limitations of online-learning and technology for refugee education and the practical and ethical dilemmas arising from the provision of Westernized higher education in non-Western refugee contexts.

"Start ins Deutsche – Students Teach German to Refugees at Goethe University Frankfurt" by Marika Gereke and Subin Nijhawan spoke about the German language program. In September 2015, the world witnessed an unanticipated migration movement of refugees toward the EU. The German government decided for an open-border policy to harbor everyone who could make it on German territory. In large, the civil society joined efforts to create a so-called Willkommenskultur (welcome culture) during the "summer of welcome." The chapter introduces the project "Start ins Deutsche" (German language kick-off) of Goethe University, Frankfurt as one ambitious example of civil society initiatives. Start ins Deutsche was founded on the premise of "integration by language learning." Within Start ins Deutsche, the university students currently enrolled fulltime volunteer to teach German to refugees, in many cases with the perspective to enroll into fulltime studies at Goethe University at a later stage to pursue academic degrees. In the chapter, they have outlined the project and its main aims. Based on this, the authors, thereafter, analyze evaluation data about Start ins Deutsche with regard to the perceptions of German language teachers and their language learners, respectively. The data reveal that the German language teachers interpreted their role beyond being just teachers, while the learners appreciated the effort of their teachers in every aspect. The authors believe that the project serves as a best practice example for a civil society project toward establishing a Willkommenskultur in Germany.

The chapter "Creating a Borderless World of Education for Refugees" by Enakshi Sengupta, Shai Reshef, and Patrick Blessinger showcases the role of technology to create new and sometimes unexpected opportunities for pathways to education for refugees. In a refugee camp, most of the inhabitants if not all are economically poor and access to a mobile phone is considered to be an asset, which helps them to connect to the outside world as well as become a key component to the knowledge sharing and creating higher education pathways in refugee camps (Dahya et al., 2016). Mobile phone based access to internet communication opens up a new world for them in different realities of time, space, and possibilities. Barriers to space, time, and mobility disappear empowering the refugees with hand-held, inexpensive ready-to-use devices to access the vast pool of knowledge lying outside the high boundary walls of the refugee camps. Founded in 2009, The University of the People (UoPeople) is an Education Revolution. It is the world's first tuition-free, non-profit, American accredited, online university. UoPeople is working with the refugees to enable access to quality education for those living in camps and most of the time as non-entities in host countries. With the generous assistance from the donors, the university has set up the Emergency Refugee Scholarship Small, the Giants Scholarship Fund, and the Myanmar Scholarship Fund. These resources provide access to education to hundreds of refugees and asylum-seekers from Syria, Myanmar, Somalia, Democratic Republic of Congo, Afghanistan, Iraq, Nigeria, and many other countries.

CONCLUSION

This book is focused on the core areas of imparting education to the refugee population and highlights the recent developments intended to meet an urgent need: that of the refugees who have no or very little previous schooling and who are in need of language learning and furthering their studies for higher education. This book is designed to provide recognition to those who are working relentlessly toward imparting education to vulnerable people and giving them the tools they need to help withstand and recover from the effects of conflict and displacement.

REFERENCES

Agamben, G. (1998). In D. Heller-Roazen (Ed.), *Homo sacer: Sovereign power and bare life.* Stanford, CA: Stanford University Press.

Allwright, D. (1998). *Learning and teaching as well as you know how: Why is it so very difficult?* Lancaster: Centre for Research in Language Education.

Bawden, D. (2001). Information and digital literacies: A review of concepts. *Journal of Documentation, 57*(2), 218–259. Retrieved from http://dx.doi.org/10.1108/EUM0000000007083

BBC News. (2018). Myanmar Rohingya: What you need to know about the crisis. *BBC News,* April 24. Retrieved from https://www.bbc.com/news/amp/world-asia-41566561

Blake, V. (2003). *An investigation into the experiences of refugee women in adult education.* London: University of East London.

Blessinger, P., & Sengupta, E. (2017). Inclusive higher education must cater for refugees. *University World News,* August 25, Issue 00471.

Bloch, J. (2007). Abdullah's blogging: A generation 1.5 student enters the blogosphere. *Language Learning and Technology, 11*(2), 128–141.

Brand, T., & Earle, L. (2018). The global compact for refugees bringing mayors to the table: Why and how. Brookings Foreign Policy. Retrieved from https://www.brookings.edu/wp-content/uploads/2018/01/fp_20180125_global_compact_refugees-final.pdf

Bryer, D., Winstanley, B., & Cooke, M. (2014). Participatory ESOL. In D. Mallows (Ed.), *Language issue in migration and integration: Perspectives from teachers and learners* (p. 31). London: British Council.

Caidi, N., & Allard, D. (2005). Social inclusion of newcomers to Canada: An information problem? *Library & Information Science Research, 27,* 302–324.

Carling, J., & Hernández-Carreterob, M. (2011). Protecting Europe and protecting migrants? Strategies for Managing Unauthorised Migration from Africa. Retrieved from https://onlinelibrary.wiley.com/doi/abs/10.1111/j.1467-856X.2010.00438.x

Chen, R. (2010). Computer-mediated scaffolding in L2 students' academic literacy development. *CALICO Journal, 28*(1), 74–98.

Cincurova, S. (2015). Ukraine: Europe's forgotten refugees. Retrieved from https://www.opendemocracy.net/can-europe-make-it/sara-cincurova/ukraine-europes-forgotten-refugees

Data and Information. International Organization for Migration (April, 2018)

Dahya, N., & Dryden-Peterson, S. (2016). Tracing pathways to higher education for refugees: the role of virtual support networks and mobile phones for women in refugee camps. *Comparative Education, 53*(2), 284–301. Retrieved from http://dx.doi.org/10.1080/03050068.2016.125987

Employability Forum. (2003). English spoken here? In *Report on a Conference to Review the Teaching of English to Asylum Seekers in the UK.* London: *Employability Forum.* Retrieved from http://www.universityworldnews.com/article.php?story=20170823063722674

IOM. (2018). *Mixed migration flows in the Mediterranean.* Retrieved from: https://rovienna.iom.int/publications/mixed-migration-flows-mediterranean-june-2018

Kleinmann, H. (1982). External influences and their neutralization in second language acquisition: A look at adult Indochinese refugees. *TESOL Quarterly, 16*(2), 239–244. Policy Development and Evaluation Service, United Nations High Commissioner for Refugees, Geneva, Switzerland.

Leung, L. (2011). *Taking refuge in technology: Communication practices in refugee camps and immigra-tion detention*. New Issues in Refugee Research, Working Paper No. 202.

Meredith, S. (2018, June 28). Europe's migration crisis is 'make-or-break' for the EU, Germany's Merkel says. Retrieved from https://www.cnbc.com/2018/06/28/europes-migration-crisis-is-make-or-break-for-the-eugermanys-mer.html

New York Declaration for Refugees and Migrants. (2016). Resolution adopted by the General Assembly on 19 September 2016. Retrieved from http://www.un.org/en/ga/search/view_doc.asp?symbol=A/RES/71/1

Rygiel, K. (2011). Bordering solidarities: Migrant activism and the politics of movement and camps at Calais. *Citizenship Studies, 15*(1), 1–19. Retrieved from https://doi.org/10.1080/13621025.2011.534911

Schuman, F. (1982). In H. Kleinman (Ed.), *External influences and their neutralization in second language acquisition: A look at adult Indochinese refugees*. Retrieved from https://doi.org/10.2307/3586795

Sengupta, E., & Blessinger, P. (2018). *An introduction to refugee education. Refugee Education: Integration and Acceptance of Refugees in Mainstream Society*. Bingley: Emerald Publishing

Shiferaw, D., & Hagos, H. (2002). *Refugees and progression routes to employment*. London: Refugee Council.

Sumon, S. (2018, June 25). Monsoon in Bangladesh adds to Rohingya refugees' plight. Arab News. Retrieved from http://www.arabnews.com/node/1327826/world

The Australian. (2018). Row deepens over Europe's refusal to take refugees. *The Australian*, June 24. Retrieved from https://www.theaustralian.com.au/news/world/row-deepens-over-europes-refusal-to-take-refugees/news-story/2d1b26bee27b3d4bec2a3ce87f9ba2b4

Thorne, S., & Reinhardt, J. (2008). "Bridging Activities," new media literacies and advanced foreign language proficiency. *CALICO Journal, 25*(3), 558–572.

UNHCR. (2016). *Left behind refugee education in crisis*. UNHCR. Geneva. Retrieved from: http://www.unhcr.org/59b696f44.pdf

Vanegas, H. (1998). Humanistic task-based language learning and the ESOL learner; towards a truly learner-centred approach. *Language Issues, 10*(1&2), 21–23 and 22–27.

Warschauer, M. (2002). Reconceptualising the digital divide. *First Monday, 7*(7). Retrieved from http://dx.doi.org/10.5210/fm.v7i7.967

Zahirovic, E. (2001). *Problematizing low acquisition of English among Bosnian refugees in Lothians*. London: University of East London.

CHAPTER 1

ASYLUM-SEEKING STUDENTS' EXPERIENCE OF HIGHER EDUCATION IN THE UK

Damian Spiteri

ABSTRACT

This chapter is dedicated to presenting and analyzing the accounts of young men in the UK from an asylum-seeking background about how they experience a university. The chapter has been written with the goal of contributing to existing literature about how to promote an understanding about the active engagement of refugee students in higher education in the UK. It focuses on understanding the meaning that these young men assign to their studies in the UK, their overall experience of attending university, and the personal meaning that they assign to their lives in the UK. It explores the different personal and structural factors that they believe enable them to reach their goals – as well as the factors that they believe constrain them from doing so.

Keywords: Higher education; immigration policy (the UK); racism; discrimination; student life; migration

INTRODUCTION

Since the 1990s, the British immigration policy has been subject to an increased number of limitations on people seeking asylum in the UK. The ongoing preparations that were put into place for Brexit to take place on March 29, 2019 are likely to be an influencing factor. More direct limitations, however, have included cuts in funding for agencies that have promoted the integration of refugees to the British

Language, Teaching and Pedagogy for Refugee Education
Innovations in Higher Education Teaching and Learning, Volume 15, 17–26
Copyright © 2019 by Emerald Publishing Limited
ISSN: 2055-3641/doi:10.1108/S2055-364120180000015002

society and the progressive limiting of the rights that are associated with the issuing of humanitarian visas to individuals who are granted protection by the UK. There has also been the closure, in 2012, of the UK Border Agency-backed Refugee Integration and Employment Service (RIES). RIES had been set up to prevent the marginalization of asylum-seekers and refugees living in the UK (Ager & Strang, 2008, 2010), and its closure could be interpreted as a statement that government involvement in support for refugees who were granted the right for longer term settlement in the UK had to be discontinued. Since 2005, except for the relatively small number of refugees, who were granted immediate permanent leave via the United Nations Refugee Agency Gateway Protection Program, refugees have been granted a limited leave to remain which is of five years' duration. This is in contrast to the relatively more permanent nature of the refugee status that had been granted prior to that year. From 2005 onward, cases have become subject to a review and it is only after that review takes place that a decision is taken about whether an indefinite leave to remain in the UK is to be granted.

These changes are of concern to university students for various reasons. Primarily, the award of refugee status means that, normally, a person will not be forcibly repatriated at least in the short term, in consonance with non-refoulement principles. Second, the award of the refugee status means that they are entitled to social security benefits, National Health Service (NHS) health care, employment, and family reunion. Third, on a symbolic level, when people are granted refugee status, this means that they are being informed that they have every right to be in the country. In other words, it is being acknowledged that they are in the UK due to socio-political factors (usually a politically and/or economically unstable country of origin) – and not because of something (for instance) that "they" have done. Consequently, their migration is not associated with "an inner, pathological condition of the displaced" (Malkki, 1992, p. 33). The common use of the term "clandestine" can be used, for instance, as a social construction by governments to monitor and control immigration – sometimes in a more restrictive way than would be otherwise socially acceptable. "Clandestine" is a derogative term which suggests that people have done something wrong and thereby have something to hide in leaving their country of origin, something which is probably rooted in an idea that they did not enter the country through traditional routes. It is, however, a loosely applied term and a colloquialism … and can thereby be applied to other migrants, too. In more realistic terms, people who seek asylum, and thereby some form of national or international protection, come from a rich variety of social backgrounds, family structures, ethnic groups, racial identities, belief systems, and religions. Consequently, the label of clandestine does not do justice to the complexity of the lives of university students which, in any case, could not be readily framed within any discourse (Lather, 2008, 2009) – even ones that do not bear such negative connotations as "clandestine."

This chapter explores the meanings which students from refugee backgrounds, in UK universities, attribute to their status and the different significant events that they experience as a part of their daily lives. It gives importance to acknowledging their voice and capturing their own subjective viewpoints, while, at the same time, ensuring that their voice is not reified. Due recognition needs to be given to the changes in their understanding and self-representation of their experiences as they acquire new skills, knowledge, and competencies – while carrying out their university studies. King (1999) observed how ethnically and culturally mixed groups of English as a Second Language students in North America did not only learn language skills and competencies but had also undertaken personal and cultural transformation due to their interactions with the other people they had met while in North America.

Having said this, the Refugee Council (2012) points out that people who arrive in the UK and ask for asylum are among the most marginalized in the UK society. This is likely to be due to their lack of power, relative to nationals, which makes it more difficult for them to bring about purposeful change. However, as is clearly shown in this chapter, such generalizations do not necessarily apply to all people with the same bearing, as the university students around whom this chapter has been constructed, are eagerly looking forward to graduating and moving on with their lives. This might mean that certain disadvantages may not be prevalent in structured and meritocratic university settings; particularly, if they have specific policies in place whose goal is that of promoting social equity (Spiteri, 2016).

THE RESEARCH PARTICIPANTS

The chapter is informed by a research study that took place between February 2016 and January 2017. During that time, I interrupted my lecturing duties in Malta for an academic year to lecture in social work at the University of York in the UK. In Malta, I lectured in Health and Social Care at the Malta College of Arts, Science, and Technology, or, as it is more commonly known, MCAST (pronounced M-cast). I initially thought that I would contact the research participants, who would provide me with data for my study which I could then use when writing up this chapter through refugee organizations in the UK. Finding participants through this route proved to be more difficult than planned, however. I lacked a well-established network of contacts with local refugee organizations in the UK. This meant that I could not establish, at a glimpse, which of these organizations would give my study priority (since they would see it aligned to their own objectives), as I would have been likely to have been in a position to do, had I been conducting this study in Malta where I had lived practically all my life. I thereby opted to create a snowball sample, starting out by inviting participants who I met at the University of York (and thereby came to know personally) to participate in my study; rather than asking organizations to identify potential participants for me.

Although, ideally, I would have liked to have research participants who included both men and women, the people who accepted to take part in my study were men. Five men were interviewed in all. The first two participants whom I approached were two Nigerian refugee university students who were attending various events during the Lesbian, Gay, Bisexual and Trans-sexual (LGBT) awareness week at the University of York in February 2016. These two young men appeared enthusiastic about participating in my research initiative and besides accepting to be interviewed, also put me in contact with another four men, whom they knew were refugees. Two of these participants were from Somalia, and the other was from Iraq. All participants were in the 22 to 25 age-bracket. The participants from Africa were black and the Iraqi man was white. They were all undertaking undergraduate studies in courses with a vocational inclination including teaching and dentistry.

As is to be expected of university students in the UK, all the participants could all speak English; although this ranged from fluent (the Nigerian students explained that they had spoken English since babyhood) to hesitant (both the Somali students and the Iraqi student appeared to be looking for the "right words" when they were speaking – sometimes it seemed to me that they were thinking in their native language and translating the words into English before speaking out loud). Both the Nigerian and the Somali participants had been in the UK since they were in their mid-teens and had been granted leave to remain in the UK prior to starting university. The Iraqi participant's case was different. He explained that he had been offered a temporary humanitarian status (discretionary leave), and as a result did not have a clear asylum-seeking status to enable him to apply for university without problems. Discretionary leave is granted to asylum seekers who do not qualify for humanitarian protection; yet, the Home Office deems it appropriate to allow the person to stay in the UK, usually for three years or less. The university that the Iraqi participant attended told him that, unless he could rectify matters, he would be liable to pay the fees of a foreign fee-paying candidate, which was well beyond his financial means. He thereby thought at the time that he might be better off not attending university at all. He explained that he felt totally helpless at this point in his life. Not only did he have no control over how the Home Office would decide his case, but he also did not know when they would decide it. He explained further that, thankfully, things worked out for him. He had a positive answer one week after the university academic year had started, and the university accepted his "late application" after taking into consideration the facts of his case.

RESEARCHER INVOLVEMENT

In research studies that adopt an in-depth approach with a small number of participants, it is normal for researchers to say something about themselves in the overall context of the study. In virtue of this, I would like to start out by saying I have never been through the experience of being a refugee or seeking national or international protection at any time in my life. I have been brought up in the European country of Malta, which has a long history of democracy, political stability, and the upholding of the rule of law. It is the smallest member state of the European Union, having joined in 2004. My interest in refugee issues was triggered by happenings in Malta. From 2001 onward, boat-loads of people that were fleeing from different parts of Africa to reach Europe landed in Malta. This is understandable since geographically, Malta is centrally positioned between North Africa and mainland Europe (Italy). Some drifted to Malta, others mistook the Maltese shores for Italian ones, and some were brought to Malta as the nearest country by search and rescue personnel. Very few chose Malta as their destination since Malta is an island cut off from the European mainland by sea and also a very small country and thereby not characterized by the large cities of what they would probably consider as "typical" European countries.

My initial active engagement with young people from asylum-seeking backgrounds came about when they were placed in my classes at MCAST. Initially, I was at a loss about how to adapt my lectures to make them more interesting for them, while catering for the remaining students at the same time. This led me to conduct my own research about the teaching of young people from an asylum-seeking background and this led me to eventually publish my book *Multiculturalism, Higher Education, and Intercultural Communication* with Palgrave Macmillan in 2016.

I was neither a novice to interviewing nor I was a novice to conducting and publishing research on asylum seekers in Malta; and this prior experience led me to be informed that – in the UK context, I needed to build up a holistic appreciation of the occurrences, in the lives of the participants – if I were to succeed in my goal of promoting an understanding about the active engagement of refugee students in higher education (in the UK). I thereby knew, from the outset, that I had to be careful to be self-reflexive enough not to see the participants as different from me. For instance, by classifying them as "the refugees" and myself as "the non-refugee," or else, by classifying them as "the students" and myself as "the lecturer," I would have been clearly differentiating myself from them making it more difficult for me to empathize with them. Stated otherwise, had I approached the participants with an attitude that they were different, I would have created an artificial dichotomy between "the participants" and "myself." In Bennett's (1986) terms, I would have adopted an ethno-centric outlook, which tends to generate distance between myself and those that I perceive as different from me. There was a risk that this would have come about since I might have created perceptual biases wherein I would have denied, or I would have justified differences rather than appreciating reality for what it was.

Bennett (1986) believes that people would be enabled to become closer to one another (and thereby in a position to come to common understandings) if they adopt an "ethno-relative" outlook. Adopting an "ethno-relative" outlook entails both acknowledging and accepting differences; and thereby creating a sense of unity among people who are in some way different from one another. As a researcher, adopting this outlook meant critiquing my own outlook and problematizing the things I am most likely to take for granted. For instance, my idea of a family meal is sitting around a table with both men and women present and eating one or more plates using forks, knives, and what I consider the "ordinary" utensils. However, in certain cultures, I would be expected to eat with the men, and eat with my hands. Problematizing the things that I take for granted, enabling me to obtain a deeper understanding of events and circumstances in people's lives, is an integral part of bracketing. Bracketing is the "reframing of the classifications and constructs that we impose on our perceiving" (Heron & Reason, 2001, p. 150). Through using bracketing, I was further enabled to explore the participants' subjective viewpoints about being in university – without projecting my own understanding of either university life, or my beliefs about what university life should be like, upon them. Bracketing also enabled me to empathize with the participants when they spoke about other aspects of life that had a relatively indirect impact on university life, including intimate relationships, family-life, friends, pastimes, and work.

I carried out one interview with each participant and while it may have been beneficial to carry out more interviews, since this would have given the participants a longer overall time span in which to express themselves, based on my years of experience as a lecturer, I assumed that they were most likely to be under pressure with their studies, and would be reluctant to meet me more than once. I also considered the additional expense that carrying out more than one interview would involve for me, most especially since the participants were studying at different universities in different parts of the UK. Each interview lasted around 60 minutes in total even though some were slightly shorter, and some took a slightly longer time to carry out. The interviews were conducted in suitable spaces located on or around university campuses, which included the study rooms in libraries, empty lecture halls, or, in one case, on a relatively quiet table at the far corner of one of the university canteens.

When carrying out research leading to the writing up of this chapter, I sought an ethical approval from the MCAST, since this was the institution where I was working on a long-term basis. I was also conscious that at the time of publishing the study, I would have resumed working at this institution and would have returned to Malta. My application considered such aspects as negotiation of consent, anonymity of participants, and carrying out research with vulnerable persons. The MCAST approved my request but recommended that I refer people to the appropriate sectors if the participants threatened harm to themselves or to others.

I proceeded to discuss ethical matters with the participants in the start of the interview and presented them with a consent form. I clarified with them that they did not have to answer any question if they did not want to. I also told them that, if they thought that a question was inappropriate, they were perfectly free to say so; and that they were free to end the research at any time, if they wanted to. I also promised that if they ended the research prematurely, I would not use their data in the study. I assumed that if they were to leave the interview in this way, they would probably be feeling distressed about something they said, and I did not want to further add to their stress by publishing it. I explained to them the scope of the research, mentioning to them that it was focused on the active engagement of students from refugee backgrounds at universities in the UK and for this reason could have a participatory character, wherein they could liberally bring up issues that they thought were relevant and could enrich the interviews.

THE FINDINGS – "WHAT DOES ATTENDING A UNIVERSITY MEAN TO ME"?

When exploring the active engagement of refugee students in higher education in the UK, and the meaning that the young men described in the previous parts of this chapter assign to their studies in the UK, their overall experience of attending university was influenced by their perceived transition to the labor market after graduating. Even though this chapter has highlighted the methodological challenges that I confronted when carrying out the underlying research as a person from Malta (who had never been a refugee) and it has also, at great length, contextualized the participants, in describing where they come from and who they are; certain macro-level factors need to also be given mention if a holistic picture of their situation is to be presented. For instance, racism, even if not manifested at universities, can still have an impact on people if they witness it in the wider community. Racism can leave them fearful that they may be vulnerable to being discriminated against sometime in the future. Poverty is also an issue of concern, since all the participants reported that, to succeed at university, they had to make numerous sacrifices so that they would not run out of the little money they have. Potential unemployment is also an issue of concern most especially, since some people do not succeed in getting jobs immediately after graduating and there are likely to be greater challenges ahead, since technology is likely to take over many of the jobs that are assigned to people in today's world (Giddens, 1999).

The participants claimed that there were moments when they felt discouraged when they felt that life was too expensive; particularly, if they lived far away from the university campus and could not cope with travel costs. They also thought that costs of daily living were not cheap; and they had little cash in hand to participate in any recreational pursuits if they were not offered at a discounted rate to university students, or, in some cases, if they were not offered free of charge. The Somali participants mentioned their obligation to send money home in the form of remittances. They said that they worked to acquire some form of income while at university as well as to send money back home to their families in Somalia. Even though this was stressful, it gave them a sense of honor to send money home in this manner, because they believed they were meeting social and familial obligations. It is likely though that the aspiration to make money was reflected in the courses of study that they chose, which, as pointed out earlier on in this chapter, included teaching and dentistry. The participant who had taken up university studies in dentistry thought that dentistry offered him a high promise of employment upon graduating and explained that this was why he chose this line of study rather than the performing arts. He explained that this would have been his preferred choice, career-wise, had he to have had his mind at rest about money.

All the participants shared a common conception that was articulated by Abeo, one of the Nigerian participants, who explained that:

> You have one enemy. That enemy is fear. Fear of thinking when you think about the past. Fear of thinking when you think about the future. Life is so uncertain, so very uncertain.

In terms of life at university, refugee students may be particularly vulnerable if they know that their case is eventually set for review and they may face possible deportation and repatriation. This was expressed by the Iraqi participant, who said that, while he was encouraged by his admission to university, he did not feel that he was welcome. He explained that he believed that "the people of the UK are not my people." He was scared that since he was not truly comfortable, this would reduce his ability to concentrate on his studies. His emphasis is on his emotional, psychological, and social positioning, and shows a possible conditioned association with the stress he is experiencing. On the one hand, what he is saying reflects what Arnot, Pinson, and Candappa (2009) highlight – namely that asylum-seekers are in effect both "physically and symbolically 'out of place' – the 'other in our midst'" (p. 249). This is connected to macro-level considerations, which place nation states as central features in the governance of modern-day societies. On the other hand, it reflects his overall insecurity.

The active engagement of refugee students at UK universities is strongly influenced by how they feel and some of the participants spoke about their traumatic past, and about how their efforts to leave their past behind them did not always succeed. One of the Nigerian participants complained about sporadic flashbacks resulting from the intense emotional injuries he had previously suffered in Nigeria. Mental health is a factor that impacts significantly on educational performance (Hodes, 1998). One of the participants also mentioned that he had spent time in a refugee camp and had a feeling of being "severely locked in without the possibility of building a future," when at the camp. In the context of the camps, there is likely to be an onset of

> depression, apathy, delinquent behaviour; or aggressive acts to situational mental disturbances, drug abuse and suicide. In many cases, this may also reflect the high level of anxiety and despair within the refugee community as a whole. (United Nations High Commissioner for Refugees, 1994)

On the other hand, the participant mentioned the drive of his parents and how they always tried to give him hope. He said that he would not be where he is today, had his parents not "pushed" him there. He mentioned his fear of failing his exams and although, so far, he has done well in his university studies, he said "failing my exams would be the end of the world for me."

Apart from parental help, another participant mentioned the importance of friends, networks, and social capital. He said that these networks, particularly with people from his own country, also helped him to build up resilience, most especially since within those networks were people who he had got to know from prior to going to university. Another spoke of the competencies that he had, but also said that at university, little attention was given to these, and while on the one hand he experienced some frustration at this, on the other hand, he just "buried his head in the sand and got on with things just to fit in with what everyone else was doing." This repression of past experiences, or what Kibreab (cited in Marfleet, 2006, p. 210) has called tabula rasa comes about when "refugees [are] treated as if they were tabula rasa with no history, past experiences, culture, anticipation, skills [and] coping mechanisms to interpret new situations." The tabula rasa can generate a deficit discourse wherein people from refugee backgrounds (or for that matter any migrant backgrounds) are not seen as forming part of UK society unless they can live in a manner consistent with (what is socially constructed as) the UK way of life. Having said this, he does not see himself as having some form of transnational citizenship, whereby he foresees that he would one day return to his country of origin to promote its development. This is particularly since educated personnel would be in high demand and he consequently he might be asked to consider returning there, at some point in future. He says that he would like to live, for the rest of his life, based in the UK.

CONCLUSION

On the one hand, the years that the participants are spending at a UK university appear to have a stabilizing influence on them. The university seems to not only be a gateway to their the building of brighter possible futures, but also a means to their further fitting in with UK society, which many of them have made and see as their homeland – a belief which is likely to be consolidated by their having lived there since they were young. On the other hand, the tensions that are associated with being in a relatively insecure time of their lives, where they have not started working and are still in the process of building their future, are also clearly very real to them. One of the participants emphasized examination success, and while he may share the aspiration for examination success with students the world over, there may be greater tension due to the overall financial insecurity that refugee students tend to experience.

A core tenet that runs throughout this chapter is that all the young men who have been interviewed value higher education and all participate in it wholeheart-edly. All of them are determined to qualify and all have the aspiration that their qualifications will lead them to take up employment after graduating. All clearly have had difficult moments in life, ranging from flashbacks deriving from past traumas, the lack of resources due to cost-cutting measures at a governmental level, and the difficulty of being foreigners. The Iraqi participant mentioned that his Iraqi friends did not understand why he wanted to attend university, and in this respect, his attending university separated him from his diaspora; even though, as he said, "I have a mind of my own, and will not let other people lead me to feel broken down." (I assume that broken down is an expression for feeling under the weather – a similar expression – *nhossni mkisser* also competencies in Maltese). This shows a tension between their wanting to belong to their com-munity and wanting to forge their own goals. Yet, the essential difficulty, which all the participants faced, was how to be able to forge (and reach) their goals in the light of the constraints they faced; particularly in relation to, as one of the participants put it, "what will happen to me if I run out of money?"

REFERENCES

Ager, A., & Strang, A. (2008). Understanding integration: A conceptual framework. *Journal of Refugee Studies, 21*(2), 166–191.

Ager, A., & Strang, A. (2010). Refugee integration: Emerging trends and remaining agendas. *Journal of Refugee Studies, 23*(4), 589–607.

Arnot, M., Pinson, H., & Candappa, M. (2009). Compassion, caring and justice: Teachers' strategies to maintain moral integrity in the face of national hostility to the "non-citizen". *Education Review, 61*(3), 249–264.

Bennett, M. J. (1993). Towards ethnorelativism: A developmental model of intercultural sensitivity. In R. M. Paige (Ed.), *Education for the intercultural experience* (2nd ed., pp. 21–71). Yarmouth, ME: Intercultural Press.

Giddens, A. (1991). Modernity and self-identity. In *Self and society in the late modern age*. Cambridge: Polity.

Heron, J., & Reason, P. (2001). The practice of co-operative inquiry: Research with rather than on people. In P. Reason & H. Bradbury (Eds.), *Handbook of action research: Participative inquiry and practice* (pp. 179–188). London: Sage.

Hodes, M. (1998). Refugee children may need a lot of psychiatric help. *British Medical Journal, 316*(7134), 793–795.

King, K. P. (1999). Changing languages, cultures and self: The adult ESL experience of perspective transformation. Retrieved from www.adulterc.org/proceedings/1999/99King.pdf. Accessed on March 30, 2018.

Lather, P. (2008). *Getting lost: Feminist efforts towards a double(d) science*. Albany, NY: State University of New York Press.

Lather, P. (2009). Against empathy, voice and authenticity. In: A. Y. Jackson & L. A. Mazzei (Eds.), *Voice in qualitative inquiry* (pp. 17–26). Abingdon: Routledge.

Malkki, L. H. (1992). The rooting of peoples and the territorialization of national identity among scholars and refugees. *Cultural Anthropology, 7*(1), 24–44.

Marfleet, P. (2006). *Refugees in a global era*. Basingstoke: Palgrave.

Refugee Council. (2012). *Between a rock and a hard place: The dilemma facing refused asylum seekers*. London: Refugee Council.

Spiteri, D. (2016). *Multiculturalism, higher education and intercultural communication*. London: Palgrave Macmillan.

United Nations High Commissioner for Refugees. (1994). *Refugee children: Guidelines on protection and care*. New York, NY: United Nations.

CHAPTER 2

CONCEPTUALIZING HIGHER EDUCATION ASPIRATIONS FORMATION AMONG MARGINALIZED MIGRANT YOUTH IN JOHANNESBURG, SOUTH AFRICA

Wadzanai F. Mkwananzi and
Merridy Wilson-Strydom

ABSTRACT

There has been limited research to date that takes account of marginalized migrants' educational aspirations in the Global South using a human development lens. There is thus a need to consider where aspirations and education fit into processes of development among and for youth, particularly in the South-to-South migration context. This chapter conceptualizes the formation of educational aspirations among marginalized migrant youth. The emphasis is on higher education, with a focus on educational aspirations, because of the importance of higher education for both intrinsic and instrumental development of individuals in equipping them for multiple futures. Using the human development and capability lens for analysis, we argue that to understand educational aspirations we need to take account of material resources as well as the interaction between individual agency and structural conditions. The chapter argues that the formation of higher educational aspirations is

Language, Teaching and Pedagogy for Refugee Education
Innovations in Higher Education Teaching and Learning, Volume 15, 27–41
Copyright © 2019 by Emerald Publishing Limited
All rights of reproduction in any form reserved
ISSN: 2055-3641/doi:10.1108/S2055-364120180000015004

complex, as is the environment that shapes them. Such a complexity requires an in-depth and comprehensive analysis to take account of the lived realities of marginalized groups.

Keywords: Agency; asylum; Global South; aspirations; youth; migration

INTRODUCTION

Conceptualizing higher education aspirations, particularly for marginalized populations such as migrant youth, is important as it helps us to understand the role different factors contributing to or obstructing the potential of education as a key capability for human development (Sen, 1999). In this chapter, we conceptualize the formation of educational aspirations among marginalized migrant youth. There has been limited research to date that takes account of marginalized migrants' educational aspirations in the Global South. It is thus important to consider where aspirations and education fit into processes of development among and for youth, particularly in the South-to-South migration context. The emphasis is on higher education, with a focus on educational aspirations, because of the importance of higher education for both intrinsic and instrumental development of individuals in equipping them for multiple valued futures. There is also a need to understand current structures and systems within higher education institutions and how these may influence marginalized migrant youths' educational aspirations.

We begin this chapter by contextualizing migration into South Africa from other Southern African countries (Zimbabwe in particular), thereby highlighting the challenge of defining refugees in the context of the migrant youth in our work. Using the human development and capability lens for analysis, we argue that to understand educational aspirations we need to take account of material resources as well as the interaction between individual agency and structural conditions. As such, we show that the formation of higher educational aspirations is complex, as is the environment that shapes them. Such a complexity requires an in-depth and comprehensive analysis that takes account of the lived realities of marginalized groups. The conceptualization of educational aspirations we provide therefore intersects along the axes of agency and structural conversion factors. Based on these intersections, we argue for four types of aspirations, namely *resigned, powerful, persistent,* and *frustrated* aspirations. Finally, the chapter presents an analysis of what this conceptualization may mean for human development.

CONTEXTUAL ORIENTATION

Despite the growing significance and global scope of international migration, the South-to-South movement has been neglected in global policy debates on migration and development (Crush & Ramachandran, 2010). These authors further highlight that often the debate is focused on the South-to-North movement, evidently corresponding to the idea that what seems to matter in development is how the South can be more like the North. This is attributed to the view that there are more opportunities for work in Europe compared to Africa. Yet, marked by the long history of labor migration, Africa has also been portrayed as a continent of people that are on the move, seeking to expand their livelihoods in different ways (Van Dijk, Foeken, & van Til, 2001). In sub-Saharan Africa, migration has been an intrinsic component of the developmental process since the colonial era, notably in Southern Africa. Wentzel and Tlabela (2006, p. 74) note that at the beginning of the twentieth century, extensive migration patterns had emerged across Southern Africa based on labor possibilities around the industrial sector. Khan (2007) notes of South Africa:

> Patterns of migration observed in South Africa have become progressively more complex and diverse in recent times with South Africa attracting not only refugees and asylum seekers but also skilled professionals from across the continent as well as environmental and socio-economic migrants. (p. 1)

This complexity has, over time, affected the categorization of migrants in South Africa with categories becoming less and less definitive. These unclear boundaries are highlighted by Birchall (2006), who acknowledges the overlap in the terms that seek to classify migrants. In addition to the principal conventions[1] that govern the international refugee matters, South Africa has its own policies, themselves subject to change over time. Since democracy in 1994, a number of discussions have taken place in relation to the recognition of refugees and asylum seekers and as a result, different legal instruments in the form of White and Green Papers (see Bernstein, 1998; Handmaker, De la Hunt, & Klareen, 2001) were put in place, leading up to the current Refugee Policy (Act 130 of 1998). Grounded in the Constitution, the Refugees Act promotes self-settlement and self-sufficiency for asylum seekers and refugees. In other words, they are allowed to seek employment and live within communities, among other rights such as access to public healthcare and education services. An asylum seekers' permit (often referred to as the Section 22 Permit) acknowledges that an application has been lodged for refugee status. However, there is no clarity or official clarification of the rights that the holders of these permits have in comparison to refugee status holders. For example, although the permit allows one to work, it is not clear if it allows one to study or access other services considered necessary, especially in a self-settling environment. Therefore, there needs to be an understanding that the two documents, an asylum seekers' permit and a refugee permit (the Section 24 Permit), although they allow their holder to live in the country, confer different privileges. The Refugees Act was followed by the Immigration Act (2000), which allows permits for skilled migrants, students, and tourists as well as different categories of permanent and temporary migrants. The amended Immigration Act 13 of 2002 criminalizes undocumented migrants (asylum seekers), making it possible to arrest, detain, and deport illegal migrants. Gordon (2010) has argued that the new immigration policies are characterized by ambiguity and inconsistencies. Since the mid-2000s, South Africa has been experiencing an influx of economic migrants, many from neighboring countries, particularly Zimbabwe. The intensity of migration into the country has seen more and more youth, including minors, migrate into the country. To regularize their stay in the country, most apply for refugee recognition, and because it takes a long time to be granted refugees status, many remain with asylum seekers' permits as their only official documentation. Evidently, definitions and classification become challenging for these migrants. In this chapter, we thus use the term "marginalized migrant" to refer to refugees, asylum seekers, and undocumented migrants.

EDUCATIONAL POLICY LANDSCAPE

Refugee youths are also incorporated in the country's Youth Policy (2009–2014), which guides the approach to youth development and is based on principles of justice, human rights, and empowerment, among others (see National Youth Policy 2009–2014, 2018). Wellbeing and education are key intervention areas. However, the policy only refers to *refugees*, individuals who have been granted official refugee status and protection under the Refugee Act of 1998, which defines a refugee in accordance to the 1951 United Nations Convention (see United Nations High Commisioner for Refugees, 2018). This therefore does not include asylum seekers' permit holders, many of whom are economic migrants rather than asylum seekers by the Convention's definition. Such disparities and lack of clarity in policy make it more challenging for marginalized migrant youth to navigate their way in terms of which services they can access, including education. As such, Khan (2007) writes that despite policies being in place, refugees still face huge obstacles in converting their legal rights into effective protection. Marginalized migrants experience challenges such as lack of employment, limited access to scholarships and bursaries, and other social challenges associated with daily living. Thus, in the South African context, in addition to the everyday social challenges that marginalize these migrant youths, they may still have to meet the standard requirements for accessing higher education (e.g., the proof of availability of funds) in order to realize their educational aspirations.

CAPABILITIES, EDUCATIONAL ASPIRATIONS, AND MARGINALIZED MIGRANTS

While a number of scholars (e.g., Conradie, 2013; DeJaeghere, 2016; Hart, 2013) have conceptualized aspirations using the capabilities approach (CA), this conceptualization remains limited when it comes to educational aspirations of marginalized migrant groups, particularly in the South African context. This chapter seeks to bridge this gap. The CA allows for the assessment of individual wellbeing in terms of opportunities and freedoms that individuals have to achieve what they value being and doing. Thus, how well a migrant is doing is determined by the kind of life they are living. A substantial contribution of the CA is its ability to deepen our understanding of the complex lives of marginalized migrant youth by capturing multiple disadvantages, in this case relevant to the educational context. Using the CA to understand disadvantage in terms of available freedoms and conceptualize migrants' life experiences, we show how disadvantage influences both educational and broader aspirations of these youth. In the context of our work, an examination of migrant youth's capabilities and functionings is associated with what they are able to do and be based on the opportunities available to them. It will, however, be shown that although some functionings may be unachievable as a result of various contextual influences (conversion factors), this does not mean that they are not valued by the migrant youth aspiring to them.

It is important to consider that not everyone can convert resources into valued functionings the same way. For example, for a migrant youth to access education, factors such as documentation, finances, grades, and language come into play. Neither does the availability of all these resources necessarily result in a similar functioning being achieved. This is as a result of other influencing conditions such as environment, social connections, individual agency, and other individual differences. Robeyns (2005, p. 99) groups these various conditions into three types of conversion factors: personal (e.g., gender, age, and sex), environmental (e.g., physical environment and geographical location), and social (e.g., policies, norms, class, and race). When seeking to understand how well a person's life is going or to what extent a person is flourishing, we need to ask about both wellbeing and agency (Wilson-Strydom & Walker, 2015). Negative influences of these conversion factors may lead to limited freedom for one to exercise agency. As such, questions of agency and conversion factors will be used as a yardstick to measure the freedoms that migrant youth have.

In educational contexts, Hart (2013) stresses the ability of the CA to inform policy and practices that can enhance the capacity of young people to pursue their aspirations. On its own and for every individual, education is typically seen as a fertile functioning: it contributes to the development of other human capabilities and sets a *foundation* for additional freedoms and choices (Nussbaum, 2011). There is also evidence in the literature that education has the potential to expand people's existing capacities into developed capabilities as well as expand human freedoms (Walker, 2005). Thus, while education may be viewed as a means to practice self-sufficiency in terms of its instrumental value, particularly in a self-settling country like South Africa, it could also play an important role in human development and in the expansion of an individual's capabilities to lead a flourishing life (Sen, 2009). As such, migrants' marginalization is not only limited to documentation and shelter, but also to constraints on aspiring to lead lives that are valuable to them. The relevance, therefore, of the CA to migrant youth is that it offers a framework in which to assess their potential for living lives they have reason to value, while also identifying future educational possibilities. The value of aspirations is that they can stimulate behavior leading to advancement of capabilities; in the migrants' case, migration can then be seen as an investment opportunity, allowing the aspirational window to widen (Ray, 2006). In Section 2.5, we discuss the four types of aspirations. Owing to the limits of word count, it has not been possible to present much empirical data; as such, this chapter focuses essentially at the conceptual level.

FOUR TYPES OF ASPIRATIONS

The research presented this chapter was conducted in central Johannesburg between 2014 and 2016, focusing on migrant youth who lived or accessed services at the Central Methodist Church (CMC), services that were offered through its refugee shelter before it shut down on December 31, 2014. In total, 26 marginalized migrant youth were interviewed. There were two rounds of data collection. In the first round, purposive sampling was used to identify the marginalized migrant youth. However, during this first round, it was striking that there was only one female among 14 males. We therefore used snowball sampling to reach out to more women for the second round of data collection, during which eleven more women were interviewed. Interviews were semi-structured and usually lasted about 60 minutes each. The CMC was chosen as the location for the research for its work with refugees and asylum seekers, based on the different activities they offered and the shelter's flexible accessibility. Additionally, the church runs Albert Street School offering primary and secondary schooling to marginalized migrant children and youth. Based on the stories told by the 26 marginalized migrant youth, four types of educational aspirations were identified: *resigned, powerful, persistent,* and *frustrated* aspirations. Fig. 1 shows the interaction between conversion factors and agency in aspirations formation and provides a summary of how these two factors influence the formation of the four types of aspirations.

Fig. 1 illustrates the interconnectedness and interplay of factors influencing aspirations in the context of disadvantages, in this case, for marginalized migrant youth. Aspirations and agency are interwoven with both being influenced by personal and external factors. External factors relate to those conversion factors that are beyond the individuals' control, such as community, family background, and structural conditions (Chiappero-Martinetti & Venkatapuram, 2014). Personal factors represent those conditions that are individually determined (but always located in a social and collective context), such as skills, motivation, age, sex, and other personal traits. Financial constraints are an example of external factors that one has no control over, whereas individual agency is an example of internal factors and could be characterized by traits such as having determination or motivation to pursue one's desired functionings and achievements (Keogh, Garvis, Pendergast, & Diamond, 2012). Determination is an important internal factor, as it propels the migrant youth to achieve what is valuable to each of them. These external and internal conversion factors do not always have an either–or influence. The influence of specific conversion factors is also dependent on their interaction with other factors. In varying contexts and circumstances, an individual can experience all these forms of aspirations at different points of their lives, dependent on the interaction of resources and conversion factors at various stages. Furthermore, the lines between the types of aspirations in practice may be blurred at any one time; as such, these aspirations should be seen as ideal types.

Resigned Aspirations

Resigned aspirations can be placed at different points along two intersecting continua of positive external influences (social and structural conditions) and low

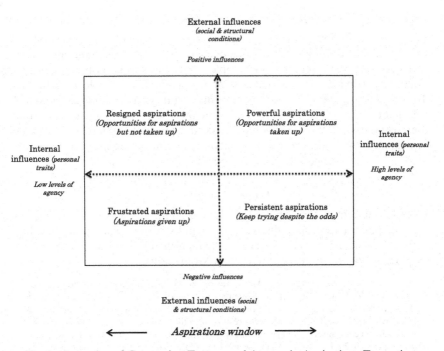

Fig. 1.   Interplay of Conversion Factors and Agency in Aspirations Formation.

levels of agency (internal influences) operating in the space of the aspirations window, as shown in the extract below:

> My sister and I had nowhere to go. It was November, then we met a guy who showed us the shelter at the church. [But] now I would rather study what is simple, I don't want a course that will take many years or months because I want to get an income fast. (Rita, female, 21, a jobseeker)

Thus, while one may have social and structural conditions in place, such as living at the church shelter and an opportunity to complete secondary schooling, the choice not to take up this opportunity may suggest that a migrant has become resigned to the fact that realizing their aspiration of studying toward a certain profession is not possible. Experiences and circumstances may lead to the belief that the opportunity to pursue their educational aspirations has passed and, thus, the marginalized migrant youth resigns their aspirations. Such resigned (potentially adapted) aspirations may be challenging for strategies or interventions that aim to use aspirations as an instrument for human development progression (Conradie & Robeyns, 2013). This is because often when individuals have adapted their aspirations, they are likely to believe that certain capabilities are not available to them, even when such capabilities and options are present (Conradie & Robeyns, 2013).

While aspirations resignation can also be seen as a result of the absence of minimal resources to at least live a decent life, the interaction of conversion factors leading to aspirations resignation is complex, and it can involve personal, economic, social, and cultural influences. The structural conditions may be in place, such as flexible policies for migrant youth to participate in education, but the immediate needs of survival lessen one's agency toward pursuing educational activities. In some cases, even the people within one's aspirations window may not motivate an individual to make use of any potentially available opportunities. To a large degree, in contexts of extreme disadvantage, a person's agency to realize what they value is often influenced more by their current state of being, than the possibilities of the future. Thus, resigned aspirations should be understood in relation to the extent to which a person's basic needs are met and within the context of a specific person's unique experiences.

Powerful Aspirations

Powerful aspirations can be placed at different points along two intersecting continua of positive external influences (social and structural conditions) and high levels of agency (internal influences) operating in the space of the aspirations window, as illustrated by the extract from Musa's story.

> The first time I arrived here [South Africa] was on the 13th of September 2007 and I was sixteen years old. I found a job helping where they were building houses. I arrived at the church in May 2008, and in July all children were called and told a school was being opened, that is when Albert Street School was opened. I realised then that there was no future in working for construction companies or doing gardening, so I decided it is better I go to school. I completed my O-Levels in 2011, I wrote five subjects and I passed them all. My parents could not take me to school [back in Zimbabwe], so this is a precious gift for me. I am doing an online course. Part of the scholarship terms and conditions are that after completing the higher certificate I will get an internship, after which I can further my studies with a degree, that is, if I qualify. (Musa, male, 23, a college student)

Powerful aspirations occur when the individual is pursuing what they value in life and the structural conditions enable this. The individual has control in different aspects of their life, such as the emotional, physical, and psychological. This is accompanied by flexible social and structural conditions in terms of policies and schooling access. Powerful aspirations explain well the positive relationship between an individual's strong agency and positive available structural conditions. However, reference to positive structural influences does not suggest that the available conditions naturally make it easy for migrant youth to form educational aspirations. Rather, it suggests that despite the circumstances, an individual may choose to see potential in an otherwise difficult environment, which is why understanding the nuanced intersections of agency and social conditions is so important. For example, while some may view migration policies and a lack of documentation as limiting, others may nonetheless find possibilities within these systems. Similarly, although lack of recognized documentation and finance may limit one's choice of studying at a first-class school, some may view the opportunity to complete their secondary schooling irrespective of the quality of the school (structural condition) to be a positive conversion factor in the realization of their aspirations. Thus, negative experiences can motivate an individual to raise their aspirations in order to overcome their present conditions. Here, the level of agency determines how far the individual goes with the hope of living a life that they value. If this expression of agency is further supported by positive individuals within the aspirations window, one may remain motivated. As such, motivation and mentorship can be viewed as important factors that have a positive impact on an individual's life (Fried & MacCleave, 2010) and for clear and powerful aspirations to be in place, different positive influences, which are not necessarily material, are required. As some of these influences may not necessarily be positive at all times, one needs to be able and willing (agency) to maneuver within these structures and conditions (conversion factors).

Persistent Aspirations

Persistent aspirations can be placed at different points along two intersecting continua of negative external influences (social and structural conditions) and high levels of agency (internal influences) operating in the space of the aspirations window. Aspirations can be viewed as persistent when an individual is exercising agency, but social and structural factors are such that it becomes extremely difficult to realize these aspirations. The following extract is an example of persistent aspirations:

> I completed my education [at Albert Street School] in 2010. I then registered for an Environmental Management program, but had to drop out due to finance problems. Its financial problems that have made me to be stuck like this, but what I know is once I get a job that can give me a stable salary, I can budget and continue with my studies. Right now I want to study Project Management; it's a short course that can give me a better job. Once I get a diploma in Project Management, then I can look for a job, and then once I get a job, I can pursue my degree. (Elton, male, 25, a jobseeker)

It can be argued that this type of aspiration is influenced by intrinsic motivation more than extrinsic motivation, although they have instrumental values tied to what they want to achieve (such as gainful employment). Regardless of present conditions, the individual maintains both high levels of agency and remains optimistic that their aspirations will be attained in the future. In some cases, an individual may have the determination to raise and/or achieve their aspirations, but structural conditions may be too restrictive. Restrictive conditions may be a result of current structural conditions or the result of one's past choices. For example, one may personally meet the necessary requirements to enroll at university, but fail to maneuver through the system due to the costs involved, and yet still remain persistent about the possibility of realizing their aspirations.

Conditions in persistent aspirations do not, necessarily, suggest that aspirations are unachievable, but rather may take a longer time, depending on changes in the structural arrangements. The interaction of high levels of agency and constraining structural conditions points to the role that personal conversion factors such as motivation and resilience can play. Thus, it is important to understand that constraining conversion factors do not always result in lesser agency but can also motivate one to exercise higher levels of agency. If the agentic individual can meet up with an opportunity, these aspirations have the potential to become "powerful." What is important is for one to actively seek opportunities, rather than assuming that opportunities will arise naturally or randomly in the future.

Individuals experiencing persistent aspiration are potentially at risk of aspirations resignation if circumstances do not change and they may give up these aspirations at a later stage.

Frustrated Aspirations

Frustrated aspirations can be placed at different points along two intersecting continua of negative external influences (social and structural conditions) and low levels of agency (internal influences) operating in the space of the aspirations window as illustrated below:

> I came to Albert Street School and tried to learn there, but I had so many personal challenges. Now I'm doing nothing. When I was still at home I wished to become a doctor. Now I think if I could do a course at college like catering it would be better, but I know it's difficult for me to get the money to go to school. Really, I don't know what I will do. In the first place I am not sure if I will finish off my schooling or not; it's very difficult to have dreams when you do not have schooling. As of now, I will take anything that comes my way because I don't have a choice, and though I want to change my life, right now I don't have a plan of how to do that. If now I am looking for a piece job [so] that I can feed and clothe myself so that even when I go out, people see me like a human being. I do wish that while I am here I could get the opportunity to complete school. It's difficult to have job security if you are not educated, but I have also seen that there are people who will not have everything in life. (Obert, male, 20, a jobseeker)

These aspirations are characterized by low levels of individual agency and negative influences of social and structural conditions. The combination and interaction of these two contexts has the potential to lead to a situation where an individual resigns their aspirations and this resignation is accompanied by the lack of belief in oneself and in the social and structural conditions present, leading to frustrated aspirations. Similar to resigned aspirations, diverse factors may lead to low levels of agency, such as lack of motivation or one's personal history. However, in frustrated aspirations, low agency is accompanied by negative structural influences such that there seems to be no room for opportunities. According to Duflo (2012), low agency may be a result of the anticipation of likely failure by an individual who may then decide to hold back his or her efforts. Where there is absence of individual motivation, absence of the capability of hope and stringent structural conditions that limit opportunities, it becomes a challenge to start imagining the crossing of paths of opportunity and action. In the event that structures change, thereby narrowing the aspirations gap, those with frustrated aspirations may not actively seek and pursue new possibilities. According to scholars such as Appadurai (2004) and Ray (2006), such a frustration of aspirations can create poverty traps.

UNDERSTANDING EDUCATIONAL ASPIRATIONS FORMATION FROM A DISADVANTAGE PERSPECTIVE

The characteristics of poverty identified by Anand and Sen (1997, p. 5), such as lives robbed of dignity, confidence, and material wellbeing, were evident in the experiences of the migrant youth interviewed in this study. While "income-based" understandings of disadvantage are simple to understand, they do not look at other aspects of disadvantage, which are important for understanding valued human wellbeing. For example, a migrant youth may enjoy the benefits of a particular economic activity, yet be illiterate and lack critical thinking skills, both of which are important in expanding the capacity to aspire. This points to the value of formulating a broader understanding of "capability disadvantage." While poverty may be viewed as capability disadvantage, experiences of disadvantage among the migrant youth provide a way to think about poverty as both a challenge and a catalyst for critically thinking about and reflecting on one's life. That most of the migrant youth realized the need to get an education in order to live a better life is an indication of their awareness that education is important in reducing poverty, in being able to provide for themselves and the rest of their families. This widens our understanding of migration from a development perspective.

Wolff and De-Shalit's (2007, p. 72) view of disadvantage as a state "when one's functionings are or become insecure" or when one has a "lack of genuine opportunities to secure functionings" (p. 84) was apt for understanding the migrants' narratives. This view of disadvantage brings together conversion factors and the impact of agency and freedoms to realize valued educational aspirations. Indicators such as the resources available and constraints on basic capabilities such as shelter and food can be used to determine the extent of disadvantage among a group of people (Wolff & De-Shalit, 2007). Migrant youths' experiences of push-and-pull factors leading to migration, together with their experiences in South Africa, may be considered evidence that these conditions place them at a degree of disadvantage and deprivation associated with poverty. This therefore calls for an understanding of how their lives could be improved.

Although the migrant experiences reported on here may enlighten us about the South-to-South migration and development and their potential to realize educational aspirations, the sample is not representative of the vast majority of migrants that come from other countries. How many migrants are actually able to pursue their educational aspirations is a question that remains unclear, as not many schools in the country cater for marginalized migrants. For the majority of South-to-South migrants who do not get the opportunity to engage in higher education, vulnerability remains very much a reality, even in a different national context. Such educational and knowledge disadvantages have the potential to increase levels of poverty, whereas access to these capabilities may in turn improve other dimensions important for valued wellbeing. Therefore, the aim of arguing for higher education for marginalized migrant youth is not necessarily to claim that university education is for everyone. Rather, it is about having meaningful educational choices, and the opportunity to progress to different types of higher education, including vocational education. In looking at marginalized migrant youths' capacity to aspire to education, a number of studies in the field of higher education are relevant (see Walker, 2012; Walker & Mkwananzi, 2015). To address inequalities, stakeholders in education should ask themselves about the kind of world and society they would want to work and live in, and then look at how education can help to create that kind of world (Walker, 2012). Such an approach would enhance freedoms and begin to address the disadvantages hindering the development of a better society, including the advancement and realization of one's aspirations.

Appadurai (2004) supports the need to advance educational aspirations among disadvantaged individuals, as better-educated people tend to have wider horizons and aspirations with the potential to lift them out of poverty. This instrumental value of education is important in bringing forth a social change directed toward justice (Walker, 2010). For the migrant youth, being in education is imperative, since the confidence, resilience, motivation, knowledge, and navigational skills that can be acquired through education are preconditions for participation in work, life, and community areas (Walker, 2012). From her earlier work, Walker (2006) suggests that education is a capability enhancer, especially for individuals from marginalized and disadvantaged backgrounds. Through education, people become better positioned to pursue what they have reason to value, which for migrant youth is first and foremost to escape poverty. In their work on disadvantaged youth, Walker and Mkwananzi (2015) further reinforce the capacity of education to reduce disadvantage. The realization of educational aspirations and use of capabilities acquired have the potential to enhance young people's quality of life and the lives of their families. Thus, the potential long-term contribution of education for marginalized migrants is significant, even though not easily measurable as it encompasses both intrinsic and instrumental contributions in a transnational sphere. Developmentally, education may well be used for self-reliance, but even more so in the longer term to rebuild the countries of origin of these migrants.

WHAT DOES THIS MEAN FOR HUMAN DEVELOPMENT?

The understanding of the formation of the four types of aspirations presented in this chapter is important for both education and human development, as it shows how potential educational aspirations could be raised among marginalized migrants for the betterment of their lives. In presenting the influence of external and internal conditions (conversion factors) on aspirations formation at different times of the migrant's lives, a foundation from which to build is provided for approaches to development, including educational interventions. As Conradie and Robeyns (2013) assert, aspirations have a role to play in small-scale human development initiatives by assuming a capabilities-selection role and an agency-unlocking role. This agency unlocking role would include capabilities identification, that is, identifying the capabilities needed and valued by the migrant youth in a given context and directing interventions toward advancing and creating these capabilities. The creation (and advancement) of such capabilities would potentially lead to the youth being active agents in the realization of their aspirations. Thus, understanding the nature and formation of aspirations is important not only for the individuals concerned, but also requires collective efforts. Structural bodies, such as governments, educational institutions, and Non-Governmental Organizations (NGOs), ought to advance policies and development initiatives that enhance the capabilities and freedoms necessary for human development. Fostering human development through aspirations formation would be characterized by the extent to which migrant youth have meaningful options for a better life and the freedoms to pursue lives they value, including opportunities for an education.

CONCLUSION

We have provided a theoretical conceptualization of educational aspirations formation among marginalized groups, in this case, migrant youth. The interaction of capabilities, conversion factors and aspirations has shown the complexity and multilevel intersections involved in aspirations formation. Hence, for the freedom of marginalized migrant youth to be enhanced, there is a need to understand these complex intersections at both individual and structural levels. At individual levels, factors such as voice and agency require attention and support. At structural levels, power relations in the form of policies need to be reworked to fit the present-day challenges of migration in South Africa. This includes promoting the freedom of voice so that marginalized migrant youth express what is valuable to them, as well as have the space to name the injustices they face. Addressing these injustices would also entail making higher education a choice that migrant youth who qualify can realistically make. Availability of educational opportunities has the potential to address a wide range of social ills that are a result of poverty, such as a high prevalence of Human Immunodeficiency Virus (HIV) and Acquired Immuno Deficiency Syndrome (AIDS), high rates of substance abuse, and high rates of criminal and violent behavior (see Mkwananzi, 2013). In so doing, the benefits of access to higher education for migrant youth would go far beyond the articulation of educational aspirations, and move toward breaking down ongoing systematic poverty faced by marginalized migrant youth.

ACKNOWLEDGMENTS

The authors gratefully acknowledge funding from the SARCHi Chair in Higher Education and Human Development at the University of the Free State, and, in particular, the funding provided by the South African National Research Foundation Research Chairs Initiative (Grant number U86540).

NOTE

1. For example, 1951 Convention relating to the Status of Refugees, the 1967 Protocol relating to the Status of Refugees, and 1969 Organisation for African Unity Convention governing Specific Aspects of Refugee Problems in Africa.

REFERENCES

Anand, S., & Sen, A. (1997). Concepts of human development and poverty: A multidimensional perspective. Retrieved from http://clasarchive.berkeley.edu/Academics/courses/center/fall2007/sehnbruch/UNDP%20Anand%20and%20Sen%20Concepts%20of%20HD%201997.pdf

Appadurai, A. (2004). The capacity to aspire. In M. Walton & V. Rao (Eds.), *Culture and public action* (pp. 59–84). Stanford, CA: Stanford University Press.

Bernstein, A. (1998). Unworkable and costly. Retrieved from http://www.cde.org.za/images/pdf/ Unworkable_and_costly_MR.pdf

Birchall, J. (2016). Gender, age and migration: An extended briefing. Retrieved from https://open-docs.ids.ac.uk/opendocs/bitstream/handle/123456789/10410/Gender%20Age%20and%20 Migration%20Extended%20Briefing.pdf?sequence=1

Chiappero-Martinetti, E., & Venkatapuram, S. (2014). The capability approach: A framework for population studies. *African Population Studies, 28*(2), 708–720. Retrieved from http://dx.doi. org/10.11564/28-2-604

Conradie, I. (2013). *Aspirations and capabilities: The design and analysis of an action research project in Khayelitsha, Cape Town.* Ph.D. thesis, University of the Western Cape. Retrieved from http:// etd.uwc.ac.za/xmlui/handle/11394/4608

Conradie, I. & Robeyns, I. (2013). Aspirations and Human Development Interventions. *Journal of Human Development and Capabilities, 14*(4), 559–580. DOI: 10.1080/19452829.2013.827637.

Crush, J., & Ramachandran, S. (2010). Xenophobia, international migration and development. *Journal of Human Development and Capabilities, 11*(2), 209–228.

DeJaeghere, J. (2016). Girls' educational aspirations and agency: Imagining alternative futures through schooling in a low-resourced Tanzanian community. *Critical Studies in Education, 59*(1), 1–19. doi:10.1080/17508487.2016.1188835

Duflo, E. (2012). *Human values and the design of the fight against poverty.* Tanner Lectures, May 2012. Retrieved from http://mahindrahumanities.fas.harvard.edu/content/lecture-2-esther-duflo-human-values-and-design-fight-against-poverty

Fried, T., & MacCleave, A. (2010). Influence of role models and mentors on female graduate students' choice of science as a career. *Alberta Journal of Educational Research, 55*(4), 482–496.

Gordon, S. (2010). Migrants in a 'state of exception': Xenophobia and the role of the post-apartheid state. In M.S. Mapadimeng & S. Khan (Eds.), *Contemporary social issues in Africa: Cases in Gaborone, Kampala and Durban.* Pretoria, South Africa: AISA.

Handmaker, J., De la Hunt, L.-A., & Klareen, J. (2001). *Perspective on refugee protection in South Africa.* Lawyers for Human Rights, South Africa. Retrieved from file:///C:/Users/UVP/ Downloads/Perspectives_on_Refugee_Protection_in_So.pdf

Hart, C. J. (2013). *Aspirations, education and social justice: Applying Sen and Bourdieu.* London: Bloomsbury.

Khan, F. (2007). *Patterns and policies of migration in South Africa: Changing patterns and the need for a comprehensive approach.* Cape Town, South Africa: University of Cape Town Refugee Rights Project. Retrieved from http://www.refugeerights.uct.ac.za/downloads/refugeerights.uct.ac.za/ patterns_policies_migration_FKhan.doc

Keogh, J., Garvis, S., Pendergast, D., & Diamond, P. (2012). Self-determination: Using agency, effi-cacy and resilience (AER) to counter novice teachers experiences of intensification. *Australian Journal of Teacher Education, 37*(8), 46–65. Retrieved from http://ro.ecu.edu.au/ajte/vol37/iss8/4

Mkwananzi, F. (2013). Challenges for vulnerable young people in accessing higher education: A case study of Orange Farm Informal Settlement, South Africa. Unpublished Masters Dissertation. University of the Free State, Bloemfontein, South Africa.

National Youth Policy 2009–2014. (2018). Retrieved from: http://www.thepresidency.gov.za/download/ file/fid/122

Nussbaum, M. (2011). *Creating capabilities: The human development approach.* Cambridge, MA: Harvard University Press.

Ray, D. (2006). Aspirations, poverty, and economic change. In A. V. Banerjee, R. Benabo, & D. Mookherjee (Eds.), *Understanding poverty* (pp. 409–421). Oxford: Oxford University Press.

Robeyns, I. (2005). The capability approach: A theoretical survey. *Journal of Human Development, 6*(1), 93–114.

Sen, A. (1999). *Development as freedom.* Oxford: Oxford University Press.

Sen, A. (2009). *The idea of justice.* London: Penguin.

United Nations High Commissioner for Refugees. (2018). *Convention and Protocol Relating to the Status of Refugees.* Retrieved from http://www.unhcr.org/3b66c2aa10

Van Dijk, H., Foeken, D., & van Til, K. (2001). Population mobility in Africa: An overview. In M. de Bruijn, R. van Dijk, & D. Foeken (Eds.), *Mobile Africa: Changing patterns of movement in Africa and beyond* (Vol. 1, pp. 9–26). Leiden, Netherlands: Brill.

Walker, M. (2005). Amartya Sen's capability approach and education. *Education Action Research*, *13*(1), 103–110.

Walker, M. (2006). *Higher education pedagogies: A capabilities approach*. Maidenhead: Open University Press and the Society for Research into Higher Education.

Walker, M. (2010). Critical Capability Pedagogies and University Education. *Educational Philosophy and Theory*, *42*(8), 898–917.

Walker, M. (2012). A capital or capabilities education narrative in a world of staggering inequalities. *International Journal of Educational Development*, *32*, 384–393.

Walker, M., & Mkwananzi, F. (2015). Challenges in accessing higher education: A case study of marginalised young people in one South African informal settlement. *International Journal of Educational Development*, *40*, 40–49.

Wentzel, M. & Tlabela, K. (2006). Historical background to South African migration. In, P, Kok., D, Gelderblom., J.O., Oucho & J, Van Zyl. (Eds). *Migration in South and southern Africa: dynamics and determinants* (pp. 71–96). Cape Town, HSRC Press.

Wilson-Strydom, M., & Walker, M. (2015). A capabilities-friendly conceptualisation of flourishing in and through education. *Journal of Moral Education*, *44*(3), 310–324. doi:10.1080/03057240. 2015.1043878

Wolff, J., & De-Shalit, A. (2007). *Disadvantage*. Oxford: Oxford University Press.

CHAPTER 3

OCCUPATION-BASED DIDACTIC MODEL FOR ENGLISH LANGUAGE TEACHING TO REFUGEES TO IMPROVE THEIR SUSTAINABILITY AND SOCIAL INTEGRATION

Haydeé Ramírez Lozada

ABSTRACT

With the purpose to contribute to the English language teaching-learning process of refugees, as part of a university linking project carried out at the Pontifical Catholic University of Ecuador, Esmeraldas Campus, to foster refugees' sustainability and social integration, an educative investigation was carried out with the help of the Applied Linguistics School at the mentioned university, in collaboration with the United Nations Refugee Agency, from 2016 to 2017. The population was formed by 20 student refugees and 4 students from the Applied Linguistics School who worked as teachers. The refugees who attended the course needed English language literacy because they were going to be resettled in other countries, which were English-speaking ones. With the empirical-analytical and hermeneutic methods, and the techniques of observation and survey, a diagnosis of the teaching-learning process was made, which revealed the necessity to teach English to the referred refugees based on their communicative needs, according to their jobs. As a result, an occupation-based didactic model for English language teaching to refugees, with its components, principles, and laws, was designed, which permitted the proposal of a didactic

Language, Teaching and Pedagogy for Refugee Education
Innovations in Higher Education Teaching and Learning, Volume 15, 43–57
Copyright © 2019 by Emerald Publishing Limited
All rights of reproduction in any form reserved
ISSN: 2055-3641/doi:10.1108/S2055-364120180000015005

methodology for fostering meaningful learning, motivation, and communica-
tive competence in English in connection with refugees' occupations.

Keywords: Education; English language teaching; refugees; social integration; communication; motivation

INTRODUCTION

The United Nations (n.d.) have stated many objectives to end poverty and ine-qualities, promoting peaceful and inclusive societies, which protect man, as a generic term, and all his rights. The sustainable development goals "recognize that ending poverty must go together with strategies that build economic growth and addresses a range of social needs including education, health, social protec-tion, and job opportunities…" (p. 1).

It is the responsibility of countries that send and receive migrants to take care of these goals, since refugees have different social needs to be solved. Therefore, many programs have been carried out under the leadership of the United Nations (n.d.) to integrally fight for the provision of sustainable lives for refugees.

When analyzing what sustainable development means, it is important to con-sider the following points:

- It has been defined as development that meets the needs of the present without compromising the ability of future generations to meet their own needs.
- It calls for concerted efforts toward building an inclusive, sustainable, and resilient future for people and the planet.
- For its achievement, it is crucial to harmonize three core elements: economic growth, social inclusion, and environmental protection. These elements are interconnected and all are crucial for the wellbeing of individuals and societies.
- It should mean that eradicating poverty in all its forms and dimensions is an indispensable requirement for sustainable development. To this end, there must be promotion of sustainable, inclusive, and equitable economic growth, creating greater opportunities for all, reducing inequalities, raising basic standards of living, fostering equitable social development and inclusion, and promoting an integrated and sustainable management of natural resources and ecosystems.

In response to this demand, the educational system has great responsibility. Precisely, the University of the twenty-first century has included four important dimensions in its formative processes: teaching, linking with the community, investigation, and management. Linking with the community projects favor the collaboration of high educative institutions with poor people, those who suffer from inequalities, to whom the population of refugees belongs.

Providing educative opportunities is one of the major priorities of the com-munities of refugees. Parents and children all over the world affirm that educa-tion is the "key for the future" since education may bring about a cultural rise and development of moral values. As Dryden-Peterson (2011) states, despite not knowing "what will happen tomorrow," education brings stability and hope, what implies peace, solution to economic and social problems, and motivation to learn, work, and live. This is a good way for eliminating refugees' poverty. As affirmed by the United Nations (n.d.), contributing to the eradication of poverty in all its forms, is an indispensable requisite for sustainable development.

The right of refugees to education (Dryden-Peterson, 2011, p. 8) is established in Article 22 of the Convention about the statutes of Refugees of 1951; the Resolution 64/290 (July 2010) of the Council of Human Rights of the United Nations General Agency about the right of education in emergency situations, and in the project of resolution on the Council of Human Rights about the right to education of refugees, migrants, and asylum applicants (June 2011).

One of the linking projects carried out by the Pontifical Catholic University of Ecuador, Esmeraldas Campus, in collaboration with the United Nations Refugee Agency, has been *Strengthening of sustainable means of life and local integration in Esmeraldas*, and one of the areas that this project has included is the English language literacy to refugees, which has been developed with the help of students from the Applied Linguistics School, who have had the responsibility to work as teachers.

Teaching English to this community of refugees has been significant because they are generally resettled in English language speaking countries, such as the United States of America, New Zealand, Australia, and others. When organizing the curriculum to teach these refugees, the lack of a didactic model, which could give support to a methodology to help teachers organize the didactic units and lessons to teach, was noticed. For this, a diagnosis of the students' language learning needs was crucial, as well as an analysis of the linguistic theory that deals with the teaching of English for Occupational Purposes.

TEACHING ENGLISH FOR OCCUPATIONAL PURPOSES

According to Hutchinson and Waters (1994), to teach with specific purposes refers to the fact that the contents and methods selected are determined by the students' learning needs. This implies the necessity to make a diagnosis of what the refugees need to learn in regards to vocabulary and communicative functions in order to cover their needs of social interaction.

Social interaction demands refugees to communicate using terms in relation to their occupations; therefore, the branch of English for Specific Purposes that must be considered is English for Occupational Purposes. It requires a diagnosis of the occupations the refugees carry out or think they will carry out to design the contents of the curriculum.

For the curriculum design, it has also been imperative to make a diagnosis of the methodological needs of the teachers of English, which should be regarding the organization of the teaching-learning process of English for Occupational Purposes to refugees, to get them to be able to communicate with native speakers of the language. Consequently, it has been important to consider some of the fundamentals of communicative teaching.

THE COMMUNICATIVE APPROACH TO LANGUAGE TEACHING

The communicative approach to language teaching demands English teachers the design of syllabuses for teaching in a way that students can communicate with the language. The advocates of a skills-based syllabus proclaimed the teaching of the four main skills of the language: listening, speaking, reading, and writing, in an integrated way, as it occurs in the real world (Richards, 2006). The advocates of a functional syllabus, on the other hand, demanded the organization of contents in accordance with the functions the students should be able to carry out in English.

Apart from taking into consideration the features of communicative competence of the Common European Framework of Reference for Languages (CEFR), as stated by the Council of Europe (n.d.), either present theoretical or empirical research on communicative competence is based on the models proposed by Canale and Swain (1980), Bachman and Palmer (1996).

In their theoretical foundations on communicative competence, Canale & Swain (1980) proposed at first three principal components, i.e. fields of knowledge and skills: grammatical, sociolinguistic, and strategic competence. In an advanced version of this model, Canale (1983, 1984) transferred some elements from sociolinguistic competence into the fourth they proposed: discourse competence.

The model projected in this study considers the development of students' communicative competence in the four dimensions mentioned above.

PEDAGOGICAL THEORIES THAT SUPPORT THE OCCUPATION-BASED DIDACTIC MODEL FOR ENGLISH LANGUAGE TEACHING TO REFUGEES

This model is supported by the Contextualized Didactics (Alvarez de Zayas, 1997) and the Developing Didactics (Silvestre & Zilberstein, 2002). Besides, the contributions of Alvarez de Zayas (1999) were considered in relation to the necessary connection that should be between school and life, and among the components of the didactic process.

To achieve competent students in a language, the use of a Humanistic Theory is of paramount importance. As affirmed by Williams and Burden (2005) quoting Rogers, there are important elements that justify a humanistic approach to education. First, they refer to the fact that human beings have a great potential to learning, what denotes that the learning process will be significant for them if what is taught is understood as important by them. It means that it is essential to involve the learners' feelings in the teaching-learning process. Taking into consideration the occupational needs of refugees and other communicative needs, for designing the English didactic process for them, shows how humanistic this process is.

To believe in man as a human being makes us consider the Liberating Theory (Freire, n.d.) in the English class. It is outstanding to reject the idea that people keep ignorant without learning the culture of the powerful, because each citizen is a carrier of culture with his/her personal vision of reality. Moreover, the provision of linguistic resources to develop the language gives the refugees a hope to express freely without being afraid of being negatively criticized.

Similarly, Hooks (2003) emphasizes the importance of promoting learning among students and teachers, so that any teacher may have the power to use the classroom as a domain. The idea is of creating a friendly and free environment to teach, where students, in this case refugees, may express their feelings, and where respect may prevail. According to Hooks (2003) the English classroom should be a place where the minds of the students can expand, doing collaborative work either students–students or students–teachers.

Refugees should feel free to speak English about their life experiences, their family, their favorite dishes, their music, and other cultural issues. Learning English as the international language of communication helps refugees not only to prepare for sustainability in their resettlement, but also to defend their own culture and learn the culture of the English language speakers, and of the speakers of other languages who live in the host countries. Therefore, they can enrich their own culture in a process of interculturality and multiculturality. This may be summarized in four important points that Magsino, quoted by Tadayon and Khodi (2016), considers in situations of multiculturalism: cultural retention, cultural sharing, equality of opportunity, and individual freedom.

One of the ways to open refugees to culture and knowledge is by means of upgrading courses, either on English or any other subjects of interest, to which they generally attend with much wish to learn. Referring to this, Martin (2016) states how refugees bring with them their capacities, their strength, and their desire of skills upgrading. He emphasizes that to invest in the education of these young people is to invest not only in their future, but also in the development of the country. This stresses the need to teach English to refugees by means of simulated social interactive activities that may resemble the ones carried out by the native speakers of the language.

The necessity to achieve learning in a social context, in the interchange of experiences, gives prominence to the Historical-Cultural Approach in this study. Domínguez (2013), quoting Vygotsky, points out the role of society in the formation of the individual's psychic and personality developmental processes. This approach defines clearly two evolutive levels in the students' learning process. One level is related to the real capacities of learning and another with the possibilities to learn with the help of other students or the teacher: Zone of Present Development and Zone of Proximal Development. The latter characterizes the prospective development of the individual to promote a new zone of development in each moment of learning, which dialectically denies the antecedent one with the application of new forms that let him/her work and look for knowledge by himself/herself, letting him/her be prepared for Self-Regulated-Learning.

Zimmerman and Schunk (2011) assert that:

> Self-Regulated Learning refers to the process whereby learners personally activate and sustain cognitions, affects and behaviors that are systematically oriented toward the attainment of personal goals. By setting personal goals, learners create self-oriented feedback loops, through which they can monitor their effectiveness and adapt their functioning (p. 1).

With English lessons, refugees may learn the language by achieving goals directed to their needs, they may feel more motivated to learn, and more proactive during the learning process, establishing good relations with their classmates and their teachers, as mediators in the teaching-learning process, being willing to communicate in English.

PREVIOUS STUDIES

Adkins, Birman, and Sample (1999) emphasize that when teaching English to refugees, it is necessary to help them cope with the new culture, which includes values, beliefs, and traditions; in this way, refugees may adjust to a new life; therefore, they can obtain mental health through stress reduction. These authors affirm that the necessary communicative functions to teach are regarding buying food and giving directions. They also express the need to create didactic materials for language learning, according to learners' needs. The contribution to mental health may be expressed with the inclusion of some communicative functions in relation to going to the doctor, looking for an adequate place to live, and buying food and drinks.

In preceding investigations with refugees, Ramirez, Perlaza, Escobar, and Lopez (2016), in PUCE Esmeraldas, Ecuador, reported how the English language can be taught in a multilevel classroom, considering the students' learning needs for the design of teaching activities, with an emphasis on the use of the Ludic Methodology to make the learning environment more flexible and pleasant, therefore more contributing to learning.

METHODS

A qualitative investigation was carried out with the empirical-analytical and hermeneutic methods, with the techniques of observation and survey applied to a population of 20 refugees and 4 students from the Linguistics School, who worked as English teachers in the linking project *Strengthening of sustainable means of life and local integration in Esmeraldas*, during the academic years 2016–2017.

The English lessons were taught in the Pontifical Catholic University of Ecuador in Esmeraldas. There were two teachers assigned per group of students, which were divided into Children group and Adults group. There was one PhD teacher-investigator, who oversaw the linking project, in the English language Literacy Program, supervising teachers and carrying out the educative research.

RESULTS OF THE EDUCATIVE INVESTIGATION

The methods of observation and survey revealed the following findings:

- The main communicative functions that refugees needed to learn were: looking for a job, buying, selling, talking to a doctor about their health status, requesting information about medications, treatment, asking and talking about directions, and ordering food.

- The vocabulary mostly needed was in relation to occupations, cell phones, clothes, food, medications, illnesses, symptoms and signs, tickets, rents, numbers, and the alphabet.
- The grammatical structures were related to the present, past, and future simple tenses, the use of modals (can, should, and must), the use of pronouns, the use of there is/there are, and how much and how many.
- The refugees under study were slow learners. They showed fear of making mistakes. Anyway, they had a desire to learn, and expressed their need of a didactic material for doing their independent work.
- The teachers of English used active methods. They expressed their need of a didactic model and methodology to teach English.

When a diagnosis about the most frequent entrepreneurships that the refugees carried out in Esmeraldas was made, it was revealed that they had relation with selling cell phones, clothes, and food. This demanded the teaching of terminology in English based on those activities.

In regard to other learning needs, it was revealed that the refugees needed the language for the following communicative functions: giving and asking for directions, spelling their names, greeting, and giving personal information, which are associated with vital needs for a job interview, besides, visiting the doctor, buying medication, knowing the parts of the body, and renting a house.

Related to the way the refugees wanted to learn English, the majority (80%) preferred to learn in groups or pairs, in communication with others. They also liked to learn with explanations, using dialogues, and by means of a Ludic Methodology, through games and songs. A reason for this could have been that most of the refugees revealed anxiety caused by living in a foreign context, with a different culture.

These previous results, and the theoretical review done, permitted the design of a didactic model for English language teaching to refugees based on their occupations, which is described as follows.

OCCUPATION-BASED DIDACTIC MODEL TO TEACH ENGLISH TO REFUGEES

Structure

Didactic Components
Personal.
The teacher of English: He/she plays an active role in the process, monitoring the language interchange among the students (refugees), when practicing and constructing new knowledge. The teacher is the monitor and facilitator, providing the students with a flexible environment, with dynamic activities. Therefore, the teacher of English not only looks for the students' cognitive development, but also for their affective growth, establishing a relationship of love among them, with a liberating approach. It will let the teacher know the students' sorrows and happiness, achievements and experiences. From this moment on, the communicative activity may be carried out.

The students: They keep an active role in the teaching-learning process, interacting with their teachers and classmates, doing pair work and group work, in a collaborative way. This will make the students communicate freely, improving their knowledge.

Impersonal.

Contents: The contents of each didactic unit should be structured according to the students' diagnosed needs, which are derived from their occupations. Apart from this, the language of survival will be taken into consideration, following a topic-based approach, with the use of some communicative functions, among which the most important are: introducing yourself, looking for a job, expressing ability and possibility, expressing existence, buying food, clothes, medications, selling food, clothes and cellphones, and visiting the doctor.

The vocabulary will be also linked to the students' learning needs. A practical activity will be carried out introducing the alphabet and numbers. The most important grammatical structures to be taught will be the use of pronouns, the use of the present, past and future tenses of the verb, the use of there is/there are, the use of the modal verbs can, must, should, and the use of how much and how many.

Objectives: The objectives will direct the process, expressing the purposes that will be accomplished in each didactic unit and each lesson. They will be expressed according to the Bloom's Taxonomy (Bloom, . et al, n.d.), in connection with the students' levels of assimilation.

In the teaching-learning process to refugees, there are some illiterate or semiilliterate adult students speaking in their mother tongue. This has an implication on the way contents to teach English should be structured, in this case from the simple to the complex.

Methods: The teaching methods should be selected according to the results of the diagnosis made to the students, who will have the freedom to choose the way they would like to learn, though it is significant to respect the teacher's methodological decision. He/she should know what methods to use according to the students' levels of learning.

The Ludic Methodology, using songs and games, may be very useful because it permits relaxation in the learning process by means of stress reduction and flexibility. Through this methodology, the students are encouraged to participate since the first day, despite their learning limitations.

The Communicative Approach to language teaching may be used because social interaction is overriding in the learning process of a foreign language. The students should interact in pairs and groups to learn. This also permits more language development in the class time assigned. When the students are working in pairs, all of them are talking at the same time under the teacher's guidance and control.

The use of the Communicative Approach does not mean that ludic activities cannot be used. On the contrary, to achieve the different dimensions of communicative competence, linguistic, discourse, strategic and cultural, games or activities using songs may be designed and put into practice. They have proven to be very much contributing to English language learning because lots of words may be used freely, different grammatical structures may be combined, and pronunciation may be practiced, as well as word order. Besides, students get prepared for the topic of the lesson: food, looking for a job, at the shop, my visit to the doctor, among others.

The Ludic Methodology in communicative activities creates an environment of liberation in the classroom, letting the students be involved in learning with enthusiasm.

Didactic Materials

To achieve freedom and communication in the classroom, some didactic materials should be designed according to the topic of the unit, and in relation to the students' learning needs. They should be designed and used in such a way that they benefit motivation, and, therefore, promote learning.

Some didactic materials that may be effective, among others, are flash-cards, pictures, board-games, videos, projector, screen, balls, boxes, posters, color pencils, and markers.

Teaching Organization Form. The English language teaching-learning process to refugees will be organized in a comprehensive practical English-language class, by means of which the teachers may facilitate the development of the four main skills of the language: listening, speaking, reading, and writing, in integrating activities. They should be designed considering the students' language learning needs in a liberating, humanistic, and communicative environment.

Evaluation. Emphasis should be made on the formative evaluation, where the progressive development of knowledge and abilities in free communicative activities will be considered. Self-evaluation, coevaluation, and heteroevaluation should be applied. They are made possible because of the flexibility of the class environment.

Each student's achievement will be reinforced by means of expressions of reassurance pronounced by the teacher. This will create a feeling of success in the students, which potentiates learning. If the students feel that they are not learning, a sense of frustration may invade them, limiting learning.

Didactic Principles

The didactic principles that rule the English language teaching-learning process to refugees are as follows:

- *Communicative interaction* consists of the collaborative interchange in pairs or groups, among the students, as well as the interchange students–teachers.

In this principle, the Socio-Cultural theory of Vygotsky is fulfilled in its asser-
tion of the primacy of the interpsychological sphere of learning, expressed by
learning in social relations, over the intrapsychological one, which refers to
learning occurring in the minds of the students.
- *Freedom in the teaching-learning process* emphasizes that in an environment
  of freedom, without being constrained to specific activities, language content,
  and topic area, refugees can learn easily with activities that may be in constant
  change in accordance with the diagnosis of learning needs.
- *Humanism in the didactic process* is expressed by a climate of respect and love
  for man generically, as a human being, full of dreams, aspirations and needs,
  no matter his origin.

Learning needs-based teaching is a characteristic of English for Specific
Purposes, directed at teaching what and how the students need to learn. In the
case of the model proposed, the teaching of English will be based on communicative functions, vocabulary, and grammar related to survival and according to the
occupations the students and relatives develop to survive.

Didactic Laws

The English language teaching–learning process to refugees should be ruled by
the following laws:

- The relationship among all the components of the didactic process, in response
  to the emergent needs of communication for survival.
- An unconditional love for the didactic process to refugees as a vulnerable
  population.
- An unconditional love for refugees and their inclusion to the English class.

These laws regulate the teaching-learning process from the epistemological
and praxiological points of view.

METHODOLOGY TO TEACH OCCUPATION-BASED ENGLISH TO REFUGEES

This methodology is a didactic tool that permits to carry the occupation-based
didactic model to teach English to refugees to classroom practice. It has one
general objective and four stages, which are described below.

General objective: To teach English for Occupational Purposes and survival to
refugees, from the communicative, humanistic, historical-cultural, and liberating
dimensions

Stage I

You are free to learn.

Objective: To provide the students with a liberating environment for learning

Procedure 1: Presentations (conversations students–students and students–teachers)

Students and teachers introduce themselves and start a social interchange, telling each other their names, making emphasis on pleasant phrases. This may be developed, at the beginning of the course, in the students' mother tongue. The teacher may also introduce phrases in English, making the students repeat them and use them in conversations either in pairs or groups.

The main communicative functions should be:

Introducing yourself/meeting people

Example:

My name is......../ What's your name?

Nice/Pleased to meet you

Nice/Pleased to meet you too

Then, the teacher may introduce the communicative function:

Requesting information about origin

I am from .....Where are you from?

I am from ......

Nice/Pleased to meet you!

Nice/Pleased to meet you too!

The students may be welcomed to class:

Welcome to the English class

Procedure 2: Systematization

It consists of the systematization of the communicative functions and lexicon studied for the presentations by means of dialogue expansion. Each of the parts of the dialogue, which have been practiced, is going to be mixed in a longer dialogue. By means of this procedure, the students may feel success in the learning process because their knowledge may consolidate. Therefore, less mistakes are going to be made. It is advisable not to finish the activity till each student can talk to each classmate and the teacher.

At the end of this stage, the students will feel that they are welcomed to the class, happy in an environment of friendly relations, relaxed and flexible.

With this first stage, being provided with a free and pleasant environment for learning English, students will feel security at being humanly treated, with love. This coincides with Hooks (2003) and Williams and Burden (2005), quoting Rogers, in the fact that this atmosphere is favorable for learning, which permits the students to expand, through collaborative work students–students and students–teachers. This is essential for preparing refugees for sustainability in English-speaking countries, where most of them are going to be resettled, since they will have to live and work in society. Consequently, they will need to make use of the English language.

Stage II

What you need to learn.

Objective: To make a diagnosis of the students' learning needs

Procedure 1: To apply a diagnostic test (survey) in the students' mother tongue. For this, the teacher should give necessary instructions to the students. In case of difficulties to write or read in the mother tongue, the teacher will read the questions and will copy the answers. This is mainly for illiterate students in their mother tongue. The teacher should not show any surprise; instead, they should help students accomplish the activity politely.

In the test, there should be items that allow students to express freely.

Procedure 2: To evaluate surveys. The teacher will check the students' answers and will evaluate their learning needs in order to design the teaching activities.

By means of this stage, the English teacher will have an accurate information about the students' learning needs, which will help him/her design the lessons and orient the English language teaching-learning process in a correct way, with the focus on the students' linguistic and occupational needs for facing their lives in English-speaking countries.

Stage III

Design of what you are going to learn.

Objective: To design the teaching activities according to the students' diagnosed learning needs

Procedure 1: To make a list of all the contents that will be included in each teaching unit.

Procedure 2: According to the contents, the teacher should organize the rest of the components of the didactic process: objectives, methods, didactic materials, teaching organization form, and evaluation. It is important to establish the role of the teacher and the students in each of the didactic units. In addition, the teacher should get the students to be involved in the elaboration of some didactic materials, such as pictures, flash cards, and objects, to make their participation active in the teaching-learning process, what enhances their leadership and therefore, benefits their language learning.

This stage permits the syllabus design and lesson planning. According to students' learning needs, the contents will be chosen, and the activities for teaching-listening comprehension, speaking, reading comprehension and writing will be designed based on those contents.

Stage IV

You are learning,

Objective: To teach the activities designed

Procedure 1: To motivate the students for the language teaching-learning process with the use of warm-ups. They may be designed based on ludic activities, such as games, songs, or poems.

Procedure 2: To introduce the new content by means of realistic situations, through which all the students may be involved with active participation. The teacher may look for the collaboration of students who have studied the English language before. Imitation will become a potential technique for learning.

It is crucial to keep a relaxing, flexible, and trustful atmosphere in the classroom, with instrumental music, pictures, colors, and flowers, to allow happiness since the very beginning of learning. To accomplish this, the teacher should keep a good mood, with a smile, and make use of polite and encouraging phrases. While the students work with others in pairs or groups, the teacher should monitor them and suggest ideas or correct mistakes with patience and very much politely.

In the free activities, when the students are using the language, the teacher should not interrupt them to correct mistakes. He/she should jot them down for further correction, which can be carried out at the end of the class, in another class, or a tutoring session.

In this final stage, the students will be taught English through realistic activities in relation to their occupations and the language for survival. The students will be organized in pairs or groups to interact since the very beginning, fulfilling the statements of the Historical-Cultural Approach to Language Teaching (Domínguez, 2013, quoting Vygotsky) about the role that society plays in the formation of the individual's psychic and personality developmental processes. When lessons are taught, the students are developing their communicative skills in the English language, in a relaxed and enjoyable atmosphere, which is required for effective learning.

CONCLUSIONS

The occupation-based didactic model for the English-language teaching-learning process to refugees becomes a fundamental didactic theoretical foundation for carrying out the didactic process of English to refugees and gives support to a methodology that permits the organization of the referred process in the classroom.

The methodology designed turns to an imperative didactic tool to improve refugees' meaningful learning, their motivation, and their communicative competence in the English language, their values as human beings, and their opportunities to be included in society.

The refugees' communicative competence upgrading will permit their empowerment in their interaction and will help them gain the same opportunities for social benefits as native speakers in their target setting of resettlements.

The methodology described may be applicable in all contexts where English is taught as a foreign language to refugees. The different stages may be used, as well, in the teaching-learning process of any other foreign language to refugees. However, in both cases, the use of the methodology should be preceded by a diagnosis of the refugees' learning needs.

REFERENCES

Adkins, M., Birman, D., & Sample, B. (1999). *Cultural adjustment, mental health, and ESL: The refugee experience, the role of the teacher, and ESL activities*. Denver, CO: Spring Institute for International Studies. Retrieved from http://www.springinstitute.org/wp-content/uploads/2016/04/culturaladjustmentmentalhealthandesl2.pdf

Alvarez de Zayas, C. (1999). *Didactics. School in Life*. La Habana, Cuba: Pueblo y Educación Editorial.

Alvarez de Zayas, R. M. (1997). *Towards a Comprehensive and Contextualized Curriculum*. La Habana, Cuba: Félix Varela Editorial.

Bachman & Palmer (1996). Model of Language Ability. Retrieved from http://www.ealta.eu.org/events/Summer_school_2016/05_handout_bachmanandpalmerLev elt.pdf

Bloom, B; et al. (n.d.). *Taxonomy of the objectives in Education*. 8th Ed. El Ateneo Editorial. Retrieved from http://aprende.colombiaaprende.edu.co/sites/default/files/naspublic/ambientes_aprendi/repositorio/aprendizaje/taxonomia_objetivos_educacion.pdf

Canale, M., & Swain, M. (1980). Theoretical Basis on Communicative Approaches to Second Language Teaching and Testing. The Ontario Institute for Studies in Education. Applied Linguistics. Vol, 1, No 1. Retrieved from https://www.researchgate.net/publication/31260438_Theoretical_Bases_of_Communicative_Approaches_to_Second_Language_Teaching_and_Testing

Canale, M. (1983). From communicative competence to communicative language pedagogy. In Richards, J. C., & Schmidt, R. W. (Eds.), *Language and Communication*, 2–27. London: Longman.

Canale, M. (1984). A communicative approach to language proficiency assessment in a minority setting. In Rivera, C. (Ed.), *Communicative competence approaches to language proficiency assessment: Research and application*, 107–122. Clevedon: Multilingual Matters.

Council of Europe (n.d.). *The Common European Framework of References for Languages: Laerning, Teaching, Assessment*. Language Policy Unit, Strasbourg. Retrieved from https://rm.coe.int/16802fc1bf.

Domínguez, L. (2013). Perspectivas del enfoque histórico cultural para la psicología del desarrollo. *Journal Amazônica*, 6(2), 169–259. Retrieved from https://dialnet.unirioja.es/servlet/articulo?codigo=4730567

Dryden-Peterson, S. (2011). *Education to Refugees. A Global Study*. Instituto de Ontario para Estudios en Educación, Universidad de Toronto. Servicio de Evaluación y Elaboración de Políticas. Alto Comisionado de las Naciones Unidas para los Refugiados. Ginebra. Retrieved from http://www.refworld.org/cgibin/texis/vtx/rwmain/opendocpdf.pdf?reldoc=y&docid=510a71b92

Freire, P. (n.d.). *Pedagogía del Oprimido*. Retrieved from http://www.servicioskoinonia.org/biblioteca/general/FreirePedagogiadelOprimido.pdf

Hooks, B. (2003). *Teaching community: A pedagogy of hope*. New York, NY: Routledge. Retrieved from file:///C:/Users/hramirez/Downloads/12009-37403-1-PB.pdf

Hutchinson, T., & Waters, A. (1994). *English for specific purposes*. Cambridge: Cambridge University Press.

Martin, M. (2016). *Jóvenes refugiados en Pichincha, Ecuador. Reforzando el acceso a educación universitaria*. Retrieved from http://noticias.usfq.edu.ec/2016/09/jovenes-refugiados-en-pichincha-ecuador.html

Ramirez, H., Perlaza, M., Escobar, J., & Lopez, B. (2016). Teaching English to refugees in a multilevel classroom. *International Congress on the Didactics of the English Language Journal*, 2(1), 1–11. ISSN 2550-7036. Retrieved from http://revistas.pucese.edu.ec/ICDEL/index

Richards, J. (2006). *Communicative language teaching today*. Cambridge: Cambridge University Press. Retrieved from https://www.professorjackrichards.com/wp-content/uploads/Richards-Communicative-Language.pdf

Silvestre, M., & Zilberstein, J. (2002). *Towards a Developing Didactics*. La Habana, Cuba: Pueblo y Educación Editorial..

Tadayon, F., & Khodi, A. (2016). Empowerment of refugees by language: Can ESL learners affect the target culture? *TESL Canada Journal/Revue TESL du Canada, 33*(10), 129–137. Retrieved from https://files.eric.ed.gov/fulltext/EJ1134423.pdf

United Nations (n.d.). *Sustainable development goals*. Retrieved from https://www.un.org/sustainabledevelopment/

Williams, M., & Burden, R. (2005). *Psychology for language teachers: A social constructivist approach*. Cambridge: Cambridge University Press.

Zimmerman, B. J., & Schunk, D. H. (2011). *Handbook of self-regulation of learning and performance*. New York, NY: Routledge, Taylor & Francis Group. Retrieved from https://books. google.com.ec/books?hl=es&lr=&id=XfOYV0lwzGgC&oi=fnd&pg=PP1&dq=self+learning +&ots=4KzjKjkQ8H&sig=AVhk8R05pZRkBlFOmuvnZ6V4xAM#v=onepage&q=self%20 learning&f=false

CHAPTER 4

POST-SECONDARY EDUCATION AND THE FULL INTEGRATION OF GOVERNMENT-ASSISTED REFUGEES IN CANADA: A DIRECTION FOR PROGRAM INNOVATION

Donald Reddick and Lisa Sadler

ABSTRACT

Canada's immigration goals are multifaceted and ambitious, reflecting both a desire to attract those who can contribute economically and culturally and offer protection to the displaced and the persecuted. Alongside these goals is a pledge that newcomers will receive the services and supports they need to fully integrate into Canada's cultural and economic landscape. This chapter argues that post-secondary institutions, working in partnership with community organizations and primary/secondary schools, are well positioned to facilitate economic and cultural integration, particularly for otherwise vulnerable refugee groups. However, the authors' previous research illustrates the many barriers refugee youth face in accessing Canadian post-secondary education. The authors hypothesize that efforts to increase post-secondary access – and, thereby, facilitate the accomplishment of immigration goals – will be most effective when specific age groups within the refugee demographic are targeted; in particular, younger children who have spent more time in the Canadian education system. This approach requires a shift in settlement practice from

Language, Teaching and Pedagogy for Refugee Education
Innovations in Higher Education Teaching and Learning, Volume 15, 59–73
ISSN: 2055-3641/doi:10.1108/S2055-364120180000015007

that of meeting only initial, urgent settlement needs, to one that enables the development of economic and cultural capacity. The authors envision a program that, on the one hand, helps refugees to value and gain the broad benefits of post-secondary education, while, on the other hand, directs post-secondary institutions to offer programs and pathways that are more inclusive to the unique challenges faced by this vulnerable demographic.

Keywords: Post-secondary education; cultural integration; resettlement; refugees; bicultural identity; education pathway

ECONOMIC AND CULTURAL INTEGRATION OF GOVERNMENT-ASSISTED REFUGEES IN CANADA

The world's growing refugee crisis has led to unprecedented numbers of refugees living in precarious situations for protracted periods. While international organizations and affected countries search for long-term solutions, a partial means of alleviating the crisis – available to less than 0.5% of the world's refugees – is the opportunity for resettlement in a third country. Working with the United Nations High Commissioner for Refugees (UNHCR), Canada has played a leading role in this effort, resettling an average of 10,000 Government-assisted Refugees (GARs) each year (Canadian Council for Refugees, 2017).[1] In the past decade alone, Canada has resettled 3,900 Karen, 6,600 Bhutanese, and 23,000 Iraqi GARs, along with thousands of others from Africa, South America, and the Middle East. More recently, between November 2015 and January 2017, the Canadian government spearheaded the resettlement of 40,081 Syrians (Immigrants, Refugees and Citizenship Canada, 2017a)

The Canadian government resettles GARs based on UNHCR priorities, which change from year to year. As a result, GARs typically arrive in groups or "waves" from a shifting set of countries and regions. While Canada's refugee resettlement programs give refugees an opportunity to rebuild new lives away from the shadow of war and insecurity, the challenges for refugee integration are considerable. Refugees face many significant barriers to integration, including trauma, poverty, lack of English language skills, and employment skills that are not commensurate with Canada's job market. Nevertheless, the successful social, economic, and cultural integration of newcomers, including GARs, is a priority for the Canadian federal government. It has set ambitious integration goals, earmarking close to 1.2 billion dollars each year for settlement and integration purposes (Immigrants, Refugees and Citizenship Canada, 2017b, p. 22). Given the complexity of the integration challenge, the government is prioritizing innovation and experimentation in its approach to funding integration activities, indicating it

will consider new and bold approaches, such as settlement funding that drives social innovation as well as other experiments whose aim is not to simply make improvements, but rather to add new value to the kind of results [it] already achieves. (Immigrants, Refugees and Citizenship Canada, 2017b, p. 5)

Education represents an important, but sometimes overlooked, aspect of the resettlement and integration process. It is our belief that post-secondary education,[2] in particular, provides the greatest opportunities for refugee families to both improve their economic livelihood and successfully become part of a community's social and cultural fabric. However, our previous research (Reddick, Dooley, & Sadler, 2013) and experience working with Karen GARs in British Columbia's Lower Mainland reveal a troubling gap; 10 years after arriving in Canada, Karen youth continue to struggle to access post-secondary education. The struggle is in some ways understandable because Karen GARs arrived in Canada as a vulnerable group (Sadler, 2013). Most youth were born in refugee camps and had little formal education experience. Likewise, their parents also lacked education experience, and many were illiterate even in their own Karen language.

In this chapter, we draw from our experiences with Karen GARs to present a vision for refugee integration built on successful access to post-secondary education. We argue that programming should target arriving pre-teen refugee children, a group who arguably possess the greatest potential to establish a legacy of economic and cultural integration within Canada. The suggested approach is primarily designed for vulnerable groups like Karen GARS, and has application to other refugee communities facing either economic or cultural integration challenges.

THE JUXTAPOSITION OF CANADA'S INTEGRATION GOALS AND HUMANITARIAN ADMISSION POLICY

Canada's admission policy for GARs is based on assisting those in greatest need of protection, *regardless of their potential integration capacity* (Presse & Thompson, 2008). At the same time, immigration policy seeks to ensure newcomers – including refugees – have the services and supports necessary to "fully integrate into Canada's cultural and economic life" (Immigrants, Refugees and Citizenship Canada, 2017b, p. 2). The juxtaposition of Canada's humanitarian admission policy with its ambitious post-settlement goals reveals the extent of the integration challenge and makes clear the need for innovative settlement and integration programming.

For Canada's settlement and integration of refugees to be successful, initiative must be undertaken by both the refugee and host Canadian communities. We agree with Hyndman and Hynie (2016), who note that full integration of refugees should culminate in the joint development of the refugee *and* host communities. From the perspective of refugee development, successful integration implies refugees take steps to be gainfully employed, participate in host-community activities and civic organizations, and progress toward the formation of bicultural identity.[3] From the perspective of the host communities, successful integration implies a broad celebration of multiculturalism, and the recognition and support for the culture and causes that refugee communities carry with them to Canada. But two-way integration cannot end at celebration and broad cultural support; rather, local communities must adapt services and programs to meet the unique needs of refugees.

POST-SECONDARY INSTITUTIONS AS THE INTEGRATION CATALYST FOR RESETTLED REFUGEES AND HOST COMMUNITIES

Canada's federal government recognizes the importance of education opportunities for resettled refugees (Immigrants, Refugees and Citizenship Canada, 2017b). Education is seen as an indicator of wellbeing in Canada, enabling knowledge acquisition, participation in job markets, and a higher quality of life. With this in mind, post-secondary institutions have significant potential to facilitate the full integration of refugees in their host communities.

Post-secondary education provides the knowledge, values, and skills that can improve refugee livelihoods and foster economic contributions to the local community. Such competencies can also serve other purposes, including capacity for effective intercultural exchange, and the increased ability for the refugee diaspora to make contributions in their war-torn home countries (Anselme & Hands, 2010). As argued by Dryden-Peterson and Giles (2010),

> given the uncertainty of the future for refugees, the increasingly globalized realities that most of them face, and the promise of knowledge-based economies, education – that is adaptable and portable – is critical. (p. 3)

At the same time, post-secondary education facilitates integration in subtler ways. It has the potential to extend the academic and social peer support that refugee students can experience during high school; these peer relationships facilitate cultural exchange between refugee youth and others, advancing cultural appreciation and the development of multicultural values. Likewise, post-secondary institutions are traditionally recognized as places where diversity is welcomed and supported. This provides an ideal environment where others will recognize and learn from the unique perspectives and experiences possessed by refugees, facilitating greater awareness within the university community and beyond.

As noted by the World University Service of Canada (2016), post-secondary institutions are respected "idea" leaders within their communities. They can call attention to the benefits of refugee participation in society; in addition, by working to identify best-practice policy and programs, they make refugee/community integration more attainable. As respected leaders, post-secondary institutions are also well placed to connect key community stakeholders in effective integration partnerships.

For all of the aforementioned reasons, we believe a successful integration model requires increased refugee access to post-secondary education. However, higher education institutions must embrace their capacity to facilitate the economic and cultural integration of refugees, partnering with schools and community organizations. We recommend that such partnerships contribute to a refugee student's readiness for post-secondary, as well as facilitate successful post-secondary transitions.

IDENTIFYING THE POST-SECONDARY ACCESS CHALLENGES FACED BY KAREN GARS

Our convictions concerning an effective model for successful refugee integration have emerged from our 2013 study on post-secondary access barriers faced by

Karen GARs in the communities of Langley and Surrey, British Columbia, and subsequent developments within the communities. A summary of the 2013 study results and follow-up observations provides a helpful context for our recommendations in this chapter.

Karen GARs arrived in Langley and Surrey between 2006 and 2012. The group's initial settlement needs prompted a significant response by settlement workers, community organizations, and volunteers. After their early settlement needs were addressed, Karen youth indicated aspirations for post-secondary education, but expressed frustration when attempting to access programs. Recognizing the frustration of Karen youth, concerned support groups joined with several faculty from Kwantlen Polytechnic University (KPU) to establish a steering committee with a mandate to address the barriers being faced. The committee determined that, as a first step, a study be undertaken to explore access barriers, and the authors of this chapter took up the challenge.

We chose the Active Community Engagement Model (ACEM) as a means for inquiry (Dooley, Gagnon, Bhatt, & Tweed, 2012). The model seeks to build capacity within the community being studied by including community members in the development of research questions and conclusions. The study was informed by a literature review that identified many barriers faced by refugee students in accessing post-secondary education (Sadler, 2013). Karen youth with effective intercultural capacity were selected as research assistants and collected survey data by interviewing sample groups of Karen youth, Karen parents, and settlement workers in Langley and Surrey areas.

Interview results confirmed the barriers to post-secondary education identified in the literature review. These barriers fell into the following three categories:

1. Skill/ability preparation for post-secondary (e.g., language skills, literacy, numeracy, study skills)
2. Support services available when undertaking post-secondary (e.g., registration, tutoring, mentoring, financial assistance)
3. Awareness of post-secondary options and pathways (e.g., program selection/advising)

In response to the study, the steering committee worked with representatives from KPU admissions, advising, and counseling areas to raise awareness regarding GAR challenges. Committee representatives also worked alongside the KPU's Future Students Office to provide community information sessions regarding existing university pathways and available support services for groups such as GARs.

The use of the ACEM proved effective for increasing both knowledge and understanding of post-secondary education pathways and programs in the Karen refugee community. A number of Karen refugees have subsequently applied successfully to KPU, attending classes and programs. In particular, Karen that arrived in Canada at a younger age and have spent more time in the Canadian school system are demonstrating greater high school graduation rates and moving on to KPU trades, and other general programs.

The relatively greater access of younger Karen GARs is direct evidence that greater exposure to the Canadian education system increases the likelihood of successful entry to post-secondary education. However, these emerging Karen youth still struggle with specific aspects of education transitions, including a continuing need for guidance when navigating program choices and application procedures, and the requirement to improve academic qualifications. Other challenges are also coming to the forefront, including the need for ongoing cultural integration in secondary schools, obligations that maturing youth face to provide financial support to their families, and pressure to act as linguistic and cultural intermediaries between parents and the host community.

FACILITATING ECONOMIC AND CULTURAL INTEGRATION: LEVERAGING THE POTENTIAL OF YOUNG GARS

Reflecting on the aims of the Canadian resettlement policy and the challenges faced by the Karen and other refugee groups, we feel strategic programming should leverage the economic and cultural potential of pre-teen GARs. This view is based on the belief that arriving pre-teens hold the greatest capacity to develop and preserve the economic and cultural assets essential for the integration of refugee groups and host communities.

Developing Economic Integration Capacity

We define a particular age group's *economic integration capacity* as its average member's possession of, or ability to develop, the language, knowledge, and employment skills necessary to compete on par for well-paid jobs with members of the host community.

Arriving GAR groups contain individuals across the age spectrum. We argue it is important to recognize this spectrum, and to strategically focus programming on age groups within an arriving GAR cohort. In the case of refugees from protracted and precarious situations such as the Karen, life skills and economic assets are generally lacking across all age groups. However, capacity for economic integration into Canadian society varies; research indicates the capacity to develop the language, knowledge, and employment skills for well-paid jobs is greatest in the very young, diminishes but remains significant in pre-teen youth, then drops significantly in older age categories (Hou & Bonikowska, 2016). This pattern arises because the very young and pre-teen youth hold two key advantages over older-aged members of a cohort – they have a greater capacity to learn a new language, and benefit from longer time spent in local Canadian education systems. This leaves very young and pre-teen youth in a better place to access post-secondary education.

This view of economic integration potential is exemplified by the Karen community. Since 2006, almost all Karen arriving in Surrey and Langley after the age of 14 have not achieved high school graduation (Sadler, 2013). Likewise, many youth that arrived between the ages of 10 and 14 have either not graduated from high school, or graduated through an alternative track like an adult diploma completion program. While on paper these students "graduate," they still lack the courses and skills needed to enter post-secondary education. Courses such as English 12, where there is a requirement for large amounts of English reading and writing, are particularly challenging. Meanwhile, refugee children that have arrived between the ages of 8–10, while still facing many challenges, have fared much better in the education system.

Preserving Cultural Assets

Given Canada's indicated commitment to full cultural integration, we underline the importance of refugees maintaining and sharing their cultural assets – that is, their home-country language, values, beliefs, and practices – with the broader community. Maintaining the cultural assets of resettled refugee groups is important, both because resettled refugees indicate they value their culture heritage (Wilkinson, 2002)[4] and because Canada has made a strong commitment to cultural diversity. In regard to the latter, the federal government has indicated that efforts to create space for the cultural contributions of newcomers are what "set us apart as a people who value the contribution of every individual and community across our country" (Immigrants, Refugees and Citizenship Canada, 2017b).

The tangible presence of cultural diversity within a host community requires intercultural dialogue and a mutual respect for other ways of life (UNESCO, n.d.). However, the first requirement for such dialogue and mutual respect is the preservation of refugee cultural assets that are often threatened in former home countries. As discussed by the Dali Lama during a 2010 visit to Canada:

> In our own land, there is real danger [for Tibetan culture] if the present situation remains for a long period .... Without freedom, it is difficult to have meaningful preservation of Tibetan culture .... So the refugee communities in free countries have a special responsibility to preserve [the Tibetan language and Buddhist religion]. (Contenta, 2010)

Cultural preservation brings a number of benefits to resettled communities. It can instill a sense of purpose in future generations. Amara Chin, a former refugee who now works with the United Nations recounts that:

> I saw that cultural heritage could instill a sense of purpose, fulfillment and accomplishment in my people in the dawn of a new cultural era. This experience provided an example of how cultural preservation can promote healing, improve economic well-being and repair lives. I foresee a cultural renaissance that advertises Cambodia for its arts instead of its killing fields, in which I must participate. (Chin, n.d.)

The first language fluency is a particularly beneficial cultural asset – it promotes a sense of belonging and cohesion within families and communities that facilitates healthy adjustment throughout the resettlement process (Hamilton, 2016). Research shows that first language skills increase brain development and academic proficiency, and help children maintain their cultural identity (Belanger, 2014).

However, cultural assets are at risk during resettlement. Pressures for language assimilation, especially for the very young who spend much of their time in public schools, can lead to a failure to obtain first-language fluency. Because refugee adults and seniors find it difficult to acquire the English language, a communication gap can emerge between age groups. As a result, significant cultural assets can be lost to the very young, and the generations that follow. In the void, host culture assets can become dominant, and the social benefits of cultural diversity are lost (Hamilton, 2016).

Based on our observations of the Karen community, the potential for cultural assimilation cannot be understated. Karen GARs that arrive in Canada as young children have a very different set of challenges than the older age groups in their refugee communities; they adapt to Canadian culture quickly, often at the expense of their own culture. Almost all Karen children no longer read or write Karen. Non-English speaking Karen parents are particularly troubled when their children become so immersed in English that they no longer even speak Karen, a situation that creates challenging family communication dynamics (Devadas, 2017).

These considerations imply the need for cultural preservation and transmission within resettled refugee communities. We believe that arriving pre-teen youth, relative to other members of an arriving GAR cohort, are uniquely endowed with the combination of pre-developed cultural assets and a capacity to share them within Canadian society. The very young in a GAR cohort lack the capacity for cultural transmission because they come of age outside of their home culture – home culture assets need to be transferred to them by older age groups. Arriving youth, adults, and seniors, while possessing significant cultural assets developed in their former home countries, are more apt to struggle when it comes to cultural integration. Language limitations constrain their ability to transmit their culture to members of the larger host community, and limit interactions that facilitate their development of a bicultural identity. Arriving pre-teen youth, however, have experience with home-country culture, and the capacity to develop the language skills necessary for cultural asset transfer. This capacity for cultural transmission makes arriving pre-teen youth a critical resource for the full integration of refugees and the host community.

Because arriving pre-teen refugees have much to offer, the importance of developing their economic and cultural capacity cannot be understated. However, this age group is often overlooked in settlement programming, overshadowed by the more urgent settlement needs of their parents.

IDENTIFYING THE CRITICAL CHALLENGES TO FULL GAR INTEGRATION

In addition to the barriers to post-secondary education we identified in our previous study, we've identified further challenges that must be addressed to facilitate the successful integration of pre-teen refugees on the pathway between elementary, middle, secondary, and post-secondary schools.

Building Higher Education Culture

Research has shown differences in educational attainment among different immigrant ethnic groups (Abada, Hou, & Ram, 2009). For example, immigrant Chinese, Korean, and Japanese students often achieve higher test scores and move on to university at rates that surpass not only other immigrant groups, but also Canadian-born students. Researchers refer to this as "ethnic capital," which can in part be attributed to differences in "higher education culture," that is, differences in family awareness and valuation of the broad benefits of post-secondary education.

Despite spending more time in the Canadian school system, younger Karen refugees still lack the guidance, support, and a higher education culture that assures the path to post-secondary education. A primary source for these key ingredients is found within the family. Research by Ross Finnie (2012) suggests that parents' experiences and views regarding higher education drive their children's motivation to pursue post-secondary training, so much so that other barriers – such as financial means – become secondary to access. However, refugee parents often lack the backgrounds that create positive cultural support for post-secondary goals. Gunderson's (2007) research supports the view that youth from challenged refugee families are more likely to disappear from school systems because parents do not ultimately prioritize education. Furthermore, our 2013 study of the Karen community revealed that, even when families do value higher education for their children, their inexperience with post-secondary systems often leaves them at a loss to advise or provide assistance. Karen parents reported that besides providing food, shelter, transportation, and encouragement, they felt unable to directly assist their children. Parents traced inability to provide further support to inadequate language skills, education, and experience. As one interviewed parent responded, "All I tell them is to go to the library and read many books" (Reddick et al., 2013).

As Finnie (2012) points out,

> If we want to increase the overall participation rate in PSE [post-secondary education], or to level the PSE access playing field for under-represented groups, we must adjust our policy levers from their past emphasis on affordability to focus on these newly identified cultural factors. (p. 4)

We believe these cultural factors are particularly important to impart to young refugees whose families lack post-secondary experience.

One solution to the absence of a post-secondary culture within families is to intentionally create it for refugees within the school system. Hyndman (2014) refers to research by Hynie (2014) that suggests young refugees particularly benefit from support in high schools. Support comes from guidance counselors and school activities that "(a) reinforce their integration linguistically or culturally; (b) facilitate access to employment opportunities through student internships and summer jobs; and (c) directly provide access to university education" (Hyndman, 2014, p. 20). Our experience is that school systems are often caught off-guard by the sudden arrival of vulnerable, multi-barriered refugee youth, and lack the mandate or the funding for programs that specifically facilitate a higher education culture. While the absence of such refugee-tailored programs in secondary schools is a problem for GARs who arrive at older ages, we believe it is particularly problematic when considering the needs of pre-teen refugee arrivals who possess the most potential for economic and cultural integration.

Barriers to Cultural Integration

Another challenge concerns the long-term likelihood of full cultural integration. Older Karen youth continue to exhibit a limited capacity for full cultural integration due to insufficient English language skills and a resulting desire to live life mainly within the GAR community. Conversely, pre-teen GAR arrivals have subsequently acquired sufficient English language skills, opening the door for cultural engagement with their peers. However, while facing head-on the challenges of living in a bicultural environment, these youth lack the support necessary for the formation of healthy bicultural identities. As is commonly reported for other immigrant groups (Anisef, 2005), pre-teen arrivals are eventually caught between cultures, and feel ill-equipped to engage their peers on matters that distinguish them culturally. This is concerning because the likelihood of long-term cultural representation within the larger community arguably rests with this age group – older age groups lack the communication capacity to facilitate cultural representation, while the youngest age groups lack the unique experiences and cultural memory necessary for full cultural representation.

The Weight of Family and Refugee Community Responsibility

The third remaining challenge to full integration is the significant family and community responsibilities we observe being carried by pre-teen GARs as they mature. Because many of their families live in poverty, youth are expected to provide income support to their families, as well as to use their language skills to act as language brokers for family members and others. At the same time, their parents and other refugee community members are concerned about the degree of cultural assimilation being exhibited by the pre-teen group and their younger siblings. The combination of these expectations can be overwhelming, making the additional demands associated with accessing post-secondary education seem insurmountable.

RECOMMENDATIONS EMPOWERING PRE-TEEN GAR ARRIVALS

The barriers and recommendations discussed in this chapter require settlement programming that goes beyond what is generally provided to GARs in their first few years in Canada. There are significant barriers that stand in the way of full refugee integration that require a long-term lens on programming starting with refugees that arrive as pre-teens. We have argued that, if effectively supported, this group possesses not only the capacity to achieve personal economic success and bicultural identity, but also to facilitate wider economic and cultural integration objectives. Furthermore, we believe the support necessary for such success would be most effective if coordinated through the community leadership of post-secondary institutions; post-secondary institutions are best-placed to deliver the complex summative skills and experiences necessary for successful integration. Moreover, achieving success in post-secondary education is important for the economic and cultural integration of refugee youth.

With this in mind, the following components are necessary for an effective post-secondary pathway program:

1. *A pathway built on strategically directed partnerships*
   Building the economic and cultural capacity of arriving pre-teen GARs requires the cooperative support of many parties; an effective pathway must involve partnerships built on communication and coordination between post-secondary institutions, primary and secondary schools, settlement organizations, and refugee community members who can advocate for the unique needs and challenges of different refugee groups.

   We believe the capacity for such partnerships already exists in Langley and Surrey where our previous research has taken place. GARs in these communities are supported in public schools through the Settlement Worker in Schools (SWIS) program, which is funded by Immigrants, Refugees, and Citizenship Canada. At the same time, post-secondary institutions such as KPU have both the mandate and desire to welcome and serve under-represented GAR communities. Our work with the Karen has identified individuals willing to act as community representatives. What is missing is a strategy that coordinates the actions of the various parties. Such a strategy should leverage the unique opportunities and resources available along the education pathway, with the intent of achieving the ultimate goal of economic and cultural integration.

   In regions with significant refugee populations, we recommend the formation of a steering committee composed of representatives from refugee communities, affiliated settlement organizations, primary and secondary schools, and committed post-secondary institutions. The steering committee should be headed by a post-secondary-affiliated chair, and be tasked to identify and direct sequential pathway actions that assist waves of arriving pre-teens as they move from primary to post-secondary education.

2. *Building a higher education culture along the pathway*
   The steering committee should ensure activities that build a higher education culture within GAR communities. Post-secondary representatives need to be a part of the initial settlement process, teaming with settlement workers to present to arriving refugee families the economic and cultural benefits of higher education. The message should be continuously reinforced along the education pathway. Supported by local post-secondary institutions, settlement workers either within or connected to the local school system can provide targeted group sessions, workshops, and field trips aimed to increase knowledge and understanding of the importance of post-secondary education and the variety of options and pathways available to students.

3. *Providing holistic support along the pathway*

The steering committee, in partnership with community service providers, must ensure holistic support for pre-teen arrivals as they move along the pathway. Refugee parents without formal education experience are not adequately equipped to support their child's education in Canada. As such, the steering committee should link schools, community agencies, and post-secondary institutions in an effort to provide homework clubs, tutors, post-secondary mentors, workshops on organization and study skills, intensive guidance counseling, and other activities that prepare students for post-secondary academic success. Students with refugee backgrounds in particular require more academic support in middle and secondary school to ensure that they have strong numeracy and literacy skills. It is important to highlight the need for first-language support in the midst of these efforts. This is presently being done in several local school districts, where SWIS connect GAR youth and families to their schools in their first language.

When first-generation refugees reach the age of post-secondary transition, they especially need assistance with post-secondary applications, registration for courses, familiarization with campuses, application for scholarships, bursaries, loans, etc. Financial support is a significant barrier for refugee students living in poverty. Further, they need supportive advocates/navigators that are based in the post-secondary institution. Ideally, this kind of support would be provided in their first language, recognizing the importance of language and culture preservation. Our work with bilingual research assistants has demonstrated the capacity of gifted young GARs to provide peer support, and highlights the importance of generating GAR post-secondary successes so that self-sustaining support network for post-secondary GAR arrivals is in place.

4. *Ensuring intercultural exchange along the pathway*

Cultural integration is an important objective of Canadian immigration policy. Intercultural exchange and multicultural appreciation are facilitated by common experiences over time that build cultural affinity between peer groups. This can begin in primary schools, be intentionally strengthened in secondary schools, and be brought to fruition in post-secondary institutions. Post-secondary programs enable cultural reflection and dialogue at the highest levels. Such reflection and dialogue can be intentionally spread to the wider community through post-secondary outreach initiatives. All newcomers experience strong pressure toward cultural assimilation, and if Canada is to stand behind its commitment to cultural diversity it should support initiatives that foster intercultural exchange.

SUPPORT FOR A PATHWAY APPROACH

While there is little research that addresses the complex education needs of young refugee students, we make these recommendations with the awareness that successful programs do exist that aim to help vulnerable students move on to post-secondary education. For example, *Pathways to Education* is a program helping vulnerable youth succeed in school in communities across Canada, many of them facing similar barriers to refugee students, including poverty, lack of positive role models and parent support. Notably, many students that participate in Pathways to Education programs are in fact refugees (Pathways to Education, n.d.). Their model is supported by years of research and evidenced by successful cohorts that graduate high school and move on to post-secondary.

Pathways to Education contains many of the elements we endorse. It is a collaborative approach that leverages academic, social one-on-one, and financial supports through partnerships with schools, community services, and the funding of private, corporate, and government sources. Each of these components addresses significant barriers to post-secondary education.

Another program, Partnership for the Advancement and Immersion of Refugees (PAIR) based in Houston, Texas uses similar tactics to empower refugee students to meet their full academic potential and become community leaders. PAIR offers unique after-school programs that specifically target middle school refugee students and high school students through educational mentoring and academic support. This program is "designed for students to explore opportunities for their future and develop the leadership and life skills necessary to attain higher education and employment" (PAIR, n.d.).

In sum, education – especially, as it reaches a post-secondary level – must be the primary medium for the successful integration of refugees. Education and integration are intertwined – success in school is contingent on successful settlement and integration, and successful settlement and integration is contingent on success in school. The two thus build on one another, creating all the more reason to consider settlement support programming that is stretched over a longer period of time to achieve better results in terms of economic and cultural outcomes.

CONCLUSION

Our work with Karen refugees over the last 10 years has been incredibly rewarding. Karen people are courageous, kind, hospitable and have a strong desire to succeed in Canada and give back to the community. As youth have graduated from high school, we have celebrated their accomplishments with them. At the same time, our work in the community has given us an inside view of ongoing challenges. To address these challenges, programs that foster settlement and integration should be based on a commitment to support a longer-term education pathway.

We believe the integration pathway should be built with pre-teen GAR arrivals in mind – this group holds the greatest potential for facilitating the economic and cultural integration of GAR communities in Canada. Partnership between post-secondary institutions, primary and secondary schools, settlement organizations, and GAR community representatives are key to ensuring that vulnerable refugee youth receive holistic support throughout their education and integration journey. A steering committee led by a post-secondary representative should identify and support initiatives that ensure a higher education culture within GAR communities, provide holistic academic support, build intercultural exchange, and alleviate the pressure of expectations felt by GAR youth. Such actions will demonstrate Canada's commitment to achieving its ambitious refugee integration goals, and afford vulnerable GAR groups like the Karen the greatest likelihood of finding economic and cultural integration success.

NOTES

1. Canada's refugee system includes several categories, including Privately Sponsored Refugees, Blended Visa Office Referrals (BVOR – a blend of GAR and PSR programs) and Refugee Claimants. While all refugees that arrive in Canada face challenges, we focus our attention in this chapter on program innovations that can primarily assist the most vulnerable refugee groups which are usually GARs (but increasingly PSRs or BVORs).

2. We are using the term "postsecondary education" to refer to higher education in general, and could include undergraduate programs at colleges or universities, but also skills training, trades, and career programs that have significant value and potential for economic improvement.

3. We define bicultural identity as acceptance of both the dominant and home cultures that are within an individual's identity. The person is able to embrace values from the host and home cultures and engage in positive intercultural exchange (Wu, 2011).

4. In a study of the integration of 91 refugee youth in Alberta, Canada, Wilkinson (2002) notes that 70% indicated keeping their cultural heritage was important to them.

REFERENCES

Abada, T., Hou, F., & Ram, B. (2009). Ethnic differences in educational attainment among the children of Canadian immigrants. *Canadian Journal of Sociology*, *34*(1), 1–28.

Anisef, P. (2005). *Issues confronting newcomer youth in Canada: alternative models for a national youth host program.* Toronto: Join Centre of Excellence for Research on Immigration and Settlement.

Anselme, M. L., & Hands, C. (2010). Access to secondary and tertiary education for all refugees: Steps and challenges to overcome. *Refuge*, *27*(2), 89–96.

Belanger, R. (2014, July). *Language acquisition in immigrant and refugee children: First language use and bilingualism.* (C. P. Society, Producer). Retrieved from https://www.kidsnewtocanada.ca/screening/language-acquisition

Canadian Council for Refugees. (2017). *2017 Immigration levels: Comments.* Retrieved from http://ccrweb.ca/en/2017-immigration-levels-comments

Chin, A. (2017). *Cultural relations through the artful lens of a former refugee.* Retrieved from https://www.unspecial.org/2017/02/cultural-relations-through-the-artful-lens-of-a-former-refugee/

Contenta, S. (2010, October 23). *In Canada, Tibetan refugees can preserve a culture threatened back home.* Retrieved from https://www.thestar.com/news/world/2010/10/23/in_canada_tibetan_refugees_can_preserve_a_culture_threatened_back_home.html

Devadas, Z. (2017, September 15). *Informal conversation.* (L. Sadler, Interviewer) Langley, BC.

Dooley, S., Gagnon, N., Bhatt, G., & Tweed, R. (2012, May). The active community engagement model: Fostering active participation in evaluation projects among diverse community stakeholders. *Training workshop submited to the Canadian Evaluation Society Conference.* Nova Scotia, Canada: Halifax.

Dryden-Peterson, S., & Giles, W. (2010). Introduction: Higher education for refugees. *Refuge*, *27*(2), 3–9.

Finnie, R. (2012). *Access to post-secondary education: The importance of culture.* Ottawa: University of Ottawa.

Gunderson, L. (2007). Where have all the immigrants gone? *Contact*, *33*(2), 118–128. Retrieved from http://www.teslontario.org/uploads/publications/researchsymposium/ResearchSymposium2007.pdf

Hamilton, T. B. (2016, May 16). *Losing identity during the refugee crisis.* Retrieved from https://www.theatlantic.com/education/archive/2016/05/balancing-integration-and-assimilation-during-the-refugee-crisis/482757/

Hou, F., & Bonikowska, A. (2016). *Educational and labour market outcomes of childhood immigrants by admission class.* Statistics Canada. Ottawa: Minister of Industry.

Hyndman, J. (2014). *Refugee research synthesis 2009–2013.* Citizenship and Immigration Canada. Ottawa: CERIS.

Hyndman, J., & Hynie, M. (2016). *From newcomer to Canadian: Making refugee integration work.* Retrieved from http://policyoptions.irpp.org/magazines/may-2016/from-newcomer-to-canadian-making-refugee-integration-work/

Immigrants, Refugees and Citizenship Canada. (2017a, May 4). *#WelcomeRefugees: Canada resettled Syrian refugees.* Retrieved from http://www.cic.gc.ca/english/refugees/welcome/index.asp

Immigrants, Refugees and Citizenship Canada. (2017b). *Departmental plan 2017–2018.* Retrieved from http://www.cic.gc.ca/english/pdf/pub/dp-pm-2017-2018-eng.pdf.

PAIR. (2017). *Programs.* Retrieved from http://www.pairhouston.org/programs/

Pathways to Education. (2018). *About us.* Retrieved from https://www.pathwaystoeducation.ca/about-us

Presse, D., & Thomson, J. (2008). The resettlement challenge: Integration of refugees from protracted refugee situations. *Refuge, 27*(2), 94–99.

Reddick, D., Dooley, S., & Sadler, L. (2013). *Zipporah's dream: Postsecondary access to Kwantlen Polytechnic University for the Karen and other government assisted refugees in the South Fraser Region.* Surrey: Kwantlen Polytechnic University, Centre for Interdisciplinary Research.

Sadler, L. (2013). *Overcoming barriers to post-secondary education for Karen refugee youth in Langley and Surrey, BC.* Victoria: University of Victoria.

UNESCO. (2016). *Convention for the safeguarding of the intangible cultural heritage.* Retrieved from https://ich.unesco.org/en/convention

Wilkinson, L. (2002). Factors influencing the academic success of refugee youth in Canada. *Journal of Youth Studies, 5*(2), 173.

Wilkinson, L., & Garcea, J. (2017). *The economic integration of refugees in Canada: A mixed record?* Washington, DC: Migration Policy Institute.

World University Service of Canada (WUSC). (2016). *The Canadian post-secondary education community's response to the refugee crisis.* Ottawa: WUSC.

Wu, T. (2011). Bicultural identity. In S. Goldstein, J. A. Naglieri (Eds.), *Encyclopedia of Child Behaviour and Development*, Boston, MA: Springer.

CHAPTER 5

LITERACY INSTRUCTION WITHOUT BORDERS: IDEAS FOR DEVELOPING BEST PRACTICES FOR READING PROGRAMS IN REFUGEE SETTINGS

Matt Thomas, Yuankun Yao, Katherine Landau Wright and Elizabeth Rutten-Turner

ABSTRACT

This chapter contends that to meet the needs of refugees, we must go beyond addressing only safety and security by including education as well, specifically, literacy development. The authors suggest that in order to support refugee education, generally, we need to identify best practices for supporting reading programs in refugee settings. The authors discuss basic design and assessment of literacy education programming in refugee settings that parallels the designs for traditional school-wide literacy programs, which we have in place in more stable regions of the world. The authors attempt to converge the fields of literacy education with refugee studies to make recommendations for supporting refugees' literacy education with the goal of preserving their native language and literacy while preparing them for the future.

Keywords: Literacy; education; comprehension; storytelling; refugees; United Nations

Language, Teaching and Pedagogy for Refugee Education
Innovations in Higher Education Teaching and Learning, Volume 15, 75–89
Copyright © 2019 by Emerald Publishing Limited
All rights of reproduction in any form reserved
ISSN: 2055-3641/doi:10.1108/S2055-364120180000015006

INTRODUCTION

We are living in times of considerable refugee crises. There are currently more displaced people in the world now than at any other time since the Second World War (Brangham, 2016), and the future is uncertain if we consider how and when things may improve. World leaders, such as those working through the United Nations (UN), are trying to proactively plan to meet the needs of refugees, both now and into the future. Although obviously not hoping for an ever-present refugee crisis, we are realizing that our "new normal" may involve a percentage of our global citizenship always being displaced at some time, and that we need to plan accordingly to make the best of these difficult realities, especially for those going through them. This was made evident in the UN General Assembly's recent "New York Declaration," where all the states in the world have issued a pronouncement committing themselves to not only protecting and assisting refugees, but also finding new ways to better organize the responses to refugee crises (Grandi, 2016). So, how can we manage this refugee reality well, in a way that proactively seeks to meet the special needs of those in refugee settings? It will likely involve moving past meeting the lower levels of Maslow's Hierarchy of Needs (Maslow, 1954) focused solely on safety and security, reaching toward the higher levels of personal fulfillment as well. As Filipo Grandi, UN High Commissioner for Refugees said, "We have been able to give the basics to refugees, like blankets, medicine, some food, but what refugees want also is a future, is education, is jobs" (Grandi, 2016, para. 10).

Relatedly, the International Literacy Association (2017) argues that literacy is a fundamental, inalienable human right. Literacy opens doors to educational opportunities and empowers individuals to take charge of their own learning. However, literacy development is not any easy process in the best of settings, and it is even more difficult when under duress. Montero, Newmaster, and Ledger (2014) suggested that children who have been forced into exile have gaps in formal schooling, which includes the lack of age-appropriate print literacy skills in their dominant language. Second-language acquisition research has demonstrated that when literacy in a native language is supported, students are better able to acquire reading and writing skills in a new language (Cummins, 1981; Shum, Ho, Siegel, & Au, 2016; Sparks, Patton, Ganschow, & Humbach, 2009). Therefore, we argue that in order to support refugee education, generally, we need to identify best practices for supporting reading programs in refugee settings.

The present chapter will address this aspect of education related to the general global refugee crises. More specifically, this chapter will discuss the basic design and assessment of literacy education programming in refugee settings that parallels designs for traditional school-wide literacy programs, which we have in place in more stable regions of the world, such as in the US. We attempt to converge the fields of literacy education with refugee studies to make recommendations for supporting refugees' literacy education with the goal of preserving their native language and literacy while preparing them for the future.

LITERACY EDUCATION UNDER DURESS

Reading requires readers to be "attentive, analytical, purposeful, flexible, self-aware, world aware, and emotionally sound" (Manzo, Manzo, & Thomas, 2009, p. 22). If your world has recently been turned upside-down, as is clearly the case for refugees, growth in literacy is simply very difficult to accomplish. Fear and anxiety are known to have profound psychological and physiological impacts, which can be devastating to learning (Manzo & Manzo, 1993). Any discussion of literacy programming in refugee settings should keep these kinds of challenges and struggles in mind.

CURRENT STATE OF REFUGEES

In 1951, world leaders gathered together to agree on a definition of "refugee," outline basic rights for the displaced, and state legal obligations each member nation would agree to (United Nations, n.d.). Refugee policy has changed in the US depending on national and global trends. Nevertheless, the US legal definition of a refugee has remained fairly consistent: to be considered for resettlement to the US, the person must be of specific humanitarian concern, currently outside the US, have proof of persecution based on their race, religion, nationality, political opinion, or membership in a particular social group, meet health and security guidelines, and never have participated in the persecution of others (US Citizenship and Immigration Services, n.d.). The US has been committed to supporting displaced persons overseas in a variety of ways including: providing funds for basic needs, offering medical care, and educational support.

Although each modern-day, refugee-producing situation is unique, there are some common themes worldwide. Refugees generally face a traumatic situation that forces them to leave quickly and have limited time to gather personal items or important documents such as identification, travel documents, or medical or school records. Often while in flight, individuals are separated from family or other community members, and chased or harassed, causing further trauma. When crossing international borders, people often fear being returned, imprisoned, or forced to pay bribes to continue on their journey. Once in a host country, people may be restricted from pursuing education or jobs due to their lack of documents or inability to leave a refugee camp. These typical stressors, along with others specific to a particular conflict, cause physiological and psychological changes that can affect cognitive functioning and healthy development (National Capacity Building Project, 2005).

The stereotypical mythical image of refugees being poor, illiterate, and from desert camps is beginning to change. The UN High Commission for Refugees (UNHCR) (2016) documents that over 60% of refugees live in urban centers, which provide some opportunities not available to people living in camps, and additional challenges. Some host countries allow urban refugees to obtain work permits to aid them in their survival. In many countries, however, discrimination results in being unable to acquire employment or being paid extremely low wages. Furthermore, urban refugees may be required to locate and pay for housing, food, clothing, and other personal supplies on their own or with small stipends from the UN, which can cause great stress on individuals and families. Life in urban areas can also be unsafe for refugees due to harassment by unwelcoming locals or police.

Both the international and the US refugee resettlement programs have changed over time causing the modern-day refugee context to be very different from the historical context. For example, the current procedures often require extensive interviewing, security checks, and health screenings to ensure the integrity of the program. The slower processing of applications causes people to live in unstable situations for longer periods of time, which can increase physiological and psychological trauma symptoms. In 2016, the UNHCR reported that of the 22.5 million refugees in the world only 189,300 people were permanently resettled to a third country (UNHCR, 2016). The small number of permanently resettled individuals and families is due to a variety of financial, political, and social factors in the global community. Regardless of the reasons, the effect on the individual can be symptoms of anxiety and depression. The extensive, compound trauma that displaced people endure can have drastic effects on cognitive and developmental functioning. Neurobiological studies have shown decreased memory capabilities, frozen development, and decreased daily functioning in people who have endured a traumatic event at a young age (National Child Traumatic Stress Network, n.d.).

REFUGEE LITERACY EDUCATION

While not widely explored, some scholarship exists, from both the fields of reading and refugee studies, which generally discusses literacy issues related to refugees. Furthermore, many non-government organizations have worked to develop and implement programs to promote literacy in refugee settings (see Table 1 for examples). Next, we review research focused on providing literacy-education opportunities to refugee populations.

Focusing on the Congolese refugees in Uganda, Dryden-Peterson (2006) suggested how education may be perceived as a tool for ensuring stability for displaced children, as well as a hope for ensuring a better future for displaced families: "Refugees see the education of their children as a way to prevent the recurrence of violence and to create economic opportunities that allow them to become self-reliant" (Dryden-Peterson, p. 90). The author suggests that the language of instruction was central to the success of education for the refugee children. It is an important stabilizer in the lives of refugee children. The author also suggested that ability in a language does not always equate to a child's level of education, and that children in displacement have a more urgent need for stability before they can think about their future.

Oh and Van Der Stouwe (2008) argue that the choice of language of instruction can be politically as well as educationally motivated, with the decision being rather sensitive in certain cases. The authors suggested that "The choice of

Table 1. Sample Existing Literacy Programs for Refugees.

Providing Resources		
Program	Description	Website
Book Aid International	Provides new books, donated by publishers, to refugee camps in Kenya	Bookaid.org
The Ideas Box	Ships the equivalent of a small-town library (with both print and digital resources) to refugee camps	ideas-box.org
Building Educational Capacity		
Program	Description	Website
Karen Women Organization (KWO)	The Literacy and Non-Formal Education Project was established in 2001 to help illiterate Burmese refugees in the camps to learn to read and write	karenwomen.org
We Love Reading	Trains adults inside camps to become storytellers and receive books to start libraries	Welovereading.org
Teachers Without Borders	Provide professional development and resources to teachers worldwide	teacherswithoutborders.org

language represents refugees' opposition to and/or desire to overturn the oppressive and violent circumstances they experienced" (Oh & Van Der Stouwe, p. 607). Although the refugees, in their study, came from the same ethnic background, they often spoke different languages, which necessitated the use of different languages for instruction for different refugee groups at the lower grades. The use of different languages for instruction, however, resulted in some challenges, including students dropping out when an advanced grade level utilized a foreign language for instruction.

Despite these challenges, education in refugee settings is essential to prepare children for their future. As mentioned earlier (Montero et al., 2014), children who have been forced into exile have gaps in formal schooling, and often lack of age-appropriate print literacy skills in their dominant language. As such, when they reach their first country of asylum, they come across a number of difficulties. Among those is the lack of professional development for teachers to prepare the students for the academic rigors of secondary schools. There is also a lack of age-appropriate and culturally responsive texts suitable for the students. The Montero et al. study documented how guided reading and running records (a formative literacy assessment approach) helped the students to develop their English print literacy as well as improving their behaviors.

Perry and Hart (2012) explored perceptions of teachers of adult refugee learners. The study found that although most of the teachers were certified, they were not adequately prepared to teach adult English as a Second Language learners, especially those who have limited English proficiency. The participants of the study clearly indicated a need for pedagogical content knowledge: what to teach and how to teach it effectively. The participants also indicated a need to have access to expertise in the form of mentoring, a reference person, and social networking among educators. Sarroub, Pernicek, and Sweeney (2007) examined a high school boy's experiences, as a Yezidi Kurdish refugee, in an English Language Learner language-acquisition program, at home and in the workplace. The study found that reading instruction works for students when certain support structures are in place. Despite the attempts by several teachers to connect the boy's literacy learning to the outside work world, the student saw little in school that could help him earn a living to support his family. The study suggested that literacy instruction is important and meaningful when students see value in reading, and when teachers make explicit connections to those realities and validate students' ideas.

Stewart (2015) gave an account of her experience in teaching a four–week-long summer literacy course to high school refugee students in the US. The author felt the need to get to know the students but not the time to do so. She ended up using texts that focused on life stories of refugees, and students made connections with the reading based on their own experiences. The author learned a lot from reading the responses of the students to those stories. The study pointed out "the promises of teaching refugee youths when literacy activities are designed to draw on students' own lived experiences to facilitate the teacher's knowledge and understanding of them" (Stewart, 2015, p. 157).

Dwyer and McCloskey (2013) studied a 1-month intensive summer literacy camp in developing the literacy of teenage refugee boys from Afghanistan, Bosnia and Herzegovina, Burundi, Cuba, the Democratic Republic of the Congo, Ethiopia, Eritrea, Iraq, the Karen region of Burma, Kosovo, Liberia, Nepal, Rwanda, Sierra Leone, Somalia, and Sudan. The study took place in a suburban community of Atlanta in the US. The program combined physical training and reading/writing workshops. The participants expressed increased enjoyment for both reading and writing. In addition, the data suggested that the program largely avoided summer literacy regression, a common problem in traditional nine-month school calendar settings.

Van Der Stouwe and Oh (2008) described how learning programs for refugee camps along the Thai-Burmese borders have evolved over 20 years. There has been a change from the relief model of emergency solutions to longer-term strategies of building camp communities and education systems that emphasize quality and sustainability of the services. Elmeroth (2003) studied adult immigrants from a Kurdish refugee camp in Sweden in terms of their learning of a second language: Swedish. The interviewees in the study suggested that their lack of contact with speakers of the target language led to isolation and marginalization.

Carrara, Hogan, De Pree, Nosten, and McGready (2011) examined the potential relationship between literacy and pregnancy in refugees and migrants along the Thai-Burmese border. The study reported a significant reduction in the proportion of premature births and low birth rate in the camp population. The ability to read was found to correlate with three health behavior habits: less likelihood to smoke, less malaria during pregnancy, and a greater likelihood to deliver in a health facility.

BEST PRACTICES FOR LITERACY PROGRAMMING

Despite the noteworthy research in the previous section, very little conventional scholarship seems available related to organized literacy planning at refugee camps that would parallel good school-wide literacy programming in more stable school settings. Therefore, our goal is to take what we believe to be best practices for literacy in traditional education settings and make adjustments to fit the needs of refugee populations. We do not propose to develop a comprehensive program for literacy education that would be appropriate for all refugees, but instead make four recommendations for best practices that could be implemented in a variety of settings and literacy programs.

There is a solid amount of scholarship in the reading field about ideas for best practices in school-wide literacy programming. We have found, from both theory and in practice while helping with school-wide literacy programming efforts, that effective school-wide literacy programs are typically built around these components as identified and addressed by Manzo et al. (2009): (1) leadership (Literacy Leadership Committee) made up of the principal, literacy specialists, grade-level and content area teachers, library media specialists, and literacy consultants; (2) a grounded/sound ideology or philosophy of literacy development; (3) objectives and goals; (4) clear roles and responsibilities for all involved; (5) special services for various segments of the student body; (6) ongoing needs assessment and literacy program evaluation; (7) a curriculum plan; (8) a staff development program that provides consultation, in-service training, and sharing opportunities involving literacy best practices; and (9) literacy activities that are results oriented and promote collaboration and cooperation. See Table 2 for these components from Manzo et al. (2009) that we put into an assessment chart format. While many literacy programming details are subsumed by these nine components, these do provide a basic overview and overall structure of what is needed for good school-wide literacy programming. Clearly, sustained resources and basic commitment to the enterprise are also required for school-wide literacy programming of this kind to be successful.

When we then consider how a lens such as this can be modified and applied to a refugee educational setting, we confess that our knowledge and understanding of providing educational services in refugee setting realities is only academic and speculative at best, rather than lived and experientially understood. In addition, due to the low numbers of people that are permanently resettled and the inability to predict where someone may be offered resettlement, it's difficult to recommend a particular second language in an educational setting catering to displaced people. In cases such as this, recommendations should be seen only as outside perspectives, needing the refinement that can be provided by those with more first-hand experience, perhaps especially leaders among refugees themselves. Nevertheless, there are several things we suggest for consideration of applying the literacy program characteristics to refugee settings for comprehensive literacy program planning. In Table 3, we hypothesize challenges of applying these components directly to refugee settings.

Table 2. Assessment of School-Wide Literacy Programming Components,
Traditional Setting.

	Literacy Program Component	Assessment
1	Leadership (Literacy Leadership Committee) made up of the principal, literacy specialists; grade level and content area teachers, library media specialists, and consultants	Evident? Yes / No Quality Low Medium High 1 2 3 4 5
2	A grounded ideology or philosophy of literacy development	Evident? Yes / No Quality Low Medium High 1 2 3 4 5
3	Objectives and goals	Evident? Yes / No Quality Low Medium High 1 2 3 4 5
4	Clear roles and responsibilities for all involved	Evident? Yes / No Quality Low Medium High 1 2 3 4 5
5	Special services for various segments of the student body	Evident? Yes / No Quality Low Medium High 1 2 3 4 5
6	Ongoing needs assessment and program evaluation	Evident? Yes / No Quality Low Medium High 1 2 3 4 5
7	A curriculum plan	Evident? Yes / No Quality Low Medium High 1 2 3 4 5
8	A staff-development program that provides consultation, in-service training, and sharing opportunities	Evident? Yes / No Quality Low Medium High 1 2 3 4 5
9	Activities that are result-oriented and promote collaboration and cooperation	Evident? Yes / No Quality Low Medium High 1 2 3 4 5

Further examination of Table 3 suggests that some of the hardest to meet items relate to high-quality faculty staffing and having appropriate assessment and curricular materials available. On the other hand, it seems that some of the components could be reasonably approximated with good advanced planning, while certain family literacy opportunities could, interestingly enough, perhaps, be strengthened in a refugee setting better than in a traditional school setting. Advances in available technology might also allow for surprisingly valuable gains. In all of these cases, it is our hope that Tables 2 and 3 provide educational leaders in refugee settings a structure or framework by which they can consider the construction of their literacy programming.

Table 3. Hypothesized Challenges and Possibilities for Applying Literacy
Program Components in Refugee Settings.

Literacy Program Component	Refugee Setting Challenges and Possibilities
Leadership (Literacy Leadership Committee) made up of the principal, literacy specialists; grade level and content area teachers, library media specialists, and consultants	– Leadership committee needs to have representatives from different community stakeholders, including parents, community leaders, and educators. – When possible, should include physical and mental health specialists. – Linguists/L1 to L2 expertise needed for this team.
A grounded ideology or philosophy of literacy development Objectives and goals Clear roles and responsibilities for all involved	– Needs to align with challenging realities on the ground, aligning ideals with what is optimally obtainable. – Clear objectives (e.g., supporting L1 prior to L2) need to be articulated to all involved.
Special services for various segments of the student body	– Very challenging to provide, in some ways, especially for expertise in special education, literacy intervention, second language learning. – Some related special services may be more readily available in the areas of physical and mental health.
Ongoing needs assessment and program evaluation	– Could be very hard to provide traditional literacy assessments that lead to instructional and/or remediation plans. – Student profiles may be created to identify educational background and literacy levels. These profiles could be carried to future educational settings to inform teachers of student needs.
A curriculum plan	– Must match the student population and be targeted at developing first language proficiency. – Challenge of resources and stability could loom large. – Important to consider sustainability.
A staff-development program that provides consultation, in-service training, and sharing opportunities	– Volunteers or temporary and flexible staffing can support community leaders and develop the skills of teachers.
Activities that are result-oriented and promote collaboration and cooperation	– Coordination between stakeholders and clear, agreed upon, objectives would allow for collaboration and a focus on results.

RECOMMENDATIONS FOR LITERACY PROGRAMS IN REFUGEE SETTINGS

Based upon our combined knowledge of best practices in literacy programming and the reality of refugees in the modern context, we provide four key recommendations for supporting literacy development in refugee settings. We understand that very few refugees will be permanently resettled, and, for those who are, it is nearly impossible to predict what language will be spoken in the resettlement country. Therefore, rather than focusing on second language (L2) acquisition in refugee settings, our goal is to promote native language (L1) literacy and foundational literacy skills. It is our belief that these efforts will support individuals' global education as well as their ability to learn a new language.

Teach the Importance of L1 Literacy and Value of Biliteracy

It is not unusual for a bilingual child to misuse a word or grammatical structure from one language when speaking in another. These mistakes have frequently been blamed on language confusion, with many educators suggesting that children should only be taught one language at a time. However, these instances of misspeaking are developmentally appropriate, and akin to a monolingual English-speaking child saying they "sawed the cat" to describe something recently seen (Escamilla & Hopewell, 2011). In the previous example, the child is not "confused," but simply over applying a linguistic pattern they have learned. Likewise, if a bilingual child incorrectly pluralized an adjective (as may be expected with bilingual Spanish/English speakers), they need to be gently corrected, not told to speak only one language.

These types of misunderstandings regarding language acquisition have led many to devalue the development of native language and literacy skills (Escamilla & Hopewell, 2011). This belief is based upon what Cummins (1981) called the *Separate Underlying Principle*, which suggests that the content and skills learned in one language cannot transfer to another. However, as Cummins argues, there is little research to support this model. In fact, learners with stronger literacy skills in their native language (L1) tend to acquire second language (L2) literacy at a faster rate. This fact holds true regardless of the linguistic similarities between the first and subsequent languages (Ovando, Carol, & Collier, 2006). Cummins called this the *Common Underlying Principle*, and this model has been used to support native language literacy acquisition and explain the difficulty of L2-only educational settings.

These research findings naturally led us to our first recommendation for promoting literacy in refugee settings: *teach the importance of L1 literacy and biliteracy*. Deepening learners' native language literacy skills (or literacy skills in native languages for plurilinguals) is likely to be not only more practical than attempting to teach a second language in a refugee setting, but will better prepare individuals to be successful in future environments. However, it is easy to understand how native language proficiency may seem less vital considering the many stressors present for refugees. A parent's implicit beliefs about literacy influence their interactions with their children (DeBaryshe, Binder, & Buell, 2000). Therefore, it is logical to assume that if families are unaware of the value of their native language, they may not realize the importance of emphasizing native language development in crisis settings. Explicitly teaching families the value of their native language will not only help overcome future challenges, but also empower individuals to support the education of those in their communities.

Foundational Literacy Knowledge

Our second recommendation is to *support the acquisition of foundational literacy knowledge*, including the concepts of print and phonemic awareness. Many children acquire concepts of print knowledge at a young age. Their parents read to them, pointing to the words in the book, indicating that the symbols on the page hold a deeper meaning. They quickly learn to recognize common words, such as their names, and know those patterns. This is why you will see very young children picking up books and pretending to read, or others "reading" store logos they can recognize (Tracey & Morrow, 2017). These children understand what print is, and that writing can contain messages and information.

However, acquiring these concepts of print requires meaningful experiences with text. Depending upon their situation before and during refugee status, individuals may not have had sufficient opportunities to interact with texts and acquire these foundational skills related to print. Finding authentic opportunities for individuals to have hands-on interactions with the written word is essential for developing this foundational literacy knowledge. In settings where traditional books may be limited, concepts of print can be taught using available materials, such as the labels on food packaging. A child can learn that the symbols on the outside of the package indicate the contents, and much like their like-aged peers in non-refugee settings, these children can begin to "read" the packaging and develop the value of text.

In addition to concepts of print, we need to develop individuals' phonemic awareness, which will lead to an understanding of phonics. Phonemic awareness is the ability to hear, identify, and manipulate sounds in words. Developing this skill is essential for future reading, as an individual who cannot isolate sounds in words will struggle to identify the corresponding letter (or letters) to represent that sound in words. This is one reason why so many children's books contain rhyming words – when children can identify rhymes, they are hearing the similarities and differences in words.

Helping a learner develop phonemic awareness in their first language will make learning a second language easier. Developing phonemic awareness does not require specialized tools or materials – activities can be completed orally. At the earliest stages, learners can be asked to identify pairs of rhyming words. As that becomes too easy, they can begin to produce rhymes of their own, and begin to classify words that have similar beginning, medial, and ending sounds. Finally, learners can begin to isolate, delete, and substitute sounds in words to make new words.

Focus on Comprehension

Our third recommendation is to *focus on the importance of comprehension*. According to the "Simple View of Reading," reading is composed of an individual's ability to decode the words on the page and understand their meaning (Gough & Tunmer, 1986). Unfortunately, often the first aspect of that model – decoding (the process of understanding how sounds are represented by letters on the page) – becomes the focus of reading instruction. This is likely because it is easy to determine a child's decoding skills – simply have them read words on a page. It is very possible to decode fluently without ever learning the meaning of the text; simply consider the number of individuals who learn a foreign language for religious purposes (e.g., Hebrew or Arabic) without being able to discuss the meaning of text without a translation. However, a primary purpose of reading is to comprehend, and it is possible to build comprehension skills and strategies even when learners have limited access to print.

Throughout most of human history, cultural knowledge has been passed through the generations orally, not through text. Entwined with these traditions are the passage of cultural identity, the survival of which can be threatened when families are removed from their native countries. We can use these oral traditions to not only help groups preserve their identity, but also build comprehension skills, which may translate to later reading development.

As an example, one of the earliest reading comprehension strategies in typical settings is teaching students to monitor their own comprehension. The National Reading Panel (NRP) (2000) suggests that learners must be taught to (1) be aware of what they do understand, (2) identify what they do not understand, and (3) use an appropriate strategy to mend their comprehension difficulties. In other words, we want students to practice metacognitive monitoring and to apply fix-up strategies as needed (Manzo et al., 2009). While these suggestions are made for a text-based setting, children can also be taught to actively engage comprehension monitoring during oral storytelling.

As children age, their understanding of stories (be they printed or oral) moves from the explicit to implicit; that is, comprehending a story shifts from simply being able to explain what happened to "reading between the lines" and understanding more than what was just explicitly stated (NRP, 2000). The same is true of oral tales. Adults can use these stories to scaffold children's inferential comprehension skills by moving from asking questions about what happened in the story, to why the event happened, and, perhaps, to why it mattered that it happened. This would be an example of a maturing picture of literacy as a "reading the lines," "reading between the lines," and "reading beyond the lines" (Manzo et al., 2009, p. 6) activity. Children can be encouraged to connect their own lived experiences and background knowledge to what happened in the oral stories to explain character motives and, thus, develop a deeper understanding of the tale. These skills will later transfer when reading traditional texts.

Encourage the Creation of Texts

At the highest level, being literate does not just mean one is able to understand what is said or written, but one is able to engage in the conversation and contribute toward its further development. This is where writing becomes both an essential, and intimidating, piece of literacy education. Writing requires exposing one's thoughts to others. It is expressive, and requires a certain amount of bravery to, as novelist Jhumpa Lahiri (2011) states, take "the leap from listening to saying, 'listen to me'" (para. 11). This leads us to our final recommendation, *encourage creation of texts*. In essence, we argue that engaging children in the process of creating their own text can give them a voice in an otherwise oppressive setting.

While reading instruction has traditionally taken a more prominent role in educational settings, some current researchers are now arguing for writing instruction to, perhaps, come first. Peter Elbow, for instance, argues that writing is actually a more developmentally appropriate literacy task for young children, as they can write (albeit non-conventionally) any word they can say, whereas they can only read words they have learned to decode (Elbow, 2004). Proposing a child needs to read fluently before he or she can produce a text assumes that the child has nothing worth saying until they are taught how to say it.

While word processors and formal writing tools may be at a premium in refugee settings, children can create other, less traditional texts. Stories can be written on the backs of scrap paper or drawn in chalk. If these materials are not available, children can begin to create oral stories modeled after those told by their families. Regardless of how the text is produced, children can share their stories with each other and their families, allowing for their authorship to be celebrated.

This practice will also support their later reading comprehension, as engaging in the creation of text helps children to recognize that there is an author behind all texts with specific motives, opinions, and purposes for writing. Understanding that texts are created by individuals allows children to better critically analyze what they read and comprehend the materials at a deeper level.

CONCLUSIONS

Earlier in this chapter, we presented nine characteristics of successful literacy programs in traditional educational settings (Manzo et al., 2009) that could guide literacy practices in refugee settings. The first was to establish a clear leadership team. We argue that, in refugee settings, the leadership needs to be primarily comprised of those who make up the population – that is, the refugees themselves. We believe the recommendations we propose here could be conveyed to adults in refugee settings with relative ease, building capacity for individuals to develop literacy in their own community.

The next two literacy program components, a grounded ideology of literacy development and objectives and goals, also underlie our recommendations. We believe that developing individual's first-language skills as well as foundational literacy skills that will translate to other languages will best prepare individuals for their future. Less than one-half of one-percent of all refugees will be permanently resettled (UNHCR, 2016); therefore, emphasizing a second language is unlikely to serve most refugee populations. Instead, our goal must be to build the capacity within refugee settings for individuals to become literate in their first language, and develop skills that will promote success in any language they later need to acquire.

As the world prepares to proactively plan for refugee crises, we will ideally move past only providing food and shelter (as vital as those are) to providing things such as education as well. This chapter discussed concepts involved with the design and assessment of literacy education programming in refugee settings that parallels designs for best practices in school-wide literacy programs that we have in place in more traditional settings. Some theoretical background on literacy development while under duress was also provided, along with a brief listing of a few projects taking place in refugee settings around the world that focus on the reading and literacy development needs of those in those settings. The purpose of this chapter has been to shed some light on this one particular small, but potentially important part of refugee education, with hope that it opens up opportunities for others to get involved and provide relevant aid and educational leadership where possible. Future research should involve furthering the development and assessment of literacy programming in refugee settings that, as much as possible, mirrors best practices in school-wide literacy programming in traditional and more stable settings. Through time and effort in this direction, best practices in refugee literacy programming can be established and then carried out under programs such as the UN General Assembly's recent "New York Declaration," allowing us to make good on our commitment to not only protecting and assisting refugees, but also finding new ways to better organize the responses to refugee crises; in this case, through continually improving literacy education provisions.

ACKNOWLEDGMENTS

The genesis for this chapter was an abbreviated and unpublished paper presented by the first two authors: Thomas, M. M., & Yao, Y. (2016, October). *Reading in refugee camps*. Presentation given at the Consortium for Transatlantic Studies and Scholarship Conference: Uprooted – Refugees/Migrants/The Displaced, October 10–12, University of Central Missouri, Warrensburg, MO.

REFERENCES

Brangham, W. (2016, September 19). Interviewer comments in "UN issues unprecedented declaration on refugee crisis," aired during The PBS NewsHour. Transcript of interview. Retrieved from http://www.pbs.org/newshour/bb/un-issues-unprecedented-declaration-refugee-crisis/

Carrara, V. I., Hogan, C., De Pree, C., Nosten, F., & McGready, R. (2011). Improved pregnancy outcome in refugees and migrants despite low literacy on the Thai-Burmese border: Results of three cross-sectional surveys. *BMC Pregnancy & Childbirth*, *11(45)*, 1–9. doi: 10.1186/1471-2393-11-45

Cummins, J. (1981). The role of primary language development in promoting educational success for language minority students. In California State Department of Education (Ed.), *Schooling and language minority students: A theoretical framework* (pp. 3–49). Los Angeles, CA: National Dissemination and Assessment Center.

DeBaryshe, B. D., Binder, J. C., & Buell, M. J. (2000). Mothers' implicit theories of early literacy instruction: Implications for children's reading and writing. *Early Child Development and Care*, *160*, 119–151.

Dryden-Peterson, S. (2006). The present is local, the future is global? Reconciling current and future livelihood strategies in the education of Congolese refugees in Uganda. *Refugee Survey Quarterly*, *25(2)*, 81–92. doi: 10.1093/rsq/hdi0127

Dwyer, E., & McCloskey, M. L. (2013). Literacy, teens, refugees, and soccer. *Refuge*, *29(1)*, 87–101.

Elbow, P. (2004). Writing first! *Educational Leadership*, *62(2)*, 9–13.

Elmeroth, E. (2003). From refugee camp to solitary confinement: Illiterate adults learn Swedish as a second language. *Scandinavian Journal of Educational Research*, *47(4)*, 431–449.

Escamilla, K., & Hopewell, S. (2011). When learners speak two or more languages. In D. Lapp, & D. Fisher (Eds.), *Handbook of research on teaching the English language arts: Sponsored by the International Reading Association and the National Council of Teachers of English* (pp. 17–21). New York, NY: Routledge.

Grandi, F. (2016, September 19). Interviewee comments in "UN issues unprecedented declaration on refugee crisis," aired during The PBS NewsHour. Transcript of interview. Retrieved from http://www.pbs.org/newshour/bb/un-issues-unprecedented-declaration-refugee-crisis/

Gough, P. B., & Tunmer, W. E. (1986). Decoding, reading, and reading disability. *Remedial and Special Education, 7*(1), 6–10.

International Literacy Association. (2017). Why literacy? Retrieved from https://www.literacyworldwide.org/why-literacy

Lahiri, J. (2011, June). Trading stories: Notes from apprenticeship. *The New Yorker*, June 13 & 20. Retrieved from http://www.newyorker.com/magazine/2011/06/13/trading-stories

Manzo, A. V., & Manzo, U. C. (1993). *Literacy disorders: Holistic diagnosis and remediation.* Orlando, FL: Harcourt Brace Jovanovich.

Manzo, U. C., Manzo, A. V., & Thomas, M. M. (2009). *Content area literacy: A framework for reading-based instruction* (5th ed.). Hoboken, NJ: John Wiley & Sons.

Maslow, A. H. (1954). *Motivation and personality.* New York, NY: Harper Brothers.

Montero, M. K., Newmaster, S., & Ledger, S. (2014). Exploring early reading instructional strategies to advance the print literacy development of adolescent SLIFE. *Journal of Adolescent & Adult Literacy, 58*(1), 59–69. doi: 10.1002/JAAL.318

National Capacity Building Project. (2005). Working with torture survivors: Core competencies. In *National Capacity Building Project's Healing the hurt* (pp. 19–38). Minneapolis, MN: The Center for Victims of Torture. Retrieved from https://www.cvt.org/sites/default/files/u11/Healing_the_Hurt_Ch3.pdf

National Child Traumatic Stress Network. (n.d.). *Impact of complex trauma.* Retrieved from https://www.nctsn.org/sites/default/files/resources//impact_of_complex_trauma.pdf

National Reading Panel (US), & National Institute of Child Health and Human Development (US). (2000). *Report of the National Reading Panel: Teaching children to read: An evidence-based assessment of the scientific research literature on reading and its implications for reading instruction.* Washington, DC: National Institute of Child Health and Human Development, National Institutes of Health.

Oh, S. A., & Van Der Stouwe, M. (2008). Education, diversity, and inclusion in Burmese refugee camps in Thailand. *Comparative Education Review, 52*(4), 589–617.

Ovando, C. J., Carol, M., & Collier, V. P. (2006) *Bilingual and ESL classrooms.* Boston, MA: McGraw Hill.

Perry, K. H., & Hart, S. J. (2012). "I'm just kind of winging it": Preparing and supporting educators of adult refugee learners. *Journal of Adolescent and Adult Literacy, 56*(2), 110–122. doi: 10.1002/JAAL.00112

Sarroub, L., Pernicek, T., & Sweeney, T. (2007). "I was bitten by a scorpion": Reading in and out of school in a refugee's life. *Journal of Adolescent & Adult Literacy, 50*(8), 668–679. doi: 10.1598/JAAL.50.8.5

Shum, K. K., Ho, C. S., Siegel, L. S., & Au, T. K. (2016). First-language longitudinal predictors of second-language literacy in young L2 learners. *Reading Research Quarterly, 51*(3), 323–344. doi: 10.1002/rrq.139

Sparks, R., Patton, J., Ganschow, L., & Humbach, N. (2009). Long-term crosslinguistictransfer of skills from L1 to L2. *Language Learning, 59*(1), 202–243.

Stewart, M. A. (2015). "My journey of hope and peace": Learning from adolescent refugees' lived experiences. *Journal of Adolescent & Adult Literacy, 59*(2), 149–158.

Tracey, D. H., & Morrow, L. M. (2017). *Lenses on reading: An introduction to theories and models.* New York, NY: The Guilford Press.

United Nations. (n.d.). *Refugees.* Retrieved from http://www.un.org/en/sections/issues-depth/refugees/index.html

United Nations High Commission for Refugees (UNHCR). (2016). *Global trends: Forced displacement in 2016.* Retrieved from http://www.unhcr.org/5943e8a34.pdf

US Citizenship and Immigration Services. (n.d.). *Refugees.* Retrieved from https://www.uscis.gov/humanitarian/refugees-asylum/refugees

Van Der Stouwe, M., & Oh, S. A. (2008). Educational change in a protracted refugee context. *Forced Migration Review, 30*, 47–49.

CHAPTER 6

"*START INS DEUTSCHE*" – STUDENTS TEACH GERMAN TO REFUGEES AT GOETHE UNIVERSITY FRANKFURT

Marika Gereke and Subin Nijhawan

ABSTRACT

In September 2015, Germany witnessed an unanticipated migration of refugees toward the European Union. The government established an open-border policy that meant Germany would harbor all refugee arrivals. In large, the civil society joined efforts to create a so-called Willkommenskultur *(welcome culture) during the "summer of welcome."*

This chapter will introduce the project "Start ins Deutsche" (German language kick-off) of Goethe University Frankfurt as an ambitious example of civil society initiatives. Start ins Deutsche *was founded on the premise of "integration by language learning." Within* Start ins Deutsche, *university students volunteer to teach German to refugees. In many cases these refugees have a realistic perspective to enroll into fulltime studies at Goethe University at a later stage to pursue academic degrees.*

In this chapter, the authors outline the project and its main aims. Based on this, the authors thereafter analyze evaluation data about Start ins Deutsche *with regard to the perceptions of German language teachers and their language learners, respectively. The evaluation data of* Start ins Deutsche *reveal that the German language teachers interpret their role beyond being just teachers, while*

Language, Teaching and Pedagogy for Refugee Education
Innovations in Higher Education Teaching and Learning, Volume 15, 91–105
Copyright © 2019 by Emerald Publishing Limited
All rights of reproduction in any form reserved
ISSN: 2055-3641/doi:10.1108/S2055-364120180000015008

the learners appreciate the effort of their teachers in every aspect. Hence, the authors believe the project serves as a best-practice example for a civil society project toward establishing a Willkommenskultur *in Germany.*

Keywords: Long summer of migration; welcome culture; civil society engagement; integration by language learning; refugee support; academic welcome; female refugees; labor market

THE LONG SUMMER OF MIGRATION OF 2015 – A NEW GERMAN *WILLKOMMENSKULTUR?*

On August 31, 2015, German Chancellor Angela Merkel's famous reaction toward voices critical of the skyrocketing numbers of refugees, who had successfully reached Germany, was *Wir schaffen das!* (Yes we can!). Only five days later, amid the overall dimension of the European Refugee Crisis, she even decided to announce an open-border policy to harbor more than a million refugees, according to Eurostat (2017) figures. In other words, to avert a humanitarian catastrophe, Germany decided to provide shelter without red tape when there was no time for deliberation. As a result, Mrs. Merkel was celebrated not only among the liberal press and human rights activists, but also by large parts of the civil society in Germany and beyond. *The Economist* (2015) even went so far as to call her "The Indispensable European."

We should note that this liberal policy toward the sudden and steep increase of refugees was initiated in a country with a legacy of regarding migration only for its own economic benefit. In the past, Germany had few existing supports or provisions for the successful integration of refugees into society. The renowned German author Max Frisch (1965, p. 7) once commented on the history of post-Second World War migration with his famous words: "We called workers, however humans arrived." Thus, the more recent German decision has often been described as the new German *Willkommenskultur* (welcome culture). Subsequently, in an act of unprecedented humanitarianism, German civil society put itself together and founded myriad initiatives and projects showing solidarity, with the ultimate goal to render the *Willkommenskultur* into practice and give Germany a humane face.

These initiatives were preceded by large crowds gathering at train stations to zealously welcome thousands of refugees who had boarded any of the overcrowded trains from *Budapast Keleti* station via *Vienna Westbahnhof.* Pictures from these two train stations revealing devastating humanitarian conditions have sparked a fire in world media about the dimension of this mass exodus toward entering the "Fortress Europe" as a safe and protected space. Consolidation during the "summer of welcome" gradually started after a *de facto* state of emergency with the help of many different actors, including politicians, bureaucrats, activists, and citizens. The question "what next?" echoed after a deep breath in the aftermath of one of the most emotional moments in the German post-Second World War history.

Amid the shortage of mainly – but not only – skilled labor in Germany's economy, long-term prospects for successfully integrating into German society can be classified as reasonably good. Language education for refugees has been identified as indispensable for being capable of entering the labor market and, more importantly, becoming active members within the local society. To support the successful "integration by language learning," Goethe University Frankfurt launched an ambitious program *Start ins Deutsche* (German language kick-off) in 2015,[1] where university students currently enrolled fulltime decided to volunteer teaching German to refugees. Since its beginning, 340 students participated in the project on a voluntary basis, and about 1,200 refugees attended the German language courses provided by *Start ins Deutsche*.

In the following, we firstly give an overview of the history and aims of *Start ins Deutsche,* and describe its main organizational cornerstones. Secondly, we provide quantitative and qualitative data from the evaluation of *Start ins Deutsche*. The evaluation requested students and refugees to indicate their perspectives on the project. We amended this evaluation data with our reflections as volunteer supervisors of the students, who acted as German language teachers within the project. Based on this, we finally discuss the implications of *Start ins Deutsche* for creating and sustaining a *Willkommenskultur* in practice.

START INS DEUTSCHE – AN AMBITIOUS PROJECT TO SUPPORT LANGUAGE INTEGRATION

Language learning is an essential part of integration. Correspondingly, most refugees strive for fast language acquisition. Yet, refugees mostly have long waiting times before obtaining access to professional German language courses. The process of applying for and actually starting a German language course is protracted and complex for many refugees. Moreover, open access to language courses provided by the state is not granted to all refugees per se but depends among other things on their legal status and their prospects to actually be granted asylum (Mediendienst Integration, 2016). To abridge waiting periods and guarantee access to language courses for all refugees, Tanja Brühl, Vice President of Goethe University Frankfurt, initiated the project "Start ins Deutsche – Studierende unterrichten Flüchtlinge" (German Language Kick-off – Students Teach Refugees) in October 2015.

Multiple studies have demonstrated that language skills are a central requirement for integration on various levels – from everyday communication and political participation to education and the labor market (Blossfeld, et al., 2016, p. 86; Esser, 2006). Accordingly, language acquisition constitutes the central pillar of *Start ins Deutsche*. The project provides participating refugees with either language orientation or language intensification. *Start ins Deutsche,* on the one hand, aims to deliver very elementary Basic Interpersonal Communication Skills (BICS) for the daily use of German, especially to a large group of people who have not, or only very rudimentarily, enjoyed formal schooling in their lives. On the other hand, a considerable group of highly qualified refugees can be equipped with Cognitive Academic Language Skills (CALP) in order to be able to complete vocational training or an academic degree, and thus qualify for the job market.

After *Start ins Deutsche* had been launched, an email with a call for language teachers was circulated to the whole student body of Goethe University, comprising far more than 40,000 active students. Within only a few hours after the opening of the call, the online registration system was inundated and, thus, had to be shut down because unexpectedly more than 1,000 students by then had responded and registered their application as volunteer teachers. This overwhelming response exceeded even the most optimist expectations. Thus, students were subsequently requested to include a personal statement of motivation to facilitate selection by the organizing committee.

In late 2015, a three-month pilot phase was launched as a forerunner for the first project phase with a duration of six months. Since the first project phase in early 2016, about 120 students per phase impart German language skills on a voluntary basis. As of early 2018, five project phases have been completed. The sixth phase has just started in March 2018. As about 40% of participating students have been taking part in more than one project phase, thus far about 340 students from a variety of faculties have acted as volunteer teachers for about 1,200 refugees, mainly from Syria, Afghanistan, Iran, Iraq, Eritrea, and the Balkan States.

Whereas most student volunteers involved in the project are female (about 75%, whereby the proportion of female students within the full university student body is 60%), almost all participating refugees were male in the beginning of the project. To actively incorporate female refugees into the project, an active recruitment was launched, and safe spaces provided. Because many female refugees showed discomfort with male-dominated classes, courses designed exclusively for women have been established from the third project phase onwards. These courses take place in *Café Milena*, an institution focusing on female refugees. In addition, parallel child care has been established as a part of all language courses designed for women. For these reasons, participation of female refugees has increased to 25% in a relatively short period of time.

To offer a variety of courses at different locations in the metropolitan area of Frankfurt, Goethe University closely cooperates with other institutions in Frankfurt within *Start ins Deutsche*, including the sponsoring associations of different refugee shelters (e.g., *Johanniter Unfallhilfe e. V.* or *Deutsches Rotes Kreuz – Bezirksverband Frankfurt e. V.*) and *Frankfurt hilft*, a coordination body of voluntary activities, as well as the municipal department for refugee management. All these institutions provide facilities for the language courses, or support *Start ins Deutsche* with other resources, such as organizing direct contact to refugees. In this manner, teaching teams of two or three students were assembled to teach different groups of refugees at least once a week in their shelters, in facilities of the university or in *Café Milena*. In each location, language courses take place five times a week, but are interchangeably offered by different teaching teams. Meanwhile, language courses take place in seven different locations in Frankfurt (see Table 1).

In general, *Start ins Deutsche* is financed by private donors and foundations, and supported by the close cooperation of mainly non-state institutions. Different groups of volunteers fulfilling various roles within the project (also see below) constitute the backbone of the initiative. Such civil society engagement

Table 1.   Overview of Project Locations and Courses during
the Fourth Project Phase.

Location	Background Information	Number of University Students	Number and Format of Language Courses
Location 1: Bockenheim	80 Refugees, including families and single males	42	Two intensive courses on level A1 and A2 Six open courses Daily homework supervision
Location 2: Bonames	300 Refugees, mainly families	12	Existing course offers supported by students
Location 3: Gutleut	250 Refugees, mainly single males	8	Four open courses, including one course for women
Location 4: Ludwig-Landmannstraße	440 Refugees, families and single males	13	Six open courses, including one course for women
Location 5: Rödelheim	170 Refugees, families and single males	7	Three open courses
Location 6: Café Milena	Course offers for women and girls	10 Female students	One intensive course
Location 7: Westend (University)	80 Refugees	48	Four intensive courses on levels A1, A2, and B1

has become indispensable in an area where state institutions per se lack the capacity, or even the will, to cater the necessary resources for providing refugees with the opportunities for a life with dignity.

COURSE OF PROJECT PHASES

Each of the six-month course phases has consisted of various parts, including an application period, a two-day training of the students, the language courses constituting the heart of the project, an accompanying supervision for the German language teachers and an evaluation at the end of each phase (see Fig. 1). The cornerstones of *Start ins Deutsche* are described in more detail in the following.

Two-day Training

Many student volunteers lack experience in teaching German as a foreign language. To gain basic language instruction training and be introduced to issues relevant to refugee work, participating students are obliged to take part in two-day training courses before beginning their teaching activities. These training courses are voluntarily offered by lecturers of Goethe University in cooperation with members of the *Goethe University Law Clinic*, an association of law students providing legal advice concerning questions related to asylum, and by an association for refugee academics (*Academic Experience Worldwide e. V.*). In these courses, students are equipped with basic knowledge about teaching theories and concepts and receive an insight into foreign language teaching and intercultural learning, respectively. Moreover, they are informed about legal issues related to asylum and adequate approaches to dealing with traumatic experiences.

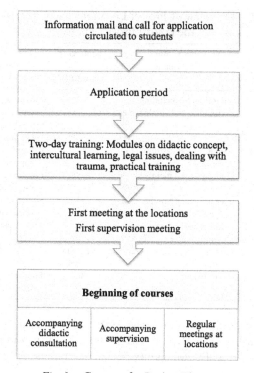

Fig. 1.   Course of a Project Phase.

Language Courses

Before the beginning of the language courses, a meeting is organized at each location involved in the project (see Table 1). During these meetings, students and staff of the locations jointly establish teaching teams, define course hours, and discuss main requirements and procedures at the respective location.

Subsequently, all teaching teams begin to offer their courses at least once a week at all of the different locations. Each course hour is independently prepared by the teaching teams based on a specialized textbook focusing on German as a foreign language. The teaching teams moreover conduct a class assessment after each course hour. The results of these assessments are provided on a virtual learning platform. In this manner, all teaching teams regularly exchange information about teaching concepts, learners' progress, and possible difficulties.

To deliver BICS as well as CALP, *Start ins Deutsche* offers language courses of different formats. Open courses, provided at nearly all locations, are not geared to a specific language level or certificate and mainly aim at providing a basic language orientation. In *intensive courses*, on the other hand, refugees are prepared to achieve a pre-identified language level (ranging from level A1 to B1 on the *Common European Framework of Reference for Languages* (CEFR)). All *intensive courses* are offered in cooperation with the *Academic Welcome*

Programme for highly qualified refugees of the International Office of Goethe University Frankfurt. These courses are intended for refugees in need of further language skills for vocational training, or to take up higher education in pursuing a University degree, respectively, allow refugees to continue studies they may have started abroad. Refugees have to apply for *intensive courses*, including the completion of an assessment test. Feedback regarding the *intensive courses* indicates that course participants appreciate the intense learning atmosphere, can develop contacts to different faculties as well as students of Goethe University and become part of university life.

A new course program – *Begegnungen schaffen* (enabling encounters) – has been established in Summer 2017. In different modules, student volunteers and refugees can deal with political, societal, or historical issues and learn from each other in an interactive way. All refugees with advanced language skills (at least equal to CEFR A2.2) are granted access to these courses provided by specifically trained students.

As described above, all course formats are also tailored for women within their safe space. Apart from language or thematic courses, *Start ins Deutsche* also offers homework assistance for children.

Supervision

To provide student volunteers with a space to reflect on their experiences in the language courses, all participating student volunteers are obliged to take part in an accompanying, professional supervision once every three or four weeks. Lecturers of Goethe University, staff of the *Psychoanalytic Institute Frankfurt,* and the *Teacher Training College Frankfurt* voluntarily act as supervisors. In all supervision groups, students can share their experiences and discuss challenges with their fellows eventually encountered in the language courses. Approaches to solving problems and difficulties as well as suggestions for further improvements of the language courses (e.g., regarding didactic concepts) are discussed together during the supervision sessions.

EVALUATION OF *START INS DEUTSCHE* BY GERMAN LANGUAGE TEACHERS AND THE LANGUAGE LEARNERS

Start ins Deutsche was pragmatically founded from scratch without any prior existing experience or masterplan in order to respond to the sudden demand for opening a perspective for the high number of refugees. All involved actors thus are committed to pioneer work and participate in the outline and planning of the project. Thus, evaluation by students for the continuous development of *Start ins Deutsche* has been identified as a cornerstone of the project, for the further improvement and even its emulation. In other words, the effort is made to foster a best-practice exercise. The following evaluation data of all four phases serve as a mirror of the perception of volunteer language teachers and refugees, respectively, and provide the basis for the discussion of the new *German Willkommenskultur*. Looking at both sides and the development of their relationship proves useful for evaluating the project's ability to act as an integrating and unifying force.

Data on German Language Teachers

Careful estimates from the data available indicate that almost 9 out of 10 local students lacked both experience as a language teacher and previous engagement in social work with refugees. The initiative served as an opportunity to attain first-hand experience. Table 2 shows selected aggregated answers of the German language teachers from all four evaluation phases. It gives an overview on main motivating factors, as well as selected qualitative responses to the open answers. More than 90% of students state more *altruist reasons*, displaying their motivation to help and contributing toward improving the overall situation of the refugees. About 80% and 70% of the students, respectively, point out that they are touched by the refugees' situation, and cannot simply serve as lone observers. These selected answers supersede more *self-interested reasons*, that is, proximity to curricular needs (40%) as well as professional CV development (16.2%).

The qualitative comments from the open response section underscore the previous aggregated responses very lucidly. A firm belief in humanism, a desire for change, and building bridges mainly appeared as categories. Also, curiosity and a positive challenge of "meeting the other," as well as a desire to counter current right-wing developments in society are noteworthy.

The students were also requested to reflect on and evaluate their overall experience in a set of different questions. Table 3 shows the average results. We will first analyze those, before in detail presenting the analysis of qualitative items that deserve careful attention, because they delineate very clearly the experiences the students made beyond being mere language teachers.

From the data, at first we learn that the language volunteers believed their students improved their German language skills significantly. But more importantly, we can infer that many of the students mostly redefined their roles firmly beyond the scope of teaching. In fact, they also offered their friendship and active support during their daily business and their attempt to cope with the new life after their struggle to arrive in Germany as their save heaven. Furthermore, students saw themselves as cultural ambassadors, serving as advisors, counselors, and even active caregivers in the effort to provide a warm welcome to Germany. The German language courses, as we learn from the data, were seen as a forum for cultural understanding. In the end, realizing the positive spirit of the program, it does not come as a surprise that 70% of the students involved in the first round continued to be engaged as language teachers and beyond within *Start ins Deutsche*.[2]

The students also gave very detailed qualitative feedback. To put the answers into a nutshell, the students assisted refugees in their daily business and errands, such as accompanying them to the supermarket, buying tickets for local transport, as well as in more formal responsibilities. This includes

Table 2. (Motivation): What were the Reasons You Registered as Volunteer Teacher for *Start ins Deutsche?*

Answer	Percentage	Population (*N*)
Because I want to contribute towards improving the situation of refugees	94	212
Because I want to help	93	213
Because the current living conditions of the refugees touch me	80	138
Because I can't tolerate just being an observer only	70	137
Because it is a useful activity for my educational curriculum	40	138
Because it is a useful extracurricular activity for my CV	16	138

Table 3. (Experience): Personal Experiences – Also beyond Teaching German at *Start ins Deutsche.*

Answer	Mean	Population (*N*)
My experience to teach refugees was positive	1.20	242
I would recommend my friends to join the program	1.60	239
German language courses contribute to cultural understanding	1.67	238
My students were able to improve their German proficiency	1.75	236
The participants benefited from the contact with me as their teacher	2.18	236
I was able to support the creation of a Willkommenskultur	2.30	51
I was able to build bridges into German society	2.54	235
It was more important to be a human than a teacher	2.78	236
I was able to provide practical life support	2.81	234
I was a cultural ambassador for Germany	2.91	233

Scale: 5-point Likert scale (1 – completely; 5 – not at all).

writing letters and emails, filling forms and applications, or doing translation work. In many cases, they even accompanied them to official appointments, to the doctor, and helped to open bank accounts. The student language teachers mentioned various times that they helped refugees to find apartments and, if they possessed an exceptional work permit, jobs. Language teachers privately collected material goods, as clothes, or toys for children. For language students enrolled in the *intensive courses*, students served as counselors with their prospective application for higher education at Goethe University. Some language teachers even initiated contact to lawyers and legal and/or psychological practitioners and thus provided valuable assistance in everyday and legal matters – and hence provided inestimable human support.

A *Willkommenskultur* definitely comprises interactions beyond formal assistance in daily and legal matters. Noteworthy is the high share of responses that indicate a deep degree of intercultural exchange in the wake of *Start ins Deutsche*. Language teachers met during their leisure time with refugees and planned activities, including cooking, playing games, or watching movies. Sports such as football provided a common ground and unifying force, as reported by a comparatively high number of respondents. They took refugees on city excursions, went to the museum, and had talks on political and cultural topics. Even reciprocal private birthday invitations were mentioned among the experiences within *Start ins Deutsche*. As the language teachers indicated, such exercises were combined with practicing the German language at such occasions.

For the language teachers, the meetings comprised more than simply voluntary language teaching. As we can infer from the responses, the language teachers mostly interpreted their role actively, offering help, but also as a time to enter into a welcoming cultural exchange. One language teacher indicates that the participation at *Start ins Deutsche* paved the way for experiences and competences which can never be emulated and learned during the course of academic study. One other comment very nicely shows the deep impact of *Start ins Deutsche* on many of the university students. The student said at the beginning that he wanted to make sure that the refugees learn German as efficiently as possible. Later, he realized that "simply having a good time together" even superseded any progress in language acquisition.

Data on Language Learners

In spite of the difficult circumstances in terms of organization and language barriers, one evaluation round was carried out with big efforts to have the opinion of the language learners on their teachers, the classes, and their improvement in German.

Table 4 includes the accumulated responses of all language learners. The satisfaction with teachers and classes is very high. Self-assessment with reference to improvement in language skills is a bit lower as compared to the teachers' perception (see Table 3), but still in the range of being rated "good." The respondents took the effort to provide qualitative feedback as well. These comments mostly consist of great gratitude, that is, saying thank you, and appreciating the diligence the language teachers exhibited throughout. The respondents of the *intensive courses*, mostly at a higher initial level of education, were also slightly more critical with their overall grading. Table 5 shows the evaluation of the participants of the *intensive courses*.

Although these numbers are slightly lower, the difference within the overall evaluation is insignificant. Qualitative comments similarly indicate a high degree of satisfaction with *Start ins Deutsche*. However, very straightforward recommendations were also offered by language learners. These included the demand for more grammar in language teaching (CALP) as well as more tailored courses for individual progress, because some of the language learners did not feel challenged enough. They can be classified as being very ambitious in their educational pathways and hence show eagerness to enter higher education at the earliest possible convenience and thus wish to finally be enrolled into a university course.

In sum, it can be said that the satisfaction with *Start ins Deutsche*, and especially with its teachers constructing a real *Willkommenskultur*, is very high. This indeed serves as a first but important step for successful integration into the German society.

Table 4. (Refugee Evaluation): How do Grade Your Teachers, the Quality of
Classes and Your Language Progress?

Answer	Grade	Population (N)
Quality of teachers	1.65	67
Quality of classes	1.87	67
Improvement of German language skills	2.38	67

Scale: German middle school grading system (1 – very good; 3 – satisfactory; 6 – insufficient).

Table 5. (Refugee Evaluation; only the Participants of the Intensive Course):
How do Grade Your Teachers, the Quality of
Classes and Your Language Progress?

Answer	Grade	Population (N)
Quality of teachers	1.84	45
Quality of classes	2.13	45
Improvement of German language skills	2.46	45

Scale: German middle school grading system (1 – very good; 3 – satisfactory; 6 – insufficient).

Impressions from Our Supervision Groups

Both of the authors were supervisors of the German language teachers from the beginning and took part in an early meeting where anticipated supervision challenges were discussed. The initiative of Goethe University along with all professional structures and resources offered an apt opportunity for us to join hands with many Germans offering their active civil society support toward the refugees. Together, we supervised one group of language teachers in every phase of the program, ranging from 10 to 22 students per group. What follows is a summary of our experiences, which, when triangulated to the evaluation data, gives a more nuanced idea about the implications the initiative had on the creation of a *Willkommenskultur*.

At the beginning of each round, we wanted to know what motivated the students to volunteer as language teachers and what challenges they anticipated. We were curious why so many young people had registered as volunteer teachers, despite the generally heavy workload associated with college education. Through questions asked during the supervision sessions, we were able to collect ample evidence from every round that most students joined *Start ins Deutsche* mostly out of *altruistic* reasons, as the evaluation data suggest. Indeed, we have the impression that the aforementioned engagement of the volunteer teachers was not based on personal gain, but instead was directed toward the ultimate goal of an active *Willkommenskultur*, and a harbinger of long-term societal change. To echo the results of the surveys, the students simply wanted to actively help in the light of the dimension the migration movement had reached.

In particular, we observed – and were impressed by – the students and their ability to enter perspective changes, and understand, feel, and talk about their emotions as a precursor to create empathy. We could witness deep reflection processes being triggered by their teaching experience, and often by their first direct contact with refugees in their lifetime. These experiences led to vivid conversations and debates within our supervision sessions. Our students were often deeply touched by the legal and organizational burdens refugees had to face to organize their life in dignity – challenges the students volunteers would never personally face in life. As already shown, these first-hand experiences were complemented by many activities outside of the classroom. We were happy to personally experience their real passion during these activities in detail.

A big part of the supervision always dealt with very common didactic and educational advice requested by the student volunteers. The questions included how to organize heterogeneous classrooms, how to balance grammar and communication, and how to organize improved learning processes. We often heard about language learners from the *intensive courses* who had high expectations and demands for properly learning the language in order to be qualified for the *Academic Welcome Programme* as early as possible – to live a normal live in dignity following the exodus.

Among the main challenges the students expressed was their general insecurity about possible cultural misconceptions and the question about the nature of the relationship *(teachers only, or friends?)*. Furthermore, we observed their anxiety having to deal with traumatic experiences of the refugee as a result of their escape to Germany. Indeed, the latter more frequently became an issue, because our students listened first-hand to narratives of human dignity and suffering from being dislocated as refugees.

Such advice seeking was further amplified by gender issues that took up a significant amount of discussion time within our sessions. As noted earlier, the majority of language teachers were female students. Volunteers were particularly concerned that female language learners often hesitated to participate in male-dominated classrooms, or were busy with providing care to children. *Café Milena* proved to be a safe space where care and assistance was improved, and also signaled that concerns of both German language teachers as well as language learners were taken seriously.

The high number of language teachers who decided to continue their engagement with *Start ins Deutsche* can be seen as the strongest evidence speaking for a *Willkommenskultur* growing from below. In the following, we will locate the project into this very discussion that has been reverberating since the "summer of welcome."

START INS DEUTSCHE – ANIMATING THE *WILLKOMMENSKULTUR*

Start ins Deutsche was founded by the university during a time that required fast and unbureaucratic responses to efficiently address the many new challenges for Germany. The aims were initially designed over and above providing emergency relief to the refugees who had been dislocated as a result of war and poverty. Language education is seen as an integrating force to establish a real *Willkommenskultur*. This includes initiatives that are directed toward not only mediating BICS, but also CALP, to subsequently enable refugees entering higher education and becoming active and equal citizens within the course of time. The program is mainly driven by the efforts of volunteer teachers who have proven to act even as friends. Rather, it has become a common custom among the group of German language teachers to pragmatically chaperone their language learners by supporting them to organize their immediate circumstances and build a foundation for future life in Germany. This idea is embodied in the overall idea of creating a *Willkommenskultur*.

In many instances, refugees stay only temporarily, often without certainty whether or not asylum will be granted at all. It is the common experience that the application for asylum is a longlasting and fraught procedure. At the same time, refugees throughout the asylum procedure only receive little integrative support by state institutions and can only enter the job market under exceptional circumstances. *Start ins Deutsche* however exists under the premise that language skills are a key step toward full integration and ultimately a transition of society. In other words, the university has established a structure that not only addresses global challenges and realities, but, first and foremost, also recognizes the identity and destiny of the refugees. We provided evidence with the data we presented, that shows how sustainable interpersonal relationships among German language teachers and their language learners have developed. This form of recognition (Taylor & Gutmann, 1992) has also been pursued by other civil society actors across Germany, albeit mostly on a smaller scale. However, more grassroots-like activism, as we have learned, can lead to a real and enduring societal change.

In the end, civil society ambition and action play an important part in addressing challenges arising from the global and social realities of postmodern globalization. The *Willkommenskultur* has, to borrow from Bhabha (1994), expedited the creation of Third Spaces for the gradual negotiation and renegotiation of identity and culture. What is more, we may be witnessing a new dynamics of transculturality (Welsch, 1998) from below – Germany could hitherto never witness. Intermingled with our current global realities, we believe that Beck's (2006) well-known *cosmopolitan vision* has become tangible at long last.

OUTLOOK

During the "summer of welcome" outlined at the beginning, an unprecedented civil engagement supporting refugees emerged in Germany, a "happening" that has even been described as a new social movement (Karakayali & Kleist, 2016). This still ongoing civil society engagement mainly consists of self-organized initiatives and organizational structures beyond the long-established associations in refugee work. *Start ins Deutsche* represents one of these newly emerged, non-traditional initiatives striving for an open and integrative *Willkommenskultur* in Germany. By initiating the program, Goethe University Frankfurt created a link for students enabling them to actively support language integration for refugees. Challenging arguments about a missing interest among refugees in integration, such offers are highly popular among refugees (Karakayali & Kleist, 2016).

Apart from the unparalleled *Willkommenskultur*, however, critical comments to openly racist voices concerning a liberal asylum and immigration policy continuously echoed in German society culminating in the electoral successes of the racist party *Alternative für Deutschland* (AfD) in 2017. For the first time since the end of the Second World War, a xenophobic party entered the *Bundestag,* mainly on an anti-refugee and anti-immigrant ticket. Moreover, the current government introduced a restrictive turn in asylum policy since the end of 2015 which is, for example, characterized by an extension of so-called "secure countries of origins,"[3] a suspension of family reunification and the negotiation of deals with Turkey and Libya to combat migration to Europe at their boarder gateways.

Against the background of this right-wing backlash, civil society engagement appears to be of utter importance, a beacon of light that reflects a *Willkommenskultur.* Such engagement is unprecedented since the beginning of the large-scale post-Second World War migration to Germany mainly during the 1960s and thereafter. All the projects and initiatives arising during the "summer of welcome" have the potential of long-lasting support for refugees, and provide spaces of intercultural encounters. Yet, while recognizing its own responsibility toward refugees, we believe the state administration should increase its sponsorship of and facilitate civil society engagement to enable projects such as *Start ins Deutsche* to foster and manifest a continuous *Willkommenskultur.* In this vein, *Start ins Deutsche* and other projects based on voluntary engagement would highly benefit from continuous state funding in order to facilitate long-term planning and sustainable support for refugees.

NOTES

1. We thank Tanja Brühl and the whole team of *Start ins Deutsche* for sharing the evaluation data and their valuable comments.
2. As other data suggest, those students who interrupted or terminated their volunteer profession, did so mostly for pragmatic reasons, for instance, their upcoming graduation, a semester abroad, and so on.
3. According to German law, refugees from so-called "secure countries of origin" may not be granted asylum.

REFERENCES

Beck, U. (2006). *The Cosmopolitan vision.* Cambridge: Polity.
Bhabha, H. K. (1994). *The location of culture.* London: Routledge.
Blossfeld, H. P., Bos, W., Daniel, H. D., Hannover, B., Köller, O., Lenzen, D., …, Wößmann, L. (2016). *Integration durch Bildung: Migranten und Flüchtlinge in Deutschland.* Münster, Germany: Waxmann.
Esser, H. (2006). *Migration, sprache und integration. AKI-Forschungsbilanz 4.* Berlin, Germany: Arbeitsstelle Interkulturelle Konflikte und gesellschaftliche Integration (AKI).
Eurostat. (2017). Asylum and first time asylum applicants by citizenship, age and sex. Annual aggregated data (rounded) *Population and Social Conditions.* Retrieved from http://ec.europa.eu/eurostat/en/web/products-datasets/-/MIGR_ASYAPPCTZA
Frisch, M. (1965). Preface. In A. J. Seiler, *Siamo italiani: Die Italiener. Gespräche mit italienischen Arbeitern in der Schweiz.* Zürich: EVZ-Verlag.

Karakayali, S., & Kleist, O. (2016). EFA-Studie-2. *Strukturen und Motive der ehrenamtlichen Flüchtlingsarbeit (EFA) in Deutschland.* Berlin, Germany: Berliner Institut für empirische Integrations- und Migrationsforschung.

Mediendienst Integration. (2016, March 8). *Herkunft entscheidet über Integrations-Chancen.* Retrieved from https://mediendienst-integration.de/artikel/bleibeperspektive-asylverfahren-asyl-integrationskurs-afghanistan-syrien.html

Taylor, C., & Gutmann, A. (1994). *Multiculturalism: Examining the politics of recognition.* Princeton, NJ: Princeton University Press.

The Economist. (2015, November 7). The Indispensable European. *The Economist.* Retrieved from https://www.economist.com/news/leaders/21677643-angela-merkel-faces-her-most-serious-political-challenge-yet-europe-needs-her-more

Welsch, W. (1999). Transculturality: The puzzling form of cultures today. In M. Featherstone & S. Lash (Eds.), *Spaces of culture: City, nation, world* (pp. 194–213). London: Sage.

PART II

TECHNOLOGY AND HIGHER EDUCATION

CHAPTER 7

REFUGEES, EDUCATION, AND DISABILITY: ADDRESSING THE EDUCATIONAL NEEDS OF ARABIC-SPEAKING REFUGEES WITH LEARNING CHALLENGES

David Banes, Carine Allaf and Maggie Mitchell Salem

ABSTRACT

Estimates suggest there are currently over 15 million Arabic-speaking refugees and internally displaced persons. The average duration of displacement has increased from 9 years in 1993 to 17 years in 2003 (Loescher & Milner 2006) and is still increasing. It is difficult to determine the precise number of people with a disability within the refugee community. Estimates vary but at least 10% of that population have some form of disability, while others suggest that this figure is around 22%, using a broader definition of needs and including those with undiagnosed disabilities as well as psychosocial trauma (Karasapan, 2016). Based on three years of intensive development including discussions with a range of humanitarian and educational organizations, government agencies, and philanthropic entities, the authors have identified the paucity of digital educational content as a significant and pressing challenge for all Arabic learners, with a major impact upon those with additional needs or disabilities. This chapter addresses the key issues to be considered in planning for and accommodating those needs within an inclusive context.

Keywords: Disability; education; refugees; education technology; access; accessibility

Language, Teaching and Pedagogy for Refugee Education
Innovations in Higher Education Teaching and Learning, Volume 15, 109–124
Copyright © 2019 by Emerald Publishing Limited
All rights of reproduction in any form reserved
ISSN: 2055-3641/doi:10.1108/S2055-364120180000015009

INTRODUCTION

The Need

This chapter outlines the lessons learned and principles developed in planning for an inclusive model of education for refugees. When we speak of the challenge of refugees and forced migrants from the Middle East, it is difficult to comprehend the scale of the issue. There are approximately 15 million Arabic-speaking refugees and internally displaced persons currently. The average duration of displacement has increased from 9 years in 1993 to 17 years in 2013 (Edwards, 2014) and the length of displacement may be increasing year-on-year, resulting in children who could spend their whole lives in displacement. Well over 50% of these populations are under the age of 20 (United Nations High Commissioner for Refugees [UNHCR], 2017). When such a movement of people occurs, traditional humanitarian responses include food, clothing, and shelter. Education, more traditionally seen as part of the development paradigm, has entered the humanitarian response, not only as a need, but also as a right. As the years of living in displacement increase above the average of 17 years, the line between a humanitarian response and the development phase is increasingly blurred. In a humanitarian response, less than 2% of aid is allocated for education (United Nations Office for the Coordination of Humanitarian Affairs [UNOCHA], 2016). When education is provided, the quality is often a variable and for those with a disability or additional learning needs there are many additional challenges to overcome.

It is difficult to determine the precise number of people with a disability within the refugee and displaced community. (For the purposes of this chapter, we will refer to refugees, migrants, and internally displaced people simply as displaced people.) Data are scarce on this issue and it is hard to formally quantify actual needs. It is likely that at least 10% of that population have some form of disability and when the impact of trauma, injury, and the general wellbeing of displaced people are considered, Karasapan (2016) reports that it is likely that this figure is estimated to be closer to 22% if using a broader definition of needs, to include those with hidden disabilities, such as those with learning difficulties such as reading and writing impairments including dyslexia.

In a report prepared by Handicap International, which is based on primary data collected from 3,200 refugees, it was found that 30% of displaced people in Jordan and Lebanon have specific needs that include:

- one in five refugees is affected by physical, sensory, or intellectual impairment;
- one in seven is affected by chronic disease;
- one in 20 suffers from injury, with nearly 80% of these injuries directly resulting from the conflict; and
- 77% of older refugees (age 60+) are affected by impairment, injury, or chronic disease.

Refugees affected by impairment, injury, or chronic diseases are twice as likely as the general refugee population to report signs of psychological distress. The report further states that 65% of older refugees present signs of psychological distress, and 45% of refugees with specific needs have problems in carrying out simple daily tasks.

It is important to understand that displaced people with a disability were always part of their home population prior to any conflict or disruption. They sought refuge like others, although some may not have been able to make the journey safely. Such conflicts inevitably lead to more people becoming disabled, not only in the conflict zone, but also in seeking escape and even within camps. This increases the number of individuals with disability significantly.

Physical disability, hearing, and sight loss are all commonplace in such conflict zones. In the immediate aftermath of seeking safety, basic humanitarian needs such as food, shelter, heating, and clothing are a priority. For those with a disability, basic aids for daily living and mobility are always urgently required, including mobility aids such as wheelchairs and aids for personal care.

However, as the crisis continues, those with a disability express the same aspirations as their peers. They seek access to employment and education, but face additional barriers if opportunities are not inclusive, and limited to begin with. While many initiatives speak of meeting the needs of all displaced people within a community, few deliver upon that for the population of those with a disability. Disability is generally an afterthought in planning and programming.

Addressing the Educational Needs of Refugees with a Disability

In seeking to address the specific educational needs of refugees with a disability, it is important to appreciate that by meeting the needs of those displaced people with a disability there are benefits to other groups seeking access to a quality education. Those who have had a severely disrupted education present themselves as having little or no literacy and find the learning of a host language extremely challenging. Many do not have the basic skills and attitudes to settle into learning if they are adolescents, while others are coping with the impact of trauma, both within the conflict areas and the host countries. There are many young people who are noncommunicative or uncooperative due to trauma and there is a need to offer tools and solutions that assist them in recovering their voice, both emotionally and sometimes literally. Many of the tools and techniques that benefit people with a disability have additional value to the wider population. For instance, text-to-speech tools that support people with low vision or dyslexia can be of great value to those learning to read a second language.

While some forms of assistance have been offered, and there are excellent examples of projects that focus upon the needs of those with a disability, such as employment projects by World Vision (Laguardia, 2017) or education projects for the deaf developed by the Holy Land Institute for the Deaf (Said Foundation, 2017), much less has been done to build inclusive projects that integrate needs within wider planning and from the beginning of the program development cycle.

One example of a project that sought to address the needs of those with a disability was undertaken by Handicap International to register displaced people with disabilities in Jordan. The project sought to address the need for humanitarian actors to have information and knowledge about available and appropriate tools for the collection of data about persons with disabilities. Such data were to provide a foundation upon which planning could take place. In many cases, such actors did not know how many people with disabilities were in camps and urban areas. Without knowing the number of people with disabilities, humanitarian actors were not equipped to identify their needs and implement inclusive projects. However, this presents its own challenge, as many displaced people in general – with or without a disability – are afraid of any formal registration processes. However, it is a step in the right direction because of its programming that targets those with a disability explicitly.

There is a major challenge in the integration of those with a disability across settings including both camps and urban settings and is well demonstrated when we consider access to education. Access to education is dependent upon many factors including policy, the quality of teaching and learning, accessible materials, and the design of inclusive schools and classrooms (Mattingly & McInerney, 2015). Moreover, people with a disability interviewed by the author in Jordan cited the need for access to the built environment, infrastructure, information, and transportation as significant in facilitating access to education. Many displaced people report the same challenges.

However, disrupted, displaced people with or without a disability bring with them expectations of learning, preferred learning styles, and their own culture into the education system. Efforts to create an educational response must build upon that prior knowledge. Even while learning the language of a host county, resources and materials are required in the mother tongue of the learners, although there may be both dialect and cultural variations between the refugee community and the host community.

When discussing the crisis in the Arab world, there is a significant lack of Arabic digital content; and when we speak of freely available and accessible Arabic digital content, we are speaking of extremely limited resources. Increasingly, approaches to addressing the needs of displaced people are founded upon the integration of digital approaches to education (Collins, 2015). Digital approaches are characterized by a series of factors including a digital device, digital content, and an infrastructure to deliver content on the device. However, few projects consider how to address the needs of those with a disability. Projects such as World Refugee School,[1] recognize the importance of a blend of digital and traditional approaches but offer no additional resources to assist those with or teaching learners with special needs.

An additional approach to meeting these demands has been offered by Rumie,[2] an education access orientated nonprofit organization that offers an android tablet-based solution that is preloaded with educational textbooks, videos, and games tailored to a student's age and curriculum. Such tablets are intended to offer interactive digital libraries in a cost-effective manner. All the learning content can be used offline, making each tablet a portable library for students to use wherever and whenever they want. Such devices offer the potential of interacting with access tools that are built into the operating system.

Education Delivery and Displaced Learners

Digital approaches to education within the displacement context may be delivered in very different ways, and might include the following:

- Formal schooling, blended into traditional classrooms with qualified teachers guiding the use of the materials.
- Nonformal schooling, offered in a range of settings within camps and urban settings and often delivered by unqualified educational facilitators.
- Self-directed learning, where there is little or no opportunity for interaction with a teacher or facilitator.

Across the life of a displaced learner, educational experience may incorporate one or all these modes. It is the fluidity of educational experience that characterizes the learning of displaced persons. As a result of such fluidity, it is often difficult to maintain the evidence of prior learning and accreditation.

For those with additional needs, we can recognize that education is also not delivered through one model only. In some cases, learners with a disability attend formal schools; however, they may not experience a full curriculum and the school may prioritize health and therapeutic needs above academic needs. The quality may be low for all learners, let all alone those who require modifications and accommodations. They may be receiving some sort of education otherwise, with informal teaching taking place, such as that facilitated by family or peers, but the lack of training and experience is likely to be acute in areas such as differentiation and those that seek to self-direct their own learning may find considerable barriers in the design and availability of learning resources.

To address the needs of such learners, the authors identified a series of key principles through discussions with stakeholders that can be applied in the design of any solution.

These include the following:

- Addressing the needs of learners with a disability from the start of the design of a project or program.
- Using technology to support and scale learning.
- Offering quality accessible Arabic digital content.
- Creating and providing content-based upon open sharing and collaboration with other initiatives.
- Aligning all content to national curricula of different countries.
- Delivering content that seeks to build the twenty-first century skills.
- Delivering content that is based upon free and open licenses.
- Offering content and platform that is usable in high, low, and no-connectivity areas through multiple devices such as a smartphone, tablet, or personal computer (PC).
- Reflecting the fluidity of experience in displaced communities in providing uninterrupted education from a variety of starting points/educational backgrounds for a variety of purposes (re-entry into formal education; entry into higher education; entry into labor market).
- Fully engaging with the affected community in the design process from the beginning.

Building a Model of Delivery

Where the educational needs of displaced people are founded upon an online-delivery model as a chain, it becomes important that at each link in that chain is based upon adequate consideration and planning for the needs of those with disabilities and special needs. In planning an inclusive model, care must be taken that any online platform is designed to interact with assistive technologies. It is likely that many learners will use mobile and portable technologies for at least some of their learning. While there may be some access to PC's, most refugees are likely to use tablets and phones for their interactions. In a recent seminar in Berlin, few of the many developers of platforms and those commissioning platforms were aware of accessibility standards. It was therefore not surprising that few of the platforms were easily used by those with additional needs. Equally, few of the platforms reviewed had incorporated English- or Arabic-Access tools into their design, severely limiting their usability for those with a disability. An introduction to tools such as ATBar,[3] an open-source browser plugin for Arabic and English, was enlightening to many. The delivery chain is made up of closely related links, each with implications for those with special needs: platform, content, and delivery partners.

THE DELIVERY PLATFORM

The delivery platform has three core elements.

Appropriate Hardware Devices

Hardware devices may include computers, tablets, and mobile phones. Discussions with refugee educators at The No Lost Generation Summit in Amman (2017) and UNESCO Mobile Learning Week in Paris (2017) would suggest that where the basis of digital learning is a computer or tablet, that access is likely to be on a shared basis and provided though a national or international initiative. In many cases however, where learners are using their personal devices, these are likely to be low-cost android smartphones or in some cases simple phones running a pre-smart phone OS such as Symbian. Many displaced learners interviewed did have access to a low-specification smartphone, but this might be on a shared basis with other family members, limiting the available time for its use for learning. However, the availability suggests an opportunity for those providing access to a digital curriculum.

In discussion groups at conferences, refugees described the immense importance of having access to a smartphone but stressing the challenge of maintaining such a phone including problems on obtaining spare parts such as chargers and funding any repairs. In discussion with the authors, the refugees and displaced persons shared their handsets around the table with examples held together with sticky tape along with many cracked screens and cases.

If such devices are to be provided, they should meet accessibility criteria such as those defined by the European Standard on "Accessibility requirements suitable for public procurement of ICT products and services in Europe," 301 549 (ETSI, 2014). This was produced by European Committee for Standardization (CEN), European Committee for Electrotechnical Standardization (CENELEC), and European Telecommunications Standards Institute (ETSI) in response to a request from the European Commission (Mandate 376). It was developed by an international team of experts, with the participation of the Information and Communication Technology (ICT) industry and organizations representing consumers, people with disabilities, and older persons.

Appropriate Learning Management System (LMS)

An LMS can be defined as a software application for the delivery of online education courses usually offering some form of eLearning. As such, it is useful to consider the use of the Web Content Authoring Guidelines (WCAG) (W3C, 2018) as the basis of ensuring the accessibility of the platform.

The guidelines are divided into three sets of priorities: A, AA, and AAA. In most cases, compliance with single "A" standards are considered the minimum level of compliance that is acceptable. Instead, procurement officers most often require AA compliance in the design of systems and web content. Some of the most important indicators of accessibility within the learning platform will include the following:

Text alternatives. It is important to provide a text alternative to describe media such as images or audio narration to support those with limited vision. In websites, the most common way to make media accessible is by creating ALT tags for images and text transcripts for audio. Such transcripts can also be used to add subtitles or captions to video.

Focus or tab order. Focus and tab order apply to those with low vision and those with physical needs such as difficulties with the use of their hands or arms. It refers to the order in which the page will be read or processed by a text-to-speech tool, and is also the order in which objects receive focus when pressing Tab on your keyboard. Purely aesthetic items, such as shapes and lines, do not usually receive focus, or announced by screen readers, since they are not essential in understanding the content.

Captioning. WCAG requires captioning for multimedia such as animated objects that are synchronized with audio and video, and video that includes audio. Such captioning is essential for those with hearing loss.

Skip navigation capabilities. Where a page or screen has a menu button, glossary button, exit button, and others appearing on every screen of your course, those using keyboard only input or text to speech will have each item announced on every screen or page they visit. This can be frustrating and interrupts learning. WCAG requires that those learners have the ability to skip all redundant navigation items so that they can get right to the main content.

Data tables. Tables that contain data, where understanding the arrangement of the data is necessary to understand the data themselves, can present a challenge to those with a range of needs. To address this, WCAG requires that data tables are labeled in a way that screen readers can interpret the data, including a logical sequence and clear headings. The ability to transform content into other formats adds to the capacity of the LMS to meet the needs of learners with a range of needs. Technologies such as "Robobraille"[4] offer the ability for learners to convert written documents into other formats such as mp3, Daisy format, large print, or Braille.

Appropriate Authoring Tools

If the platform includes tools that allow learners to create content, whether that be to write assignments, produce images, or video or record audio. The tools themselves must be accessible by users of assistive technologies and should produce accessible outputs. As with the platform itself, the WCAG standards offer a useful starting point in considering the accessibility of any authoring tools that are offered. Such standards are available in both English and Arabic to support regional developers.

Accessible Materials

The design of support services and aid should anticipate the needs of refugees with a disability. The principle of anticipation of needs should be applied. Such anticipation involves adopting a proactive approach through the design of resources, rather than reacting to needs and seeking to accommodate as they arise. In many cases, retroactively seeking to address such needs is at best a compromise and more often impossible. For the purposes of communication, literacy, and access to information, there is a need to meet clearly defined accessibility criteria and offer information in a variety of formats.

An example would be to provide information with the use of culturally and linguistically sensitive symbols or images as well as different print formats. Those who are Muslim have been shown to feel more comfortable using symbols and imageries that reflect their culture and religion. It has been found that the freely available Tawasol Symbols[5] can aid understanding of the written word with text to speech and support both literacy and verbal communication. Little has been done to recognize the need for a wide range of accessible Arabic materials that could be used on any devices. Text, images, animations, presentations, videos, and recordings are rarely designed to be inclusive, and principles of universal design unlikely to be considered. Much of the material is available in one format only, and the use of proprietary licenses means that there was no opportunity for the materials to be made accessible or converted to other formats such as Braille or mp3. By applying techniques and guidelines in the design of accessible materials, we anticipate that users will have individual needs addressed in advance. Many educational institutions offer freely available guidelines that can be applied.

One good example is published under a creative commons license by Birkbeck college as "Birkbeck for All" (University of London, 2017). Birkbeck for all[6] offers useful tutorials that address the accessible design of learning materials including tutorial on Accessibility Basics, Microsoft Word, PowerPoint, Accessible PDFs, and Video and Audio resources. Although based upon the experience of higher education, the principles can be applied for any age range and setting. The Birkbeck resources illustrate the value of the use of open licenses such as creative commons.

In developing curriculum content and resources, such licenses help to ensure that content can be further developed and enhanced to meet the needs of those with a disability or of refugees more widely. While the principle is sound, a recent review of Arabic resources found only limited materials published under such a license. Discussions with publishers within Arabic-speaking countries suggested some anxiety about the use of open licenses and limited experience of open-based business models. Many expressed concerns about widespread piracy of materials and had not considered sources of income as alternatives to direct sales.

Delivery Partners

Vital in the chain are those that would ultimately use the materials with the refugee populations. As explained earlier, such partners may, or may not, be qualified teachers. Even if qualified, their training may have poorly prepared them for the circumstances they now find themselves confronting. If they are to effectively deliver the digital content to their students, there is a need to ensure that the teachers have a good understanding of the needs of learners, and most importantly in this circumstance, the implications of disability. In addition, they must understand the content that is being delivered, how to make sure it is accessible and how it delivers the twenty-first century skills. Finally, they need to understand and be confident with the technologies that are being used – both in terms of general use of technology within the classroom and learning, and more specifically those technologies used by people with a disability. Partners may also use a delivery model that does not engage a facilitator but rather allows users to self-teach/learn. The same principles outlined here still apply.

Building Capacity in Delivery Partners

Addressing the needs of teachers to accommodate digital delivery and the additional learning needs of refugee learners is challenging. While teachers in host countries may have a qualification in their subject area, they may not ever have undertaken a formal teacher training including an understanding of child development and the impact of pedagogy. Some teachers may be poorly motivated to undertake such personal development, and hence it is important that a flexible approach to teacher development is implemented. The work of the Carey Institute for Global Good in designing the "Refugee Educator Academy" provides a useful benchmark in such a plan. The Carey Center for Learning in Practice (CLiP) is dedicated to promoting the education of all people through the advancement of a sustainable learning framework – a set of core workforce development methods and tools for use by a range of public and nonprofit organizations. The online Refugee Educator Academy uses the framework to recruit, train, and support people who teach refugees anywhere in the world. In their white paper "Sustainable Learning in Practice," the institute outlines the following four pillars of a sustainable learning framework:

- Practice communities that produce value.
- Content that is open, applied, and contextual.

- Reflection that improves performance.
- Analytics that lead to action.

As of January 2018, CLiP is offering three foundation courses for refugee educators. The courses are facilitated by experts and open and free to practitioners providing training to refugee educators. The courses include the following:

- An introduction to the community of practice for refugee educators, introducing the value of peer learning through experience-based assignments.
- An introduction to knowledge sharing for refugee educators. Participants learn how to share knowledge within and across organizations, and critical practices that can improve performance.
- An introduction to peer coaching and mobile mentoring for refugee educators. This addresses coaching methods and routines, including examples of effective lessons, and reflective practice.

While not yet directly addressing the issues of learners with special needs or a disability, this framework and training model provides a firm foundation for the integration of additional materials in the future. In the future, it is hoped that such resources for teachers have both content that specifically addressed the needs of those with a disability and seek to weave examples of the challenges faced by learners with a disability throughout the materials.

Ultimately the inclusion of students with a disability from refugee backgrounds will need to be assured within the broader context of refugee education. To do so, the application of principles of Universal Design are likely to be valuable.

INCLUSION THROUGH UNIVERSAL DESIGN

Universal design for learning (UDL) has been described as an educational framework based on research, which guides the development of flexible learning environments that can accommodate individual learning differences. The framework (Rose & Meyer, 2002) calls for creating curriculum from the outset that provides the following:

- Multiple means of representation to give learners the various ways of acquiring information and knowledge.
- Multiple means of expression to provide learners with alternatives for demonstrating what they know.
- Multiple means of engagement to tap into learners' interests, challenge them appropriately, and motivate them to learn.

The Curriculum, as defined within the UDL framework (Orkwis & McLane, 1998) has the following four parts:

- instructional goals,
- methods,

- materials, and
- assessments.

UDL is designed to increase access to learning by reducing physical, cognitive, intellectual, and organizational barriers to learning, as well as other obstacles. UDL principles also support the implementation of inclusive practice in the classroom. UDL is a proactive anticipatory model of meeting needs and it is part of the planning of educational activities and assumes that those with special needs will engage in learning at some stage.

There are initiatives that seek to implement UDL for students with a disability such as for those with hearing loss in Saudi Arabia (Al Salem, 2015). But in considering access to digital education, we may need to consider aspects of universal design, beyond UDL principles, that can be applied to the design of devices and content that will enable those with additional needs to engage in the learning process. Universal design of technology can be defined as an approach that seeks to produce buildings, products, and environments that are inherently accessible to older people, people without disabilities, and people with disabilities.

Universal design emerged from barrier-free approaches and the broader accessibility movement (Goldsmith, 1963). It both builds upon and facilitates use of adaptive and assistive technologies while recognizing the need to blend aesthetics into design. As the numbers of persons with a disability and additional needs rises globally as a result of increased life expectancy and the impact of modern healthcare on the survival rate of those with significant injuries, illnesses, and trauma, there is a growing interest in universal design (World Health Organisation, 2014).

Universal design has a strong impact upon thinking in many industries including construction of the built environment and access to information. Increasingly, universal design is also being applied to the design of technology, services, and other products and environments. In infrastructure, many people experience the impact of universal design. Curb cuts from pavement to road are common place and essential for people in wheelchairs, and are used by those with pushchairs, suitcases, etc., and are a common example. Similarly, many of the world's public transport systems offer low-floor buses that drop as they halt and bring their front end to ground level to eliminate gap, or taxis that are equipped with ramps rather than on-board lifts.

In developing technology and content that is accessible, we are increasing the ease of use for all. A recent study suggested that 85% of all videos on Facebook are viewed silently to accommodate the setting in which they are viewed (Patel, 2016). This concept of situational disability, where the user has additional needs as a result context, is useful. It is well illustrated by the need for a hands-free solution to accessing a mobile phone when driving. This is usually offered through a speech recognition solution where the functions of the phone can be controlled through voice commands. Such technologies have obvious application to those without full control of their hands regardless of setting.

By designing projects that are inclusive of people with a disability, it is likely that our projects will be more effective for all refugees seeking to engage with the content. Designing learning materials that are based upon short, simple text as content can be effective for those with a learning disability or visual impairment as the content can be accessed easily with text to speech on a mobile device. However, the same format is effective for those on older phones or with low bandwidth where richer content cannot be accessed, thus accessing all learners, not just those labeled with special needs.

In ICT, such design-for-all criteria are aimed at ensuring that everyone can benefit from a digital society and economy. The European Union refers to this under the terms eInclusion and eAccessibility (European Commission, 2017). They suggest a three-way approach: products and services which can be accessed by nearly all potential users without modification or, failing that, those that are easy to adapt according to different needs, by using standardized interfaces that can be accessed simply by using assistive technology. As a result, many manufacturers and service providers, especially in the field of ICT, produce new technologies, products, services, and applications for all. The use of graphic symbols, such as the Tawasol symbol set to enhance text and clarify meaning is effective as a tool for those with reading and writing needs, but is equally valuable in helping clarify text for those with a limited vocabulary in a specific language.

The availability of open-source access tools such as ATBar or NVDA[7] can make reading and writing easer for all. Using text to speech, color and contrast changes, and an integrated online thesaurus, learners are helped by having content delivered in a style that suits them. Experience tells us that learning delivered in a preferred format is most likely to have an impact.

APPLYING UNIVERSAL DESIGN TO THE EDUCATION OF DISPLACED PEOPLE WITH DISABILITIES

The application of the seven principles of universal design can be a beneficial process in the planning and design of digital approaches to delivery.

Principle One: Equitable Use

The delivery design should be useful and available to people with diverse abilities. This will involve not only designing a curriculum, but also ensuring that those with a disability are informed that the resources are accessible and incorporate their needs into the design. For example, webpages, documents, and apps should be capable of being accessed by people who are blind using a screen reader

Principle Two: Flexibility in Use

The design accommodates a wide range of individual preferences and abilities. The complexity of the needs of displaced people demands a flexibility in the delivery.

Displaced persons experience much of the situational disability described already, by designing for content to be delivered in a range of formats across a range of interfaces and devices we build in accommodations for diversity from the beginning. For example, presentations and documents should be able to accessed in a variety of ways such as being spoken out loud or viewed in large print

Principle Three: Simple and Intuitive Use

The design is easy to understand, regardless of the user's experience, knowledge, language skills, or current concentration level. The diversity of needs and abilities of displaced people, including both disability and context-related needs, demands the application of flexibility into the learning process. For those whose education has been significantly disrupted, an understanding that reading levels may lag behind peers needs to be taken account of. Addressing such issues will involve the use of tools and techniques that have been demonstrated to be effective for those with other print impairments such as dyslexia. For example, instructions and controls on equipment and applications should be easy to understand, using simple and easy-to-understand icons.

Principle Four: Perceptible Information

The design communicates necessary information effectively to the learner, regardless of ambient conditions or the user's sensory abilities. In many situations, displaced learners are engaging with education in far from ideal settings. They may be learning at night, on small screen devices, in low bandwidth environments. By designing to address such contexts, allowing text to be magnified, to be read out by a device, and using a range of contrast setting, we ensure that content and interfaces are perceivable both by those with sensory needs, and for those where learning in settings that are not optimum. For example, adding captions to videos supports those with hearing loss and those who are in noisy settings.

Principle Five: Tolerance for Error

The design minimizes hazards and the adverse consequences of accidental or unintended actions. As a result of both additional needs and setting, displaced learners are likely to make errors in engaging with content. Building in opportunities to review an action, to go back to where a recognized error was made and autosave content are all important techniques in ensuring the continuity of learning where individual or context-related errors occur. For example, providing an "undo" function in software to allow learners to easily correct an error.

Principle Six: Low Physical Effort

The design can be used efficiently and comfortably and with a minimum of fatigue. The experience of displaced learners is that fatigue can be an ever present. Living conditions may be poor and lighting, heating, and cooling may not be consistently effective. Designing for devices that require low physical effort, and with content that addresses glare, contrast, and ease of reading will assist those who are seeking to learn when tired, and those where a physical condition or vision impairment creates potential barriers to access. For example, the use of touch screens on tablets with word prediction can reduce pain and strain associated with extensive typing on a traditional keyboard.

Principle Seven: Size and Space for Approach and Use

Appropriate size and space is provided for approach, reach, manipulation, and use regardless of user's body size, posture, or mobility. For those engaged directly with displaced learners, there is a need to plan for all potential learners to be able to take part in education. While the physical setting of classrooms and activities may not be ideal, with careful planning and consideration we can ensure that no further barriers are created. For example, access to applications should anticipate needs such as whether someone is left or right handed, or in fact may only have the use of a single hand.

The application of universal design to the education of displaced learners with a disability has significant benefits to all learners, including those within host communities. By applying the aforementioned seven principles, we create a learning environment that supports all learners. This is crucial in addressing the argument that the scale of the issue means that we cannot think about those with a disability. A well-constructed universal design addresses the needs of all.

CONCLUSION

Looking Ahead: The Need to Build Back Better

Linking together these elements is at the heart of the approach advocated by the Qatar Foundation International from 2016 to 2018 as "Build Back Better." The approach recommended integrating Arabic-accessibility tools into any platform or tools for creating content, ensuring that content is available in a variety formats and reflects diverse circumstances and learning styles, and ensuring support to teachers and facilitators to support all students regardless of their needs.

In many cases, these were not in place for students with special needs prior to the refugee crisis, but by working together with the partners at all stages of delivery, there is an opportunity to meet not just the current needs of learners, but in truth to build back a better basis for education for the long term. Such an education will be vital for all those who seek to return home to their countries and be part of rebuilding devastated communities. Our education system must equip them with the skills to fully participate in the process, regardless of any disability they may have.

In the immediate future, technology is offering radical solutions to address the challenges of digital delivery of education to refugees. Tools and techniques such as remote support, AI and machine learning, on-demand learning, and micro certification all offer new opportunities to engage refugees in teaching and learning. However, such a technical and educational innovation must be mirrored and supported by a strategy of engagement with the audience and learners.

The importance of talking to refugees with disabilities, listening to them, and engaging them cannot be underestimated. Projects and initiatives need to move beyond the issuing statements of policy that cannot be delivered, or simply moving money around to give the appearance of action. Instead, those who wish to support education access must engage with both with those with a disability and the access community to find better ways of providing products and services that meet those needs.

The challenges faced by Arabic-speaking displaced learners with a disability are particularly daunting given the many pressing needs, chronic underfunding, and extended duration of their displacement. Yet, there are also tremendous opportunities. By addressing needs and developing solutions that are genuinely inclusive and responsive, while curating and creating quality accessible digital learning resources, we can design an inclusive education environment that far surpasses that which learners experienced previously. We can build back better.

NOTES

1. Word Refugee School (http://www.wrschool.org/).
2. Rumie (www.rumie.org).
3. ATBar (www.atbar.org).
4. RoboBraille (www.robobraille.org).
5. Tawasol symbols are a set of graphic symbols designed to support Arabic people with a disability who have a communication need. The symbols are designed in keeping with Arabic culture and values.
6. Birckbeck for All (www.bbk.ac.uk/birkbeck-for-all).
7. NVDA (https://www.nvaccess.org/).

REFERENCES

Al Salem, M. (2015). *Considering and supporting the implementation of universal design for learning among teachers of students who are deaf and hard of hearing in Saudi Arabia.* Dissertation, University of Kansas.

Edwards. (2014). *Annual report shows a record 33.3 million were internally displaced in 2013.* UNHCR. Retrieved from http://www.unhcr.org/537334d0427.html

ETSI. (2014). *Accessibility requirements suitable for public procurement of ICT products and services in Europe.* Brussels: ETSI.

European Commission. (2017). *Digital inclusion for a better EU society.* Retrieved from https://ec.europa.eu/digital-single-market/en/digital-inclusion-better-eu-society

Goldsmith, S. (1963). *Designing for the disabled.* London: Routledge.

Handicap International. (2014). *Hidden victims of the Syrian crisis: Disabled, injured and older refugees.* Handicap International.

Karasapan, O. (2016). *Disabled and forcibly displaced.* Brookings. Retrieved from https://www.brookings.edu/blog/future-development/2016/10/27/disabled-and-forcibly-displaced/

Laguardia, C. (2017). *Bringing back dignity and hope for refugees with disability through livelihoods.* World Vision. Retrieved from https://www.wvi.org/africa/article/bringing-back-dignity-and-hope-refugees-disability-through-livelihoods

Loescher, G., & Milner, J. (2006). Protracted refugee situations: The search for practical solutions. The state of the world's refugees 2006: Human displacement in the New Millennium. United Nations High Commissioner for Refugees (UNHCR).

Mattingly, J., & McInerney, L. (2015). *Education for children with disabilities improving access and quality.* London: DFID.

Orkwis, R., & McLane, K. (1998). *A curriculum every student can use: Design principles for student access.* ERIC/OSEP Topical Brief No. ED423654. ERIC/OSEP Special Project.

Patel, S. (2016). 85 percent of Facebook video is watched without sound. *Digiday.* Retrieved from https://digiday.com/media/silent-world-facebook-video/

Rose, D. H., & Meyer, A. (2002). *Teaching every student in the digital age: Universal design for learning.* Association for Supervision and Curriculum Development. Alexandria VA.

Said Foundation. (2017). *Special and inclusive education for children with disabilities in Za'atari.* Said Foundation. Retrieved from https://www.saidfoundation.org/project/special-and-inclusive-education-children-disabilities-za%E2%80%99atari-0

UNHCR. (2017). *Figures at a glance.* UNHCR. Retrieved from http://www.unhcr.org/uk/figures-at-a-glance.html

University of London. (2017). *Birkbeck for all.* Retrieved from http://app1.its.bbk.ac.uk/xerte2/play.php?template_id=468

UNOCHA. (2016). *UNOCHA FTS.* Financial Tracking. Retrieved from https://fts.unocha.org/

W3C. (2018). *Web content accessibility guidelines 2.1.* W3C.

World Health Organisation. (2014). *World report in disability.* Geneva: WHO.

CHAPTER 8

ADAPTATION OF CONVENTIONAL TECHNOLOGIES WITH REFUGEE LANGUAGE LEARNERS: AN OVERVIEW OF POSSIBILITIES

Heather Smyser

ABSTRACT

Most research on language acquisition using technology generally investigates collegiate language learners. However, it is unclear as to how well these findings apply to refugee learners, who sometimes have experienced interrupted schooling and had little exposure to technologies found in the resettlement context. Little research concentrates on the use of technology to aid language acquisition among this population. By better understanding the digital literacies refugees already possess, the author are better able to bridge this digital divide (Thorne & Reinhardt, 2008; Warschauer, 2002) and move toward researching how to capitalize on the technological skills refugees already possess in order to facilitate language learning. Therefore, this chapter reviews available literature on how refugees worldwide use multiple forms of technology, their levels of access to such technology, and considerations for pre- and post-resettlement technological options. It identifies best practices for employing technology to facilitate language acquisition in light of the multifaceted constraints refugees face. It concludes by outlining the suitability of different technologies as a means of facilitating language development within a myriad of contexts and gives recommendations for future research on using technology to facilitate language learning at all proficiency levels.

Keywords: Refugees; resettlement; digital literacy; mobile technology; language learning; software; apps

Language, Teaching and Pedagogy for Refugee Education
Innovations in Higher Education Teaching and Learning, Volume 15, 125–139
ISSN: 2055-3641/doi:10.1108/S2055-364120180000015010

INTRODUCTION: OVERVIEW OF TECHNOLOGY IN TYPICALLY STUDIED LANGUAGE LEARNERS

Research on the use of technology to facilitate second language (L2) acquisition focuses predominantly on highly educated L2 learners studying their second language in a collegiate setting (e.g., Chen, 2010, and to a certain extent Bloch, 2007). Many of these studies have found technologies such as games increase students' positive attitudes toward language use (Rama, Black, van Es, & Warschauer, 2012), raise awareness of various linguistic features in situations not easily replicated in the language classroom (Reinhardt & Ryu, 2013), promote negotiation for meaning in computer-mediated communication (Smith, 2003), and facilitate the development of academic literacy (Cheng, 2010). Technology even has been shown to mediate gestures in the L2 (Kern, 2014). However, each of these studies assumes high levels of print and digital literacies. Even those studies examining nontraditional language learning populations (e.g., Parks, Huot, Hamers, & Lemonnier, 2003) and those examining the applications of new forms of technology like social media (Lomicka & Lord, 2011; Reinhardt & Ryu, 2013) assume high levels of print literacy knowledge in at least one language. While digital literacy can help some learners overcome the challenges of becoming print literate, many digital media nevertheless require a medium to high level of print literacy (e.g., infographics, social media, websites, streaming services) in order to operate search features, clarify images, understand search results, understand the gist of the page, etc.

One of the few exceptions to the focus on university language learners using technology to learn a language comes from Bloch (2007) who examines writing development in a Generation 1.5 student, a term typically used to describe second language learners who have completed at least some schooling in the second language (Harklau, Losey, & Siegal, 1999). Some may be literate in the L1, and some may not be, depending on the amount and type of education received. The focal student of Bloch's (2007) article, Abdullah, had schooling in Somalia and in the US. However, Bloch inaccurately labels Abdullah an immigrant instead of a refugee.[1] Although this misnomer does not detract from Bloch's finding that blogs contribute to Abdullah's development of academic writing, it does minimize the challenges students like Abdullah may face when adjusting to societies that highly value print and digital literacies and when preparing to study at the college level (Matthews, 2015). That Abdullah spent time in a refugee camp is no small matter and may have exerted a profound impact on his learning. Yet, such information is only incidental in Bloch's writing. How would other individuals with similar educational profiles, both refugee and non-refugee learners, have performed with the task of blogging, a task that combines digital and print literacies in an online forum? How suitable is blogging in classrooms with learners who have had limited exposure to print or computer literacy? How much scaffolding is required for learners with unknown experiences with Western-style education in tasks that require print literacy, digital literacy, and some combination of both? Is the metaphor of technology as a bridge to language learning (Thorne & Reinhardt, 2008) flexible enough to include learners with varying degrees of print and digital literacies and not only those with education in the target culture?

Questions like these do not often find a place in literature on language learners and the conditions that promote optimal learning for them. This is despite the fact that such learners comprise a large and ever-increasing population of the US[2] and world. Many who are resettled often struggle with language and literacy learning (Dooley & Thangaperumal, 2011; Montero, Newmaster, & Ledger, 2014; *Outcomes*, 2015). Whether refugee or immigrant, their learning needs differ substantially from that of their literate, and often more educated peers – such as doctors, scientists, lawyers, etc. – who may experience faster language learning thanks in part to previous educational and literacy experiences (Burt, Peyton, & Adams, 2003; Burt, Peyton, & Schaetzel, 2008). Many refugees have experienced some combination of trauma (Finn, 2010; Halcón et al., 2004), little to no formal schooling (Montero, Newmaster, & Ledger, 2014; *Outcomes*, 2015; Refugee Children and Youth, 2006), and an education that might be vastly different from that typically experienced in the US (DeCapua, & Marshall, 2014; Matthews, 2015; Refugee Youth and Children, 2006). Therefore, this review focuses on understanding the diverse learning situations refugees find themselves in pre- and post-resettlement, with the goal of providing pedagogical recommendations regarding best uses of technology to foster concomitant language, print, and digital literacy development among these learners. The review will employ the following questions as a guide:

1. What are the experiences of refugees pre- and post-resettlement that inform the use of educational technologies?
2. How do refugees already use technology?
3. How can language instructors of resettled refugees employ media many students may already employ to facilitate language learning in pre- and post-resettlement conditions?

The choice in literature to answer these questions is informed by my experience of working with adult learners in the US refugee resettlement context. This has included in community English language classes intended only for refugees and in a job skills environment. My learners were officially resettled through the US refugee system, and my classes were heterogeneous with as many as 40 students in one class and at least 10 different languages represented in that class. Working in this context makes it extremely difficult to concentrate on the needs of refugees from only one culture or language. Therefore, this chapter will, in so much as possible, globally address trends shared by the majority of my students. However, these experiences are trends and not meant to be taken as representative of refugees as a whole or even those resettled in the US. Some statements might therefore appear controversial; however, they are included in this chapter to give voice to the concerns my students have shared with me over the years.

My choice to include some focus on employment post-resettlement derives from the challenges my learners have faced after official resettlement, including limited periods of funding and the expectation of a high level of print literacy (necessary for completing forms at school and for jobs) regardless of their level of print literacy in their first language(s). According to the US Committee for Refugees and Immigrants (2015, no page), "The U.S. government expects a working-age refugee to find a job within six months of arrival," regardless of the level of English proficiency or prior work history. This means they obtain employment and do not require assistance from social service programs within only six months. Analysis of this is beyond the scope of this chapter, but my experiences working with refugees affected by it have shaped this chapter's foci.

EXPERIENCES PRE-RESETTLEMENT

The individual experiences of each individual refugee are unique, making it difficult to identify generalities in pre-resettlement contexts.[3] This section will provide a snapshot of some of the physical realities experienced by several of my learners. It is beyond the scope of this chapter to discuss agency and the political nature of camp. Those interested in these discussions should see Ilcan and Rygiel (2015) and Rygiel et al. (this volume). What is apparent is that the need for resettlement far exceeds current capacities. In 2015, less than 1% of refugees eligible for resettlement were able to do so (UNHCR-Resettlement, 2017). Many reside in camps for years prior to being resettled (Refugee Youth and Children, 2006). Camps often have limited access to clean water (e.g., Roberts, Chartier, Malenga, Toole, & Rodka, 2001), expose many inhabitants to parasites (Abu Mourad, 2004), and may offer poor housing options (Cullison Bonner et al., 2007). Furthermore, electricity may be limited, and inhabitants may only have designated hours of electrical power (Moser-Mercer, 2014). Some living in camps may have experienced little to no or interrupted schooling (Brown, Miller, & Mitchell, 2006; DeCapua & Marshall, 2014). Even if learners have had schooling, it may have taken a form drastically different from educational models in resettlement countries, which often concentrate heavily on print literacy and scientific thought (DeCapua & Marshall, 2014; Montero, Newmaster, & Ledger, 2014). Access to various forms of technology is often limited in many camps. Despite these challenges, some learners are able to work within camp constraints and creatively use available technology to advance their learning (see Moser-Mercer, 2014, for the use of massive open online courses – MOOCs).

Because of the differences in experiences, technology may be novel for some learners or extremely familiar to others. The key to finding sustainable ways of furthering educational opportunities for refugee learners is understanding which media they are familiar with and which learners will require scaffolding prior the implementation of technology-based activities.

TRANSITIONS TO DIGITAL SOCIETIES: WHAT WE KNOW ABOUT HOW TECHNOLOGY IS USED

Only a handful of studies examine the relationship between refugees and technology (Bacishoga & Johnston, 2013; Leung, 2011; Lloyd, Kennan, Thompson, & Qayyum, 2012; van Rensburg & Son, 2010). Leung (2011), in a sample of 30 interviews and 43 surveys of refugees from all over the world and from different refugee circumstances, found that mobile technology is the most widely available form of technology for refugees in camps, and mobile phones are widely available worldwide (Nimsger, 2017). The Internet is often a major source of information for those in all stages of resettlement (Lloyd et al., 2012), and those in the early stages of life post-resettlement appear to benefit from visual and social forms of communication (Lloyd et al., 2012). This often includes pictures and movies, which reveal much about a culture without the need for a high level of language proficiency. However, access to these media often comes as a result with newer technologies, such as cell phones and computers. In early resettlement, technology may encourage newly resettled refugees to connect with speakers of their own native language(s) to the exclusion of others (Bacishoga & Johnston 2013; Lloyd et al., 2012); particularly, if learners are using technology to access media in familiar languages. When language proficiency is an issue, as in emergency situations, refugees in the Bacishoga and Johnston (2013) study relied on native speakers to make calls for them. As time progresses (and potentially proficiency in the target language improves), mobile technology appears to help foster social inclusion among immigrants and refugees into the adoptive culture (Caidi & Allard, 2005).

IMPORTANCE OF DIGITAL LITERACY

With more and more aspects of life moving to a digital platform (e.g., online education, online healthcare, use of tablets in the workplace to name a few), digital literacy – using digital tools, understanding how to access information, and understanding the social context of such information (Bawden, 2001) – is an increasingly vital skill. This is even more pronounced in the workplace where learners often need to be somewhat literate to perform their jobs. Historically, those who arrive with low levels of digital and print literacies remain in low-wage jobs even 20 years after resettlement in the US (*Outcomes*, 2015). Theoretically, technology can help many emerge from poverty post-resettlement, but it is not a panacea. What are the prerequisites for technology acting as bridge (Thorne & Reinhardt, 2008) to provide learners with the skills and resources they need to accomplish their goals in whatever linguistic, digital, and cultural contexts they find themselves?

Using Digital Technology to Promote Language Learning

How do you best facilitate the acquisition of resettlement culture literacies in a population with different literacy and cultural traditions? Literacy is by its very nature a collection of acquired attitudes and behaviors (Blanton, 2005) that represents cultural practices embedded within the linguistic landscapes (Landry & Bourhis, 1997) of any given culture. Signage permeates daily life in many Western societies and can be overwhelming to those not from the culture. When acquiring print literacy and genre awareness, students are not only acquiring the ability to decode a string of letters, but are also acquiring a cultural practice of conveying meaning using an abstract system to represent speech. Couple this with the move toward digital media in which users are required to be familiar with both digital and print literacies, what many digital immigrants and natives – those who have either become accustomed to digital technologies or those who have grown up in the age of technology, respectively – (Prensky, 2001) take for granted, and you have a veritable perfect storm of information overload in potentially unfamiliar genres. Emergent readers must overcome culture shock, develop print literacy in a new language quickly, understand the specific language of the job market, wrestle with using technology, and/or find some sort of employment before their funding runs out. Fig. 1 lists some of the skills those who have been resettled might need to overcome to obtain employment.

Technology can pose huge obstacles to refugees since many who have been resettled have not had the opportunity to develop basic skills required to operate a computer. van Rensburg and Son (2010) studied computer literacy and English language acquisition among five adult Sudanese refugee women with low levels of prior formal education over 12 weeks. Participants lacked sufficient background

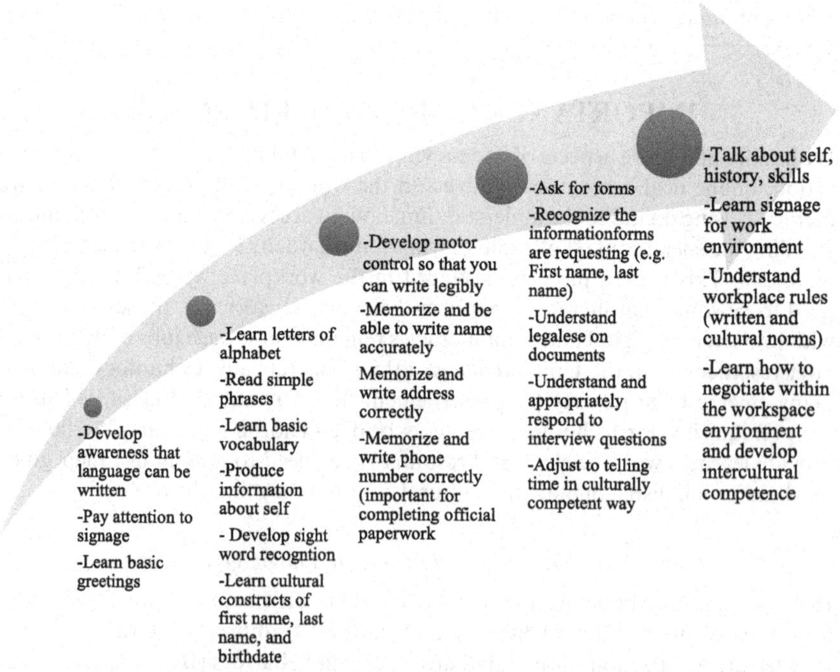

Fig. 1.   Language Skills that Facilitate Employment.

knowledge to complete activities aimed at building basic computer competency and independence. At first, the participants struggled to access free web-based learning materials. To remedy this lack of background knowledge, the participants participated in one 2-hour computer training session per week over the course of 12 weeks. These sessions scaffolded both the computer literacy and English-acquisition by introducing them to basic terminology and how to use the computer prior to introducing how to access the Internet and complete game-like language learning activities online.

During the study, the women struggled with the concept of a puzzle, something that none of them had experienced prior to resettlement but which was necessary to complete a language learning task. The instructors had the women build their own puzzles to develop genre awareness and an understanding of the mechanisms underlying the task. The participants reported that this practice with puzzles in real life helped them complete online puzzle activities that were designed to facilitate word acquisition. At the end of the study, four of the five women, with the exception of one who was more interested in playing games online, reported gains in English proficiency and newfound confidence in using the computer. This confirms previous findings of online games affording the opportunity for language acquisition (Arnseth, 2006; Cornillie, Clarebout, & Desmet, 2012; Rama et al., 2012; Reinhardt, in press; Reinhardt, Warner, & Lange, 2014) and demonstrates the flexibility technology can afford instructors if adequately scaffolded. This is especially true given that learners acquired multiple literacies over the course of the van Rensburg and Son (2011) study (computer, print, and gaming). While this chapter is the only study of its kind yet published, it highlights the challenges inherent to studying and teaching the large number of adults with low levels of print and digital literacy. Many activities that are taken for granted, such as puzzles, need to be properly scaffolded before using digital media to allow for maximum language acquisition.

My own experience corroborates the general lack of familiarity with computers and technology among the women in the van Rensburg and Son (2010) study. As in the study, many of my students, particularly learners older than mid-30s, struggled with learning how to use a computer when I included a unit on computer literacy in my job skills classes. Adopting some of the scaffolding used by van Rensburg and Son (2010) to first make learners familiar with technology before using it for language activities, I first taught learners some key vocabulary words and had them point to the major parts of the computer when I said the word. In a class of about 20 students, learning the vocabulary took at least two days of instruction, and learners struggled to identify the major parts of the computers. By the end of the unit, students required assistance to open a web browser, type sentences written on the board, use a mouse, and learn the procedures of logging on to a computer. Most had very limited English and would have struggled to make use of computer literacy courses taught in the community unless an interpreter were present, an option local libraries did not provide. Despite my best efforts, lack of time for the class and lack of sufficient computers using the same operating system (all were donated to the center) prevented full implementation of the van Rensburg and Son (2010) methods and prevented us from using web-based language activities. Fig. 2 lists some of the challenges many of my own learners have struggled with.

Given the paucity of research on this topic, future studies should concentrate on which platforms and technologies are more generalizable for digital neophytes. It should also examine effective scaffolding of digital literacy acquisition. How similar are the digital learning needs of individuals with no print literacy experience compared to those with some print literacy? How can instructors of mixed-level classrooms teach and develop digital and print literacies?

Challenges in Teaching Digital Literacy in the Classroom and for Language Programs

The group size and homogeneity used in van Rensburg and Son (2010) is not a realistic possibility for many language learning contexts in which refugees find themselves. Often, refugee education programs have insufficient computers or paid staff to provide computer instruction (Mansoor, 1993; personal communications with English instructors of refugees in my local area). Instruction efforts in US classrooms are usually left to volunteers with little or no training in how to teach either print or digital literacy (Coskun, Norton, & Spielhagen, 2011; Finn, 2010; Mansoor, 1993). Classrooms are often multilingual spaces with several different nationalities of students and literacy levels (Coskun et al., 2011;

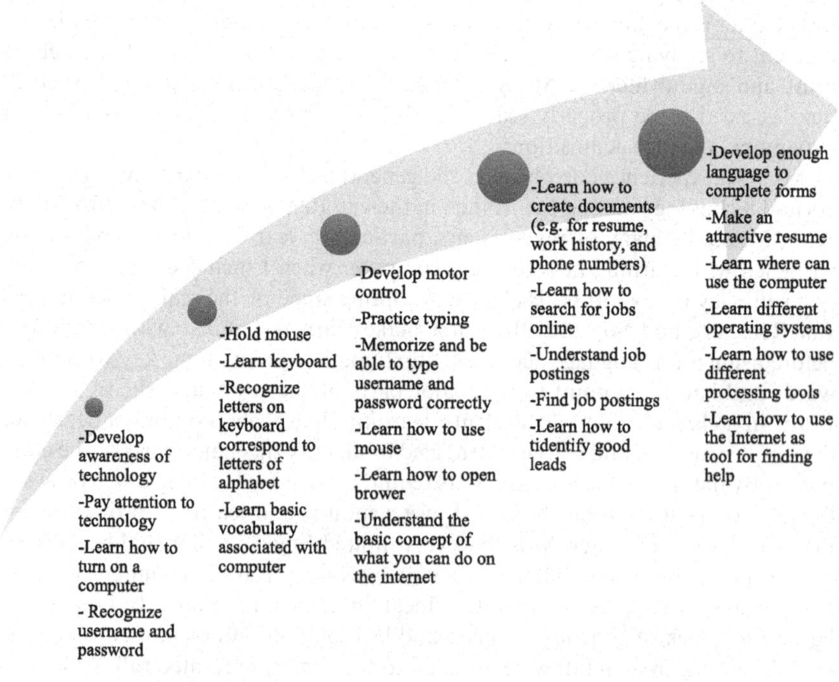

Fig. 2. Components of Digital Literacy Development.

Burt et al., 2003; *Outcomes*, 2015). Additionally, the US does not have a centralized system of education for the refugees it resettles. Often, the implementation of educational technology is left to individual programs and agencies to administer and procure, and learners may have little to no say in this process. To date, the van Rensburg and Son (2010) study is the only study to examine the simultaneous acquisition of digital and print literacies in refugees for the purpose of language acquisition. Future research should investigate the efficacy of simultaneously acquiring both digital and print, volunteer-as-teacher training programs, and factors that contribute to optimal learning to better understand how to adapt these findings to situations more likely to arise in the US.

Despite its age, the Mansoor (1993) report on selecting software for adult education programs demonstrates that the challenges of implementing technology in the refugee English classroom have changed relatively little over the past two decades in the US, although this is slowly changing with increased collaboration between programs and more awareness of the challenges individual programs face within the academic world. Mansoor writes, "The first challenge that programs face is the complexity of initial implementation" (p. 14), a problem highlighted in the need to extensively scaffold basic computer literacy. Students may need assistance in learning to type, turning on technology, and navigating different operating systems. Programs must decide which technologies to adopt, which are suitable for their students' learning needs, and which they can afford. Although not mentioned by Mansoor (1993), a crucial factor refugee educators and service providers should consider is how similar available technologies are to those in the community. Many learning digital literacy for the first time may be confused by different operating systems, as my learners were. Adapting technology into the refugee English classroom requires extensive forethought and planning since instructors often must not only teach language through technology, but also the technology itself. Making these determinations will be difficult without understanding the learning profiles of previous, current, and projected student populations. Without available research in this area, however, it is difficult to say how much students are able to do and transfer.

THE HOPE OF MOBILE-ASSISTED LANGUAGE LEARNING

Given the ubiquitous nature of technology and its positive effects on students' attitudes toward language learning in more traditional L2 populations (e.g., Lomicka & Lord, 2012), why not adapt the technologies learners are most familiar with for the classroom? Kukulska-Hulme (2009) states that use of mobile technology, "may well be aligned with strategic educational goals such as … reaching learners who would not otherwise have the opportunity to participate in education" (p. 157). Adapting preexisting online tools for the mobile platform may help address connectivity issues faced by refugees wishing to obtain a certificate from a MOOC, such as in the Moser (2014) case study, and better equip them to achieve their learning goals. The mobile (including phone and tablet technologies) platform may prove easier to use for learning. It is an all-in-one device that does not require different components, such as a mouse or keyboard, rather than several disparate parts that look and work differently on different devices (i.e., the mouse on a desktop compared to a laptop).

Mobile technology may also bridge the potential gap between camp and resettlement life. This is because it can be used to address issues of sporadic connectivity in camps (Moser-Mercer, 2014), which will hopefully be eradicated in light of developments such as the recent pledge by Facebook's Mark Zuckerberg to bring connectivity to refugee camps ("Facebook's Mark Zuckerberg pledges refugee camp internet access," 2015). However, the degree to which newly resettled refugees would require scaffolding to use apps on mobile technology to learn English is yet unknown. Would they perform as well as the refugees in the Moser-Mercer (2014) study who were able to employ mobile technology to complete a MOOC course? The combination of devices mattered greatly for them, but would that combination matter as much for students coming with little to no prior print literacy? Could instructors limit the amount of technology to only mobile forms to first familiarize students with one form of technology? Then, could instructors show them how to use this to expand their own language learning? Instructors could help learners build flashcards and find games and apps in the target language that are close to learners' level of language. Could this provide learners with more individualized attention than what's currently given?

It would certainly be easier to attempt to show students how to use mobile technology as a learning tool rather than attempt to scaffold computer literacy instruction with English instruction since an ever-growing number of refugees are exposed to mobile technology at resettlement, if not earlier. Indeed, in one of the few studies of cell phone use among refugees, Bacishoga and Johnston (2013) use interviews with South African refugees to uncover how this population uses cell phones and the ways in which their use facilitates social integration, defined as "a dynamic process that enables 'all people to participate in social, economic, cultural and political life on the basis of equality of rights and dignity'" (United Nations 2009 as cited in Bacishoga & Johnston, 2013, p. 5). They find that respondents were likely to use their cell phones to interact with colleagues and participate in study groups. From a pedagogical perspective, the Bacishoga and Johnston (2013) study is interesting in that the refugees surveyed did not view cell phones as tools. This is paralleled in Leung's (2011) study in which only a few of the respondents mentioned using this technology for educational purposes. Another potential challenge is that having low literacy levels makes it difficult to become familiar with available technologies, especially when this is coupled with some refugees escaping from remote or war-torn areas that lack access to modern amenities and technologies (Leung, 2011).

Tapping into Mobile Technologies as Tools for Language Learning

It is surprising that from these studies, few refugees explicitly associate mobile technology with learning, particularly given the plethora of free learning apps, games, and puzzles that exist. One challenge is that many of these are geared toward children, and instructors would need to spend time sifting through the number of apps. Nevertheless, some apps may be easily adapted to facilitate literacy and language acquisition. For example, one study by Verhallen and Bus (2010) investigated the use of storybooks on children's language acquisition, and this could easily be adapted to a mobile platform. Here, the authors found that four viewings of the same static picture storybook that combined audio and visuals resulted in the acquisition of fewer expressive words than when the children looked at the same storybook with video animation ($p < 0.01$). However, both groups significantly increased their receptive vocabulary on the post-test, regardless of the condition they were in. Such an easy technique of increasing vocabulary would allow refugees to be exposed to even more of the target language outside of class or even before coming to a new country, provided they had access to the technology via a smartphone or tablet and had knowledge of such a resources' existence. The challenge would be to find stories that were linguistically simple but suitable for an adult audience. Short movies from the target culture would be a way to capitalize on the desire refugees have expressed for being exposed to DVDs (Lloyd et al., 2012). While providing access to such libraries would be difficult to do in camps via mobile technology, the growth of digital libraries should facilitate access to such resources in the US, provided refugees are introduced to the resources and how to use them.

These digital stories could be optimized for language and literacy instruction by pairing the video version of stories with subtitles of the audio that play throughout. An old study by Spanos and Smith (1990) made a similar suggestion by showing refugees closed captioned television programs since many like being able to read the subtitles concurrently with hearing the audio. To date, this is one of the few studies that examines technology use and language learning in the US refugee population. With mobile technology and downloadable programs, learners would have the opportunity to have focused exposure to English while traveling on the bus, walking around town, or sitting at home. Such an increase in exposure to the target language could greatly facilitate its acquisition. Future research should investigate the use of closed captioning with digital storybooks and short films to compare acquisition of oral and written vocabulary to see if one condition affords better learning as Verhallen and Bus (2010) found.

Students could also create their own digital stories and use these as a bridge to get them to connect with textuality in a way that they had heretofore never done. These would be on topics of students' choosing, perhaps thematically limited by the instructor for larger class sizes to ensure students begin to acquire vocabulary related to the topics discussed in the classroom. Students can brainstorm in the classroom, get training on how to use a simple app on a smartphone (e.g., StoryMaker for Android, a free app that is fairly intuitive to use), and then get assistance on drafting their narratives. This can lead to the development of agency, or a notion of themselves within the broader framework of a socially constructed world according to Hull and Katz (2006). Such agency development occurred in their case of Randy, a young man from California, who interwove his passion for writing rap and poetry with images from his surrounding contexts to tackle issues such as being targeted by police. Although his videos were longer and more complex than students at early stages of literacy would be able to produce, these students could create simple videos with basic equipment to learn and explore the community.

Additionally, such a combination of mobile technology with personal experience would fit well with the Language Experience approach proposed by Bigelow and Vinogradov (2011), an approach that advocates encouraging learners to draw on their own experiences to help facilitate the acquisition of print literacy and communicative competency, and with Bhabha's (1996) idea of hybrid agency in which participants employ a partial culture to create a sense of community. By asking students to explore the world around them and create narratives of those experiences, students generate schemata for concepts such as supermarkets, libraries, malls, and classrooms that might have existed in completely different forms in the countries in which they lived prior to resettlement. In so doing, they might develop a sense of agency and have a greater opportunity explore their surroundings in meaningful ways, both of which are factors that contribute to their language learning and sense of wellbeing in a new culture. In this way, mobile technology could facilitate a burgeoning sense of curiosity and accomplishment because students are able to capture the world around them and construct their narrative of self in ways that previously would have required many disparate devices to accomplish. By storing information online, students have access to their narratives and those of others whenever they have Internet access and are thus able to increase their exposure to English that more closely matches their level of proficiency. It could also help them develop a sense of hybrid identity.

CONCLUSIONS AND FUTURE DIRECTIONS

Mobile technology could prove to be instrumental in facilitating the acquisition of digital and print literacies among refugees, both prior to and post resettlement. Apps that conform to general learning principles can easily be adapted from children's early literacy tools and reworked to be suitable for adults. Such apps would need to be adapted and adopted for use with adult learners. Instructors can also make use of the access students have to cell phones, and with some extra instructions, can help students begin to make their own stories of what they are experiencing and what they have experienced. These stories can also be uploaded into a digital library in forms that students will be able to download for viewing while going about daily activities, like riding the bus. The hope is that mobile technology will not only increase motivation in this population, but also their agency. Educators may wish to explore some of the materials available through Harvard's "Project 0" (http://www.pz.harvard.edu/) to find resources that fit the needs of their learners and learning environments. Future research should examine how effective mobile technology is in facilitating print literacy, how to scaffold digital literacy instruction, and the extent to which gaming, blogging, and collaboration aid students in acquiring a new language and the literacy cultures of a new place. The question is not so much whether or not these technologies will prove helpful, but rather what the limiting factors are for employing these technologies with a different population and how best to implement these technologies.

Currently, the literature that pertains specifically to the teaching of and learning by refugees is growing but scarce compared to that on more traditional language learners in university settings. It is hardly sufficient to make detailed recommendations for instructors or program administrators, particularly those working within the US. Despite the large numbers of refugees all over the world, relatively little has been published on their learning needs in peer-reviewed journals. It is critical that future research first paints the literacy skills in print and digital literacy of these students to guide better investigations of what they know and what funds of knowledge they possess. How familiar are students with technology when they arrive? What are they able to do with it? How well do their computer skills correlate with their print literacy abilities? Is it possible to adapt van Rensburg and Son's (2010) study to a larger, more linguistically and culturally diverse population? How effective is mobile technology for fostering print and digital literacy development? Without this, instructors and programs, particularly for resettled refugees, might flounder while attempting to determine best practices for their learners and will need to continue to develop their own materials, often with the feeling of being in isolation from others in the field. Thankfully, the success of such innovations is not limited only to programs and instructors. It lies primarily in the hands of refugees themselves who will adapt and succeed regardless of the environment, if I may generalize from my experiences. My learners found a way to use new technologies and experiences to pursue their goals, and I am hopeful that by working with communities and listening to them, we as educators can use technology to support them in their endeavors.

NOTES

1. The UN defines a refugee as "someone who has been forced to flee his or her country because of persecution, war, or violence. A refugee has a well-founded fear of persecution for reasons of race, religion, nationality, political opinion, or membership in a particular social group. Most likely, they cannot return home or are afraid to do so (UNHCR). This chapter adopts this definition throughout and is informed by the author's experiences with refugees who have been resettled in the US. It does not differentiate between different types of refugees due to the heterogeneous backgrounds and experiences of those individuals.

2. In 2016 alone (the last year for which up-to-date data was available), the US resettled almost 85,000 refugees (Zong & Batalova, 2017). However, this number is expected to be reduced to 50,000 in 2017 (Krogstad & Radford, 2017). These figures do not include the large numbers of language learners in the adult education system or those refugees in Europe.

3. The examples given here are not meant to be representative of what a refugee may experience but are rather merely snapshots of some of the larger challenges associated with life pre-resettlement that my students have shared with me.

REFERENCES

Abu Mourad, T. A. (2004). Palestinian refugee conditions associated with intestinal parasites and diarrhea: Nuseirat refugee camp as a case study. *Public Heath, 118*(2), 131–142.

Arnseth, H. (2006). Learning to play or playing to learn – A critical account of the models of communication informing education research on computer gameplay. *Game Studies*, 6(1).

Bacishogo, K., & Johnston, K. (2013). Impact of mobile phones on integration: The case of refugees in South Africa. *The Journal of Community Informatics*, 9(4).

Bawden, D. (2001). Information and digital literacies: A review of concepts. *Journal of Documentation*, 57(2), 218–259. Retrieved from http://dx.doi.org/10.1108/EUM0000000007083

Bigelow, M., & Vinogradov, P. (2011). Teaching adult second language learners who are emergent readers. *Annual Review of Applied Linguistics*, 31, 120–136. doi:10.1017/S0267190511000109

Bloch, J. (2007). Abdullah's blogging: A generation 1.5 student enters the blogosphere. *Language Learning and Technology*, 11(2), 128–141.

Brown, J., Miller, J., & Mitchell, J. (2006). Interrupted schooling and the acquisition of literacy: Experiences of Sudanese refugees in Victorian secondary schools. *Australian Journal of Language and Literacy*, 29(2), 150–162.

Burt, M., Peyton, J. K., & Adams, R. (2003). *Reading and adult English language learners: A review of the research*. Washington, DC: Center for Applied Linguistics.

Burt, M., Peyton, J. K., & Schaetzel, K. (2008). *Working with adult English language learners with limited literacy: Research, practice and professional development*. Washington, DC: Center for Applied Linguistics. Retrieved from http://www.cal.org/caelanetwork/resources/limitedliteracy.html. Accessed on August 31, 2009.

Caidi, N., & Allard, D. (2005). Social inclusion of newcomers to Canada: An information problem? *Library & Information Science Research*, 27, 302–324.

Capps, R., & Newland, K. (2015). *The integration outcomes of U.S. refugees: Successes and challenges*. Washington, D.C.: Migration Policy Institute.

Chen, R. (2010). Computer-mediated scaffolding in L2 students' academic literacy development. *CALICO Journal*, 28(1), 74–98.

Coskun, U., Norton, C., & Spielhagen, A. (2011). *Serving the Tucson refugee community: A snapshot of key issues and concerns 2010–2011*. Tucson, AZ: Bureau of Applied Research in Anthropology.

Cornillie, F., Clarebout, G., & Desmet, P. (2012). Between learning and playing? Exploring learners' perceptions of corrective feedback in an immersive game for English Pragmatics. *ReCALL*, 24(3), 257–278.

Cullison Bonner, P., Schmidt, W., Belmain, S., Oshin, B., Baglole, D., & Borchert, M. (2007). Poor housing quality increases risk of rodent infestation and Lassa fever in refugee camps of Sierra Leone. *The American Journal of Tropical Medicine and Hygiene*, 77(1), 169–175.

Facebook's Mark Zuckerberg pledges refugee camp internet access. (2015, September 27). *BBC World*. Retrieved from http://www.bbc.com/news/technology-34373389

Finn, H. (2010). Overcoming barriers: Adult refugee trauma survivors in a learning community. *TESOL Quarterly*, 44(3), 586–596.

Halcón, L., Robertson, C., Savik, K., Johnson, D., Spring, M., Butcher, J., … Jaranson, J. M. (2004). Trauma and coping in Somali and Oromo refugee youth. *Journal of Adolescent Health*, 35(1), 17–25.

Harklau, L., Losey, K. M., & Siegal, M. (Eds.). (1999). *Generation 1.5 meets college composition: Issues in the teaching of writing to U.S.-Educated learners of ESL*. Mahwah, NJ: Erlbaum.

Hull, G., & Katz, M. (2006). Crafting an agentive self: Case studies of digital storytelling. *Research in the Teaching of English*, 41(1), 43–81.

Ilcan, S., & Rygiel, K. (2015) "Resiliency Humanitarianism": Responsibilizing refugees through humanitarian emergency governance in the camp. *International Political Sociology*, 9(4), 333–351. doi:10.1111/ips.12101

International Rescue Committee. (2006). *Refugee children and youth backgrounders*. New York, NY: International Rescue Committee.

Krogstad, J., & Radford, J. (2017, January 30). Key facts about refugees to the US. Retrieved from http://www.pewresearch.org/fact-tank/2017/01/30/key-facts-about-refugees-to-the-u-s/

Kukulska-Hulme, A. (2009). Will mobile learning change language learning? *ReCALL*, 21(2), 157–165.

Landry, R., & Bourhis, R. (1997). Linguistic landscape and ethnolinguistic vitality. *Journal of Language and Social Psychology*, 16(1), 23–59. doi:10.1177/0261927X970161002

Leung, L. (2011). *Taking refuge in technology: Communication practices in refugee camps and immigration detention*. New Issues in Refugee Research. Working Paper No. 202.

Lloyd, A., Kennan, M., Thompson, K., & Qayyum, A. (2012). Connecting with new information land-scapes: Information literacy practices of refugees. *Journal of Documentation, 69*(1), 121–144.

Lomicka, L., & Lord, G. (2012). Analyzing microblogging among language learners. *System, 40*, 48–63.

Mansoor, I. (1993). *The use of technology in adult ESL programs: Current practice-future promise.* Washington, DC: Southport Institute for Policy Analysis.

Matthews, K. (2015, July 14). Refugee youth summer academy transitions students for New York Schools. *Huffington Post.* Retrieved from http://www.huffingtonpost.com/2015/07/14/refugee-summer-academy-_n_7794344.html

Moser-Mercer, B. (2014). MOOCs in fragile contexts. *Proceedings of the European MOOC Stakeholder Summit 2014*, pp. 114–121.

Nimsger, K. (2017, July 19). New technologies are part of the refugee crisis solution. *Huffington Post.* Retrieved from http://www.huffingtonpost.com/entry/new-technologies-are-part-of-the-refu-gee-crisis-solution_us_5947f238e4b04d8767077a57

Parks, S., Huot, D., Hamers, J., & Lemonnier, F. H. (2003). Crossing boundaries: Multimedia tech-nology and pedagogical innovation in a high school class. *LLT, 7*(1), 28–45. Retrieved from http://llt.msu.edu/vol7num1/parks/default.html

Prensky, M. (2001). Digital natives, digital immigrants. *On the Horizon, 9*(5), 1–6.

Rama, P., Black, R., van Es, E., & Warschauer, M. (2012). Affordances for second language learning in *World of Warcraft. ReCALL, 24*(3), 322–338.

Reinhardt, J. (in press). Digital gaming in L2 teaching and learning. In C. Chapelle & S. Sauro, (Eds.), *The handbook of technology in second language teaching and learning.* London: Wiley-Blackwell.

Reinhardt, J., & Ryu, J. (2013). Using social network-mediated bridging activities to develop socio-pragmatic awareness in elementary Korean. *International Journal of Computer-Assisted Language Learning and Teaching, 3*(3), 18–33.

Reinhardt, J., Warner, C., & Lange, K. (2014). Digital gaming as practice and text: New literacies and genres in an L2 German classroom. In J. Guikema & L. Williams (Eds.), *Digital literacies in foreign and second language education* (pp. 159–177). San Marcos, TX: CALICO.

Roberts, L., Chartier, Y., Malenga, G., Toole, M., & Rodka, H. (2001). Keeping clean water clean in a Malawi refugee camp: A randomized intervention trial. *Bulletin of the World Health Organization, 79*(4), 280–287.

Spanos, G., & Smith, J. (1990). Closed captioned television for adult LEP literacy learners. *ERIC Digest*, ED321623.

Thorne, S., & Reinhardt, J. (2008). "Bridging Activities," new media literacies and advanced foreign language proficiency. *CALICO Journal, 25*(3), 558–572.

UNHCR. (2017). *What is a refugee.* Retrieved from http://www.unrefugees.org/what-is-a-refugee/

US Committee for Refugees and Immigrants. (2015). *Frequently asked questions (FAQ).* Retrieved from http://www.refugees.org

van Rensburg, H., & Son, J. (2010). Improving English language and computer literacy skills in an adult refugee program. *International Journal of Pedagogies and Learning, 6*(1), 69–81.

Verhallen, M., & Bus, A. (2010). Low-income immigrant pupils learning vocabulary through digital picture storybooks. *Journal of Educational Psychology, 102*(1), 54–61.

Warschauer, M. (2002). Reconceptualizing the digital divide. *First Monday, 7*(7). Retrieved from http://dx.doi.org/10.5210/fm.v7i7.967

Zong, J., & Batalova, J. (2017, June 7). *Refugees and asylees in the United States.* Retrieved from http://www.migrationpolicy.org/article/refugees-and-asylees-united-states

CHAPTER 9

HOW SOCIAL MEDIA CAN PLAY A ROLE IN AN EDUCATIONAL CONTEXT, IN AN INFORMAL REFUGEE CAMP IN EUROPE

Kathy O'Hare

ABSTRACT

European policy on migration does not safeguard the rights of refugees as they travel into and across European State borders (Rygiel, Ataç, Köster-Eiserfunke, & Schwiertz, 2015). Furthermore, refugees currently in transit through Europe have little or no access to media platforms. Mainstream media frames the current migration flow into Europe with narratives of charity, sympathy, and criminality (Rettberg & Gajjala, 2016). Myths about refugees being smuggled into Europe and committing acts of violence are exaggerated by mainstream media and contribute toward shaping societies' perceptions. Little research is available in relation to how digital and social media tools can play a role in facilitating educational training for refugees in informal refugee camp settings in Europe.

The premise of this research is to explore how, if given access to a digital and social space, camp residents can develop their own digital community-led radio station. In this way, camp residents can have editorial control to create their own narratives, thus directly challenging mainstream media. Participants faced many barriers when attempting to develop digital and communication skills. The learning itself became a form of activism for participants and facilitators. The French government uses a politics of control to disrupt and prevent social

Language, Teaching and Pedagogy for Refugee Education
Innovations in Higher Education Teaching and Learning, Volume 15, 141–155
Copyright © 2019 by Emerald Publishing Limited
All rights of reproduction in any form reserved
ISSN: 2055-3641/doi:10.1108/S2055-364120180000015011

development in the camp and prevent the community from becoming a resource (Rygiel, 2011).

Keywords: Social media tools; digital learning; informal refugee camps; community radio; citizen journalism; "The Jungle" Calais; activism

INTRODUCTION

Jungala Radio is a community-led digital community radio station based in the illegitimate refugee camp in Calais commonly referred to as the "The Jungle" by mainstream media outlets in Europe.

The project was set up in November 2015 and operated until October 2016 when French Authorities demolished the whole camp. The project sought to train refugees in the ethos of community radio, broadcasting techniques, editing and production skills, narration and digital storytelling. The Jungala website, Twitter, Facebook, Soundcloud, and YouTube were used to disseminate all 24 radio documentaries that were created by participants in the project. Program topics included social, political, cultural, and creative documentation of camp life.

The project was developed under the following objectives:

- To create a digital platform using open-source, social media tools that were accessible to camp residents;
- To develop a community (of core participants) that would commit to digital learning;
- To establish a space that allows participants to challenge the dominant narratives presented by mainstream media; and
- To provide a safe learning space in the Calais Camp where cross-cultural learning and multilingualism are incorporated into the culture of the Jungala project.

The literature reviewed for this chapter includes discussion on Rygiel's (2011) single acts of citizenship, Agamben's state of exception theory (1998), and Carling and Hernández-Carreterob's (2011) acts of deterrence, direct control, and dissuasion. An overview of the camp in Calais will help to contextualize the physical and political environment that participants lived in while participating in the project, followed by a discussion on the relationship between citizen journalism and mainstream media. The research method in this chapter will describe the use of participatory action research (PAR) as a primary method in developing this project. Research findings and the discussion section will focus on the some of the core issues that arose for participants and for facilitators. Finally, the conclusion will summarize some of the main findings of the Jungala Radio project.

LITERATURE REVIEW

Governments across Europe are creating spaces for refugees that compromise the rights of refugee and asylum seekers (Salter, 2008). This challenges notions of identity, sovereignty, and citizenship, and reduces refugees to the status of quasi citizen or non-citizen (Rygiel, 2011). Important to the debate on the political reality of a refugee is Agamben's state of exception theory (1998). In ancient Rome, homo sacer (sacred man) was what happened when an individual was stripped of all his political life. He was expelled from the community of men. Nothing was greater than the political life of man. The state of exception according to Agamben (1998) is paradoxical in nature, as the nation state has been built on a dichotomy of inclusion/exclusion. International examples of the state of exception include prisoners in Guantanamo Bay, the Holocaust, the war on terror, and the treatment of refugees and asylum seekers (Diken, 2004; Salter, 2008). Sovereign law becomes suspended in spaces that refugees are funneled into including border areas, official and unofficial refugee camps, and detention centers, and is replaced with a law of exception.

The state of exception allows for a demonization process to occur within spaces that refugees occupy. Diken (2004) argues that the refugee becomes a threat to maintaining political order and thus is pushed into a state of being "non-political." The state of exception is being used globally to rebuild borders and create restrictive migration policy and laws. Over 13 European states have rebuilt partition fencing and re-established borders in along Europe's frontiers. Carling & Hernández-Carreterob (2011) argue that European migration policy is driven around three concepts, aiming to restrict movement through direct control, aiming to restrict movement through deterrence and finally, aiming to restrict movement through dissuasion. In Calais, this is evident through the building and heightening of security at borders, the use of surveillance, the use of tear gas and plastic bullets, and demolition in the camp. The entanglement of global security politics and the politics of asylum appears to be all too convenient for European States.

Sigona (2015) and Rygiel, Ataç, Köster-Eiserfunke, and Schwiertz (2015) argue that Agamben's state of exception theory does not give adequate explanation to the internal interactions of camp inhabitants in relation to how they claim rights and self-organize. Sigona (2015) proposes the notion of "campzenship" to acknowledge how camp inhabitants construct and shape relationships, create infrastructure, and develop internal political structures, thus developing an agency. This research locates itself within the agency of the camp and the project's participants.

Rygiel (2015) discusses the concept of "citizen from below." Her argument focuses on "single acts of citizenship," that is, while refugees and asylum seekers do not have access to political and civic rights, they manage to challenge authority through single acts of resistance or activism. The aim of Jungala Radio was therefore to provide a space that allowed residents to create their own single or multiple "acts of citizenship" in the form of creating and disseminating their own digital content to global audiences.

CALAIS REFUGEE CAMP IN CONTEXT

Informal and sporadic camps have been established in Calais since the late 1990s. The population in the camp fluctuates and is highly transient. Statistics from the NGO Help Refugees indicate at its peak the camp had 10,000 inhabitants. The camp is a mix of refugees, asylum seekers, and migrants. There are well-established communities in "The Jungle." Refugees have created and built businesses, homes, social spaces, and community spaces. The restaurants and coffee shops provide vibrant social and economic spaces that bring a sense of normalcy, dignity, and identity to the camp's atmosphere. These spaces can also be recognized as "single acts of citizenship" and agency.

NGOs such as Auberge des Migrants, Utopia 56, Care 4 Calais, and Help Refugees organize aid distributions, build shelters, and oversee the building of community spaces. Humanitarian aid, food, clothing, legal and illegal drugs, shoes, and mobile phones are sold on the grey/black markets in the camp. People smuggling is the most lucrative of the black markets in operation in the camp. Many people seek out smugglers as a way of getting across to the UK and reaching other destinations. Prices vary depending on time of year, political situation, and an individual's financial situation. On July 25th, 2016, French Authorities began to dismantle all the local businesses by raiding the premises and arresting the owners as a precursor to the larger eviction in October 2016. The camp has suffered from several orchestrated evictions from French Authorities including two major evictions, one in March 2016, and another in October 2016 whereby the physical camp was demolished.

There are very few academic accounts about the Calais Camp and what is available is narrow in topic (Rygiel, 2011; Rigby & Schlembach, 2013). Rygiel (2011) considers it to be a space of detention; even though it is not a closed camp, its design and capability to control the movement of refugees contribute toward a state of constant transience, which prevents them from seeking out lives elsewhere. There is a whole network of actors and policies in place to externalize and expel refugees through "pathways of expulsion." Rygiel (2011) describes the French Authorities' approach as "schizophrenic" in nature. The camp is under constant surveillance by French Authorities and exit/entry points are heavily guarded and become areas of flashpoints of conflict and violence. Calais Migrant Solidarity Group has been documenting the evidence of police brutality and violations against human rights in Calais since 2009. The 75.9% of the camp population have been subjected to police violence and brutality making this a human rights issue under The Convention against Torture and other Cruel, Inhuman or Degrading Treatment 1984 (Refugee Rights Europe, 2016).

The dichotomous power relationship between French Authorities and "the other" is entrenched with tensions and creates a volatile and hostile living environment. The camp is deemed an "unofficial" camp or "illegitimate" by the French government. This means that none of the major NGOs or governmental agencies that would normally respond to a humanitarian crisis are responding to the camp in Calais, essentially leaving this task to inexperienced volunteers.

The transient nature of the camp and its "illegitimate" status as an informal refugee camp mean that the landscape of the camp changes rapidly. Rygiel (2015) states that measures taken to demolish the camp are about removing the social and political dynamics of life and bringing it back to a level of "bare life." The CRS (French Riot Police) regularly throw tear gas canisters, shoot rubber bullets, and instigate high levels of aggression, particularly during times of eviction. Camp residents rated police violence in Calais as being the thing they feared most (The Long Wait Report, 2016).

CITIZEN JOURNALISM AND MAINSTREAM MEDIA

Similar to Rygiel's (2011) "acts of citizenship," bloggers can create "acts of journalism" (Davidson, n.d.). The internet is taking over traditional media formats as a news source. While the role of the citizen journalist gathers clarity and momentum, the role of the traditional journalist lies at a crossroads in terms of how citizen journalism directly challenges traditional media. Social media has changed how we as humans communicate with each other and how we disseminate information. Citizens are no longer heavily reliant on mainstream media for news and information as individuals now create and upload their own content using social media platforms (Holton, Coddington, & Gil de Zúñiga, 2013; Lachapelle, 2011). The consumer is now creating digital and media content for online audiences and communities of interest. Social media has democratized how we as humans communicate with each other and how we disseminate information.

Volunteers and grassroots organizations such as Care4Calais, Auberge des Migrants, and Help Refugees regularly share and update their experiences of volunteering in the camp and using social media tools such as blogging, vlogging, and live streaming, and through platforms such as Vimeo, Facebook, and Twitter. They use digital tools to fundraise, raise awareness, and organize protests and petitions. While it is important that the narratives from the volunteer experience continue to create awareness and challenge policy and governments, it is critical that that the voice of the volunteer does not become the voice of the refugee. It is imperative that these narratives remain as separate entities. Examples of disempowering narratives being used include the use of personal tragedy stories of refugees on volunteers' crowdfunding pages or the use of personal tragedy stories in mainstream media to generate charitable donations for NGOs, this behavior reminiscent of post-colonial ideology. The voice of the refugee can be safeguarded by creating and holding safe spaces for learning and education, and it can be amplified and projected to global audiences by using digital and social media tools. Thus, contributing toward a sense of agency and politicization within the camp.

Mainstream media regularly produces in print and online, articles, photographs, and footage of camp residence in the camp. This type of situation can be problematic for refugees and people seeking asylum. First, the British Home Office can use public images when assessing asylum claims. Second, these images help to shape dissentient narratives and stereotypes of refugees.

Third, images were not used in their correct context and quite often with misleading or derogatory headlines. Pinkett (2003) argues that sociocultural constructionism views community members as producers of information as opposed to consumers or receivers of information.

We encouraged participants to use their own digital platform as a way of transmitting their messages as opposed to "going public" with mainstream media due to issues of identity and future asylum cases. There is a dangerous assumption on the part of some volunteers and refugees that mainstream media can contribute toward creating positive social change for the camp.

McIntyre (2007, p. 81) states, "Anonymity, preventing exposure to danger and ensuring a safe context for individual and collective reflection and action cannot be assured in a PAR project." Holten et al., (2013) argue that web 2.0 has allowed for a rich diversity of story and narrative exchange to occur online with the help of digital and social media tools, to create social and community action and change.

RESEARCH METHOD

PAR was selected as being the most appropriate methodology for the project. PAR was chosen because of its emphasis on the participatory elements of the research.

In its simplest form, PAR is a cyclical process that involves an exploration phase, a knowledge construction phase, and an action phase. McIntyre (2007) discusses three prominent characteristics of PAR, the active participation of both the researcher and participant in co-constructing knowledge, the acknowledgement of self and critical awareness that leads to individual, collective, or social change, and the building of rapport between researcher and participant throughout the whole process. The most important aspect of PAR is to create social change. By its very nature, PAR is completely immersive as both participant and researcher actively learn together and strive for social change. The recognition of participants as co-researchers and the recognition of researchers as participants allowed a strong connection and working rapport with all involved. Fitzpatrick (2016, p. 42) states,

> cohesion is not guaranteed simply because a group congregates; it must be nurtured and promoted. Cohesiveness is the root and foundation of all group work: it is the glue that binds. Moreover, a facilitator can do what she can to develop it, but cohesion without active participant involvement is not possible.

Three facilitators operated the Jungala Radio project on a full-time basis across a 12-month period. Each facilitator had a different skill set, which complimented each other as a team. This also allowed participants to draw on the different skills sets available to them. The background of the three primary facilitators included Journalism (Film & Photography), English Literature (Narration & Story Telling), and Community Development & Community Radio. Initially, we connected with Jungle Books Library and established a working relationship with the organization. Jungle Books Library kindly allowed us to work out of one of their communal spaces. We went to a Community Leader meeting in the camp. They agreed to support the project and encouraged their respective communities to engage in the project by word of mouth.

We ran a 3-day outreach exercise to gauge interest and possible potential participants. This involved walking around the camp and talking with people. Jungle Books had given us a list of people that may have been interested in participating; however, we only had first names and thus it was a lengthy process trying to find individuals. Our first training session ran from December 27th, 2015–January 2nd, 2016. Our initial outreach exercise gauged five interested participants. Using group work theory and PAR had a direct impact on the group dynamics and created a healthy working environment. We had five participants ranging from the age of 8 to 45 years old.

The objective of the training week was to facilitate the development of digital and communication skills such as listening & talking skills, confidence, community participation & engagement, broadcasting & presenting skills, research skills, peer-engagement skills, using digital tools, digital production, and post-production skills.

Training sessions were initially scheduled for early morning. We had low attendance rates. Participants and camp residents got little sleep at night and therefore required a more suitable time later in the afternoon. Lack of sleep played a crucial role in how we ran our training sessions and the project. There are several factors at that affect the sleeping patterns of refugees in the camp in Calais. We quickly established that there was a short window of opportunity for learning in the day that peaked between 3–7 pm where people could commit to learning.

The transient nature of the camp and the will for people to leave the camp, meant at times conflicts of interests arose for participants, as they had to decide between wanting to learn new skills, which required a time commitment and the physical act of attempting to cross borders illegally. For example, after every training session participants would say "Goodbye" to all the facilitators in the hope that they would not to be returning to the camp the next day.

Analyzing camp conditions through Maslow's Hierarchy of Needs theory, Dewey (1954) reveals that many of the basic human needs required to develop self-fulfillment are not present in the camp, which makes it difficult for people to "self-actualize." These conditions make for a very hostile learning environment. Part of the role of the facilitators was to try and alleviate some of those direct physiological, and psychological needs and to "clear the path of obstacles" for participants should they decide to engage with the learning process. It was necessary to fulfill all tiers of Maslow's theory simultaneously to achieve reaching the state of self-actualization and creativity.

Simple steps were put in place to support the lack of basic human and physiological needs; for example, ensuring the availability of sugar snacks, fruits, and drinks were available, changing the training schedule to suit the needs of participants, keeping the learning space warm, listening to participants, and practicing being non-judgmental.

Methods of data collection included: field notes, participant observation, interviews, my own personal notes/diary, recordings for training purposes and recordings of participant's perspectives in terms of their personal development and training, interim and closing interviews, photos, filming, emails, Skype meetings. Participants were encouraged to keep audio diaries and a hand journal to take notes; they were also given their own audio equipment and encouraged to make note of observations, ideas, and feelings. Several participants were given their own small MP3 mini recorders with built-in cameras, so that they had equipment available to them, should they be able to capture an event happening in camp.

The camp is limited in term of its technological development. With reference to a few French residents living nearby who actively left their Wi-Fi open for refugees to access, there is little to no internet available onsite in relation the population of the camp. Internet access and internet connections in the camp were created by several volunteer-led organizations, including The Miracle Street Bus, Jungle Books Library, and The Info Bus. All provided extremely limiting connections, with no uploading or downloading capabilities. These connections were used mainly for using Snapchat, Viber, WhatsApp, and Facebook by refugees and not suitable for the demands of a training and research.

ETHICAL CONSIDERATIONS

There were many ethical issues that arose in terms of how we approached the project. Facilitators were aware that the project would be a space that generated sensitive information. We wanted participants to explore and develop their talents and creativity as opposed to "telling us" their personal stories, therefore contributing toward a space of disempowerment.

Our training sessions incorporated ethics of community journalism and community radio, anonymity, protection of their own identities, protection of others, and consent. Participants were made aware that the project was part of a university study and that the researcher was collecting data that would not compromise the identity of anyone participating in the project.

RESULTS

The new knowledge generated from the Jungala project grew from the collaboration of the facilitators, core participants, peripheral participants, and the wider camp community, and was made available to the public through social media networks. Naming the station contributed toward creating a sense of ownership, identity, and belonging for participants and the facilitators. During a group session, it was discussed as to how people felt about living in a place called the "Jungle." After a lively discussion, it was agreed by mutual consensus that the station was to be called "Jungala Radio." The project name had a political meaning.

A 12-year-old participant named the project stating, "the jungle is where animals and insects sleep, and we are not animals." "La" means "No" in Arabic; thus, "Jungle-La" means "Jungle No." We attempted to create a learning space that encouraged multilingualism and encourage participants to make programs in many languages. Participants choose English as the primary language of the project. As Facilitators, we supported this decision. The participants were actively aware of who they wanted their target audience to be and English was the primary language they chose to communicate their "single acts of citizenships" with. Making programs in English helped participants develop communications skills, confidence, to connect into the wider English-speaking network of the NGOs on the ground, volunteers, and the mainstream media.

The lack of internet connectivity seriously affected the development of the project and the development of our core participants learning. Core participants were unable to upload digital content themselves and contribute toward taking on the roles of social media administrators. This would be done by a facilitator each evening after each work session. Our social media accounts Facebook, Twitter, Soundcloud, and www.jungalaradio.com grew organically. Creating access to Jungala Radio programs for camp residents was restrictive due to lack of internet connectivity. This was overcome this by bringing MP3 files to restaurants around the camp for them to play for their customers. The biggest success, in terms of gauging and growing an audience of listenership, came from global audiences.

We set up an integrated digital platform using open-source software and digital and social media tools. The digital tools we selected worked well with each other. Core participants attended training sessions and had full access to the digital platform, while camp residents used the platform to discuss and share information with core participants. The use of open-source software meant that our core participants could access and continue to develop their digital skills once they left the camp in Calais. All content created by participants is currently available for anyone to access, download, replay, or broadcast, on the Jungala website. This promotes the open-source philosophy.

Jungala Facilitators actively challenged the ethics of mainstream media in the camp by analyzing media articles and images in print and online, finding the individuals portrayed in the images, and asking them if they wanted their images removed. Consent of the individuals who were being misrepresented was always sought and respected in these situations. Challenging the mainstream media involved a complex process of keeping the identities of our participant's safe, while both facilitators and participants learned to deal with mainstream media interest. One example from a large media network in the UK was an image taken of a child who had parents. But the article written placed beside the image was about unaccompanied minors living alone in the camp, thus alluding that this child did not have any parents and was alone in the camp. This is just one example out of many that demonstrates the unethical behavior of journalists in Calais and how this type of behavior can impede upon the safety of minors living in the camp.

Camp residents would often walk long distances throughout the night to meet with smugglers in cold weather conditions. After failed attempts with smugglers or trying themselves, to get into trucks, and trains they would arrive back in camp from 7–10 am. Attempting to jump off trucks and trains requires many physical and mental skills from hiding in cramped and wet places for extended periods of time, jumping large fences, avoiding security, police, and police dogs while trying to stay dry and warm. The activities at night are dangerous and very often lead to a whole range of injuries ranging from broken bones to death.

As mentioned in the literature review, the CRS regularly use tear gas on camp residents predominantly at night and during phases of eviction. The tear gas canisters can also cause fires in the camp. This can cause outbursts of flash violence at entry/exit points in the camp. Most volunteers depart the camp before 23.00 hours and tear gassing often started around midnight. Please listen to 10. Eviction Show (Adam & Star, 2016), 12. Tear Gas Show (Adam, 2016), 13. Eviction Day 4 (Adam & Star, 2016), and 16. Newsflash (Adam & Star, 2016) for references to tear gassing by French Authorities. Cold and wet weather conditions within the camp environment also affect how camp residents sleep. The camp is extremely active at night with many refugees choosing to sleep during the day when it is warmer and quieter as they attempt to cross the borders at nighttime.

The first radio podcast called "1. New Years in the Jungle" (Adam, 2016), was recorded and broadcast on January 1st, 2016. In this first interview, some of the core issues of the people residing in the camp are addressed by the interviewee; even though the topic is quite broad, he immediately highlights some of the political issues affecting him and other camp residents. The resident speaks about the cold weather, power struggles with Authorities, and the restrictive nature of the camp, all of which align with Rygiel's (2011) theory on direct control, dissuasion, and deterrence.

Jungala Participant:	What do you think about the situation of the camp?
Camp Resident:	It's not good because it's cold, but still thanks to the people especially from the UK people. They are helping us, they are bringing stuff for us.
Jungala Participant:	You can go to another country, so what is your difficulties that you are here now?
Camp Resident:	Actually, the difficulty is I want to go the UK, but the police they stop us, they don't want us to go the UK.
Jungala Participant:	Why you are going to the UK?
Camp Resident:	Since I know English much better than other languages.
Jungala Participant:	Yesterday was Happy New Year, so where were you and what did you do?
Camp Resident:	I was in the Jungle and at 11 pm we tried to go to the middle of the town, but the police stop us and they threw us tear gas on us and that's why we turned back and stayed in Jungle again. It was New Year…But not Happy New Year (says laughing).

The Hope Show was a political current affairs style program. This show was important in that it gave updates on meetings held by community leaders in the camp, which often involved French Authorities. This allowed for camp residents to have a direct link into the grassroots movement and internal politics of the camp. Please listen to 2. French Officials Come to the Jungle (Hope, 2016) and 3. A Response to French Officials (Hope, 2016).

Other participants digressed from the political aspects of camp life and selected to be more creative in their delivery and interpretation of having access to the platform. Muhammads' Word Cast Show (Muhammad, 2016) is about a young Syrian who learns new words in English through western pop and film culture. He uses association and observation to produce thought provoking insights about the English language. This podcast is humorous and fun.

The Save the Oceans program is particularly interesting in that the participants make connections between global displacement and the environment. This is important as it demonstrates the development of critical awareness (Adam & Star, 2016). This program highlights issues of global warming and climate refugees.

Positive outcomes of creating a cross-cultural learning space included a sense of awareness of others and a deep respect for different cultures. Participants enjoyed "being" in the space and enjoyed spending time working together. Many of the participants commented on this fact with one stating "I am really glad we are working on this project together, because I would never have met you in the camp." Participants respected the dynamics and differences and of others and used it as an advantage when working together. The space acted as a distraction from the harsh camp environment.

Some of our participants received international recognition for their work. For example, Jamil's documentary called "Journey" won Honorable Mention in Thirdcoast International Audio Festival 2016 in the Best Documentary Category. This competition is prestigious in the radio industry. The Star Show won Best Cultural Documentary for "Jungle Food" in X Ray Radio Festival 2017. The Star and Adam Show won Best Student Category for Hearsays International Audio Festival 2017. Australia's ABC Network aired several jungala programs. NPR's Invisibilia series commissioned the Star & Adam Show to create a short story; unfortunately, this story did not make it into the final cut of the Invisibilia series. Finally, Muhammad's Wordcast podcast was picked up by the ABC Australia network. A number of working relationships were also developed with the Festival of Ideas 2016 (London), Nante Radio Festival (2016), and the Migration Museum (2016). This international recognition was unforeseen and really encouraged participants and facilitators to continue with their work.

DISCUSSION

Group work theory was effective in creating a sense of community within the core group. A radio program called 9. "World Radio Day" (Adam, Hopes, 2016) demonstrated the participants' understanding of what the project is and what it means to be a part of a group. When asked the question "What does radio mean to you?" one participant responded

Radio gives me something to do here on these boring days. I learn to make the programs, I learn how to be in a group, and what is the rules of group and how to interview someone, how to use a recorder.

Another participant responded, "Jungala radio is a program that is made by Katie and Ciaran...And it's a big group that working together and talking about the Jungle." Participants engaged with facilitators and demonstrated their understanding of the political, economic, environmental, social, and cultural aspects of camp life through using their new digital skills and by creating digital content.

Cross-cultural learning was embraced by participants and facilitators and participants demonstrated this in their interactions with facilitators and each other. Making a decision as a group was based on a democratic practice, which was influenced by PAR, the ethos of community radio and group work theory. Projects that envisage themselves to be community development projects that use radio as a tool tend to be most successful.

The system we designed met with our immediate needs and requirements and was based around our three perceived areas of importance, simplicity, and affordability. We understood the limitations of being a two-three-person team of facilitators in an informal refugee camp setting and thus we consciously oversimplified our technological and digital plans. Our social media approach was different from the NGOs, grassroots groups, and individuals in the camp who use social media to voice their own opinions on behalf of refugees. Facilitators actively sought to remove their "voices" from Jungala social media posts. In doing this, it sent a clear message to all social media streams that that Jungala Radio had a strong team of participants and content creators that were competent and capable of relaying their own messages to the world; hence, contributing to agency within the camp.

Being involved in a digital project with limited internet connectivity was labor intensive, frustrating, and mentally challenging for both facilitators and participants. The lack of connectivity was due to various reasons such as running out of fuel for the generator, no electricity, too many people accessing at the same time, and equipment failure. We learned that by producing lots of content and then uploading it to Soundcloud when internet was available, we could set a timer that would release a program at specific times. This helped us overcome some of our internet connection issues. Social media sites were maintained remotely along with press interviews, potential collaborations, and general administration.

Participants created 24 podcasts covering a diverse range of topics from social, cultural, political, and artistic. Creating their own diverse digital content offered an alternative perspective and directly challenged mainstream media's negative and sensationalist reporting style. Core participants of the Jungala project crafted their own knowledge and understanding of the Calais camp and chose what information they wanted their social media audiences to know.

The "participation" (McIntyre, 2007) aspect of using PAR within the project and our participant's awareness of what "participation" means to them, became synonymous with them referencing "the group" and "cooperation" when discussing issues, helping each other with tasks and being fully immersive in the process of learning. As participants developed their new skills, their style of creating digital content also developed. They progressed from densely scripted programs to being able to critically assess and challenge their interviewees, their environment, give their own opinions while continuously thinking about technical aspects of recording, using the recorder, gauging ambient sounds, and creating a suitable environment for recording.

For example, in program 10. Eviction Show (Star & Adam, 2016), the Jungala participant challenged the interviewee in terms of his views as to why he was upset in relation to the French Authorities demolishing the camp.

Jungala Participant: What do you feel when the Jungle will be destroyed?
Interviewee: I feel so upset and so sad.
Jungala Participant: What is good in the Jungle that you feel upset?
Interviewee: Because the government remove this, our home.

Another example of the development of skills sets is in relation to production values, which is evident when comparing a progression timeline of participants programs. This example will highlight the development of The Star Shows progression and development in sequence. Program 2. Holiday Time (Star, 2016) and program 8. Jungle Food (Star, 2016) are by the same participant. The program Holiday Time is a very simple, short story read from a book using voice only and a very simple record on/off setting. The production value for program 8. Jungle Food by the same participant is much more complex. This program included multiple interviews, personal insights, and observations, fading sound clips in and out, layering sound clips over each other and defined introductions and conclusions.

CONCLUSION

The French government uses a politics of control to disrupt and prevent social development in the camp and prevent the community from becoming a resource (Rygiel, 2011). Agamben's state of exception theory (1998), acts of direct control, deterrence, and dissuasion (Carling & Hernández-Carreterob, 2011) influenced the project development and participant development daily. The barriers participants faced when trying to access the learning space were challenging physically and mentally and considered to be single acts of citizenship.

The space we established in the camp in partnership with Jungle Books Library allowed for participants to challenge mainstream media by creating their own alternative news reports, political, social, and cultural programs.

The aim of this research was to create a digital radio station in an illegitimate refugee camp in Calais, France using digital and social media tools as platform for communication and engagement. This was achieved by the provision of facilitative training in the camp, the implementation of a digital and social media platform, and the development and creation of a core group of participants that actively engaged in creating digital content and while demonstrating "acts of citizenship" (Rygiel, 2011).

Participants faced many barriers when attempting to develop their digital and communication skills. The learning itself became a form of activism for participants and researchers as new knowledge was co-constructed together.

Working on a digital project with limited internet access was extremely challenging and time consuming; however, we have established that the digital divide was much greater than originally anticipated by volunteers and NGOs on site. Digital and social media tools worked as effective tools and contributed toward disseminating information and digital content that our participants wanted to share thus challenging the dominant mainstream media narratives and offering alternative narratives based in their own realities.

REFERENCES

Adam, Hopes, S. (2016). 9. World Radio Day! – Jungala Radio. Retrieved from http://www.jungalaradio.com/portfolio/9-world-radio-day/. Accessed on December 13th, 2017.

Adam. (n.d.). 12. Tear Gas Show – Jungala Radio. Retrieved from http://www.jungalaradio.com/portfolio/12-tear-gas-show/. Accessed on December 13th, 2017.

Adam & Star. (2016a). 13. Eviction Day 4 – Jungala Radio. Retrieved from http://www.jungalaradio.com/portfolio/13-eviction-day-4/. Accessed on December 13th, 2017.

Adam & Star. (2016b). 22. Save the Oceans! – Jungala Radio. Retrieved from http://www.jungalaradio.com/portfolio/22-save-ocean/. Accessed on December 13th, 2017.

Agamben, G. (1998). In D. Heller-Razen, (Ed.) *Homo sacer, sovereign power and bare life*. Stanford: Stanford University Press. Retrieved from http://abahlali.org/files/Homo+Sacer.pdf.

Carling, J., & Hernández-Carreterob, M. (n.d.). Protecting Europe and protecting migrants? Strategies for Managing Unauthorised Migration from Africa. https://doi.org/10.1111/j.1467-856X.2010.00438.x

Davidson, A. (n.d.). The role of citizen journalism in social media & its impact on journalism. Retrieved from http://www.academia.edu/4064446/The_Role_of_Citizen_Journalism_in_Social_Media_and_its_Impact_on_Journalism.

Dewey, J. (n.d.). Modernisation of higher education new modes of learning and teaching in higher education. Retrieved from https://www.teachingandlearning.ie/wp-content/uploads/2014/10/HLG-Publication-New-Modes-of-Learning.pdf.

Diken, B. (2004). From refugee camps to gated communities: Biopolitics and the end of the city. *Citizenship Studies, 8(1)*, 83–106. https://doi.org/10.1080/1362102042000178373

Holton, A. E., Coddington, M., & Gil de Zúñiga, H. (2013). Whose news? Whose values? *Journalism Practice, 7(6)*, 720–737. https://doi.org/10.1080/17512786.2013.766062

McIntyre, A. (2007). *Participatory action research*. London: SAGE Publications.

Muhammad. (2016). 14. Muhammad's Wordcast Show – Jungala Radio. Retrieved from http://www.jungalaradio.com/portfolio/14-muhammads-wordcast-show/. Accessed on June 18th, 2018.

Pinkett, R. (n.d.). Bridging the digital divide: Sociocultural constructionism and an asset-based approach to community technology and community building. Retrieved from https://llk.media.mit.edu/papers/aera2000.pdf.

Refugee Rights Europe. (2016). *The long wait*. Retrieved from http://refugeerights.org.uk/wp-content/uploads/2016/06/RRDP_TheLongWait.pdf.

Rettberg, J. W., & Gajjala, R. (2016). Terrorists or cowards: Negative portrayals of male Syrian refugees in social media. *Feminist Media Studies, 16(1)*, 178–181. https://doi.org/10.1080/14680777.2016.1120493

Rigby, J., & Schlembach, R. (2013). Impossible protest: Noborders in Calais. *Citizenship Studies, 17(2)*, 157–172. Retrieved from http://sro.sussex.ac.uk.

Rygiel, K. (2011). Bordering solidarities: Migrant activism and the politics of movement and camps at Calais. *Citizenship Studies*. https://doi.org/10.1080/13621025.2011.534911

Rygiel, K., Ataç, I., Köster-Eiserfunke, A., & Schwiertz, H. (2015). Governing through citizenship and citizenship from below. An interview with Kim Rygiel, *1(2)*. Retrieved from http://movements-journal.org/issues/02.kaempfe/02.rygiel,ataç,köster-eiserfunke,schwiertz–governing-citizenship-from-below.pdf.

Salter, M. B. (2008). When the exception becomes the rule: borders, sovereignty, and citizenship. https://doi.org/10.1080/13621020802184234

Sigona, N. (2015). Campzenship: Reimagining the camp as a social and political space. *Citizenship Studies*, *19(1)*, 1–15. https://doi.org/10.1080/13621025.2014.937643

Star & Adam. (n.d.). 10. Eviction Show – Jungala Radio. Retrieved from http://www.jungalaradio.com/portfolio/10-eviction-show/. Accessed on December 13th, 2017.

CHAPTER 10

REACHING REFUGEES: SOUTHERN NEW HAMPSHIRE UNIVERSITY'S PROJECT-BASED DEGREE MODEL FOR REFUGEE HIGHER EDUCATION

Chrystina Russell and Nina Weaver

ABSTRACT

Higher education can offer hope and a way forward for vulnerable populations. In particular, access to internationally recognized degrees and credentials has the potential to be a key protection priority for refugee populations, opening alternative solutions to displacement through economic empowerment and increased mobility.

While innovations in online learning have opened new pathways, the delivery of higher education to refugee learners in resource-deprived settings – including camps and urban environments – remains notoriously challenging. Therefore, there is an imperative to draw upon lessons learned from existing programs in order to identify promising practices and emerging innovations.

In this chapter, we draw on our experiences of developing a higher education model for refugee and vulnerable learners to argue that successful delivery of accredited degrees to populations affected by forced displacement relies upon the following three key elements:

Language, Teaching and Pedagogy for Refugee Education
Innovations in Higher Education Teaching and Learning, Volume 15, 157–180
Copyright © 2019 by Emerald Publishing Limited
All rights of reproduction in any form reserved
ISSN: 2055-3641/doi:10.1108/S2055-364120180000015012

1)   *Flexible mode of degree delivery and assessment.*
2)   *Robust blended learning model with in-person academic support.*
3)   *Provision of adaptive and context-specific interventions and resources.*

The case study for this chapter is an initiative called the Global Education Movement at Southern New Hampshire University, which delivers accredited degrees to refugee and refugee-hosting populations in five countries. Evidence from the program in Rwanda, operated in partnership with a local partner, Kepler, suggests it is possible for a full degree program to be successful in reaching vulnerable learners, including refugees.

Keywords: Competency-based education; online learning; employment; vulnerable learners; refugee education; gender-based interventions

INTRODUCTION

The United Nations High Commissioner for Refugees (UNHCR) has prioritized tertiary education as a solution that "enhances the protection of youth and facilitates integration."[1] Evidence demonstrates its potential to build transferable skills and social capital, improve quality of life and mental health, and expand livelihood opportunities (Mitschke, Aguirre, & Sharma, 2013; Taylor & Sidhu, 2012; Wright & Plasterer, 2010). But the ongoing refugee crisis – with over 65.3 million displaced worldwide – threatens to deprive entire generations of higher education and employment opportunities. Currently, only an estimated 1% of refugee youth have access to higher education opportunities.

The imperative to expand access to higher education for forcibly displaced populations – as well as those populations affected by forced migration – has resounding economic, political, and social implications. Research has found clear economic returns for tertiary education for refugee populations: an economic analysis of refugee populations in Uganda found that acquiring an additional year of education correlates with a 3.3% higher average income, with tertiary education giving the highest income returns (Betts, Bloom, Kaplan, & Omata, 2017). In addition, recent studies by the World Bank and independent research institutions have highlighted the contributions that refugees can offer to national economies, if allowed to pursue business and employment opportunities (Betts & Collier, 2015; Betts et al., 2017; Fiddian-Qasmiyeh, Ruiz, Vargas-Silva, Zetter, 2012; Khoudour & Andersson, 2017; Sanghi, Onder, & Vemuru, 2016).

Beyond material outcomes, tertiary education offers hope to those directly affected by displacement; it also empowers individuals to engage legally and politically in long-term outcomes for their native countries. The cumulative costs of denying people higher educational opportunities are far-reaching. Disenfranchised youth are left vulnerable to radicalization and criminal recruitment, while displaced youth are often left ill-prepared to take on leadership roles which could transform their own lives and their communities' future.

There has never been a more opportune time to support refugees' access to higher education. Through the work of UNHCR and its partners, primary and secondary school completion rates among refugees have risen to 61% and 23%, respectively (UNHCR, 2017). While these rates fall short of the global averages, the steady improvement in secondary school completion is creating a growing pool of refugee graduates who are prepared for higher learning.

Meanwhile, innovations in US higher education have opened additional doors, in particular via the arrival of high quality and widely accredited options for low-cost online education. The US higher education sector has recently made significant advances in the technologies and accreditation strategies for online education, including the development of competency-based degrees and blended learning models. These innovations are diminishing the trade-off between the quality of a conventional four-year university degree and the affordability of online courses, while targeting the development of skills and knowledge most needed by employers.

Cumulatively, these opportunities demonstrate that access to internationally recognized degrees and credentials could become a key protection priority for refugee populations, opening alternative solutions to displacement through economic empowerment and increased mobility. Nevertheless, delivery of higher education to vulnerable learners in resource-deprived settings – including camps and informal settlements in host countries – is notoriously challenging. In recent years, the emergence of connected learning initiatives—including Massive Open Online Course (MOOC)-based learning solutions – has mobilized new technology-based solutions to extend opportunities for higher education for refugee and displaced youth. Inevitably, these initiatives must contend with challenges in operations and facilitating desired outcomes. Given the challenges in the face of widespread need, there is an imperative to draw on the lessons learned from existing programs delivering in order to identify best practices and emerging innovations.

In this chapter, we draw on experiences of developing a refugee higher education model to argue for three crucial program characteristics that contribute to the successful delivery of higher education degrees to refugees and populations affected by forced displacement:

1) A flexible mode of degree delivery and assessment.
2) Resource-intensive blended learning with on-the-ground access to academic support.
3) Provision of adaptive and context-specific interventions and resources.

One enduring myth that this chapter aims to dispel is that online-*only* learning can work for the majority of refugee and other vulnerable learners (Palin, 2014; Valerio, 2015). Evidence shows that even the most adaptable online learning programs cannot offer the support adequate to meet the learning gaps and logistical challenges faced by most vulnerable or disenfranchised learners. Studies have found that those that independently access and benefit the most from online and open-access educational resources are usually the least vulnerable learners – male and already well-educated (Christensen et al., 2013; Rohs & Ganz, 2015). In practice, this means online education programs must incorporate a robust blended learning model that combines online content with on-the-ground academic support and guidance in the initial phases of seeking employment (Saqib, 2014; Singh et al., 2001).

As our case study, we draw on our experiences leading a new education initiative called the Global Education Movement (GEM), which delivers US-accredited Associate and Bachelor's degrees to refugee and refugee-hosting populations in five countries. The foundation of the model is Southern New Hampshire University's (SNHU) online competency-based "College for America" (CfA) degree, through which students achieve university credits through the completion of real-world projects that are directly assessed. Evidence from the program in Rwanda – which is locally operated by our partner Kepler – suggests it is possible for a full degree program to be successful in reaching vulnerable learners, including refugees.

Section 2 of this chapter offers an overview of this model, focusing on a specific case study of a program in Rwanda, which operates in partnership with Kepler university program, an international non-governmental organization (NGO). Following an outline of the program model and key considerations of the program, we discuss the findings from program evaluations on learning and employment outcomes. We conclude with a discussion of practical and ethical implications for the broader field.

CASE STUDY: SNHU GEM MODEL & PROGRAMS IN RWANDA

This section offers an overview of the SNHU GEM model through an in-depth exploration of the program in Rwanda, which serves both Rwandan and refugee students, which operates in partnership with Kepler University Program.

The GEM is a major initiative at SNHU to bring accredited university degrees and employment opportunities to refugees and vulnerable populations affected by forced migration, including host communities. Since 2013, at SNHU, a private, non-profit, accredited institution of higher education in the United States, has partnered with the non-profit Kepler University Program in Rwanda to serve vulnerable learners and refugees. In 2018, SNHU launched GEM, a $10 million dollar initiative to bring their competency-based bachelor's and associate's degrees to communities affected by displacement in other countries. In phase I of the initiative, GEM is working with partners to launch pilots in four new locations, including Jesuit Worldwide Learning in Kenya and Malawi, Scalabrini Centre of Cape Town in South Africa, and with American University of Beirut, Multi Aid Programs and other local partners in Lebanon, as well as a global-level partnership with UNHCR (GEM, 2018).

The program run in partnership with Kepler University Program in Rwanda – henceforth called "the Rwanda program" – is a non-profit higher education program that operates campuses in the capital city Kigali as well as Kiziba Refugee Camp in Rwanda. SNHU has partnered with Kepler in Rwanda since its launch in 2013.

The program initially focused on serving vulnerable Rwandan students in Kigali; in 2015, a second campus was launched for refugee students in Kiziba Refugee Camp, in addition to serving refugee and migrant students alongside Rwandan nationals at the Kigali campus.[2] The Rwanda program pairs SNHU's CfA degree with in-person coaching, support services, and career preparation curated to meet the particular labor needs in the economic context of eastern and central Africa.

Evidence from the Rwanda program shows promising successes for student academic and employment outcomes. In 2014 and 2015, independent evaluations were conducted to measure the program's impact on student learning outcomes through a comparison of CfA students enrolled in the Kigali campus with match control groups of Rwandan students at local universities. Results showed that Rwandan students enrolled in CfA outperformed students in other higher education institutions in Rwanda at a statistically significant level in areas of critical thinking, cognitive skills, math, logic, English reading and writing, and computer literacy (IDinsight, 2015).[3] Survey findings also found that CfA students in Rwanda who engage in internships earlier in their university education receive more feedback on their internships compared to the match control group. CfA students in Rwanda also reported feeling they have a richer network of personal connections upon which to draw in their search for jobs, and are more confident about their post-graduation employment prospects (IDinsight, 2015).

In addition to learning outcomes, the program correlated with improvements attrition, gender equity, and employment outcomes for students in the program. Since 2013, attrition rates have averaged 17% and 9% for the Kigali and Kiziba refugee camp campuses, respectively. A 50/50 gender balance has been effected in Kigali since the launch in 2013; in Kiziba that balance was obtained starting from the second cohort in 2016 with the help of specific interventions to support female applicants and students and has been maintained in subsequent cohorts. Additionally, the current employment rate for graduates is at 90% across both campuses, defined as graduates that find full-time employment within six months of graduation (Kepler, 2018).

Given these promising results, particularly in the face of the many challenges presented by a camp environment, we aim to use this program as a case study through which to elucidate key lessons learned as well as to identify promising practices for the delivery of higher education to refugees and populations affected by forced displacement. We do this primarily through analysis of three components of the program that we have identified as central to its success: (1) an online competency-based degree; (2) a partner-based blended learning model; and (3) the provision of adapted resources and interventions. In this remainder of this section, we will explore these different elements of the GEM model and their partnership program with Kepler in Rwanda.

COMPETENCY-BASED DEGREE

The availability of flexible degree and assessment pathways is crucial for success in reaching refugee and vulnerable learners. In the case study considered, this flexible mode of degree delivery has been made possible by CfA, SNHU's competency-based degree program.[4]

Accredited in 2013, CfA allows students to earn associate's and bachelor's degrees through CfA by completing a series of "real world" projects with mastery-based direct assessment.[5] Faculty give instruction through direct feedback on student-submitted projects, through which students learn why they have mastered a project or what they need to improve in order to re-submit. This model of direct assessment has shown significant promise as an effective way to deliver competency-based education.[6]

Initially intended as a way to increase access to higher education for non-traditional and economically disenfranchised students in the United States via a low-cost degree option, the CfA degree has proven crucial in dealing with the cost and accessibility constraints for vulnerable learners in Rwanda as well. One reason for this is because the CfA degree is designed to be self-paced and flexible. The degree is undertaken online and allows students to progress at their own pace, without externally imposed deadlines. The project-based nature of the degree means that students do not have traditional coursework, direct teaching, grades, or credit hour requirements. Instead students demonstrate "competencies" at their own pace, earning credit toward their degrees by successfully completing projects that prove their mastery in predetermined competencies or tasks, such as writing in a business setting or using a spreadsheet to perform calculations.

In Rwanda, this adaptability often proved critical, especially for refugee learners. It means that vulnerable students are not penalized or required to repeat coursework if they miss a deadline or are forced to pause in their studies – whether due to work, electricity, or internet failures, weather events, family emergencies, maternity leave, or illness. Instead, students can pick up where they left off with their projects, without being penalized for the time lost. In early 2018, a period of insecurity in Kiziba refugee camp resulted in significant lost learning time for students; however, once the situation stabilized – and even earlier for students who were able to relocate during the crisis – they were able to resume their studies from where they left off and continued to make academic progress, without needing to take a formal leave of absence from the degree program or have any special arrangements made by the university. Similarly, if students repatriate, are resettled, or move to a new location during their studies, they can continue in the program with access to online support from tutors and coaches.

There is also evidence to suggest that completing a competency-based degree program can help to effectively prepare students for the workplace and employment in emerging economies. The basic pedagogical premise behind the CfA program – that students should rarely expect to "master" a project with a first try, but rather are taught to continuously progress toward mastery after receiving robust feedback from an expert assessor – was designed to prepare students for the twenty-first century world of work; accordingly, CfA projects are built based on market research and input from industry leaders, in combination with academic content experts. There was initial uncertainty about whether the western-centric approach to employment readiness would translate in the Rwandan context. Yet, data show that since 2013, 90% of CfA graduates in Rwanda find full-time employment[7] within six months of graduation, on average (Kepler, 2018). Additionally, feedback from employers of CfA graduates in Rwanda has focused positively on graduates' high level of technical and professional skills (Kepler, 2018), indicating a potentially broader applicability of skill sets gained in CfA in both global and local labor markets.

The project-based degree and direct assessment model have also proved compatible with low-bandwidth environments. The CfA "projects" and their accompanying academic resources can be downloaded or placed on a Local Area Network device, which allows students to work on projects offline[8]; this is ideal for low-bandwidth contexts, such as refugee camps, or even countries in which internet access can be expensive. The Kepler campus in Kiziba refugee camp makes use of a RACHEL device so that students can access educational content offline, including CfA resources. Once a student accesses a project and has the necessary electronic materials available on a laptop, desktop, or tablet, they can work offline independently until they complete the project, at which point they need an internet connection to upload the project and receive feedback from assessors.

It is also worthwhile to note the advantage of the generally widespread recognition of US degrees globally. Refugee students who earn degrees at institutions in hosting country can run the risk of not being able to transfer or have those degrees recognized by institutions or employers in their home countries or countries of resettlement. In many cases, by receiving a US-accredited degree, refugee learners have an increased chance of successfully applying for equivalencies or having their degrees recognized by institutions, governments, and employers. In addition, students who earn their degree through CfA receive the same degree as students who attend the physical campus or enroll in the traditional online program at SNHU. This is useful in contexts where governments or employers might be unfamiliar with online learning or where there is skepticism toward online degrees.

Finally, it would be remiss not to recognize the significance of CfA's comparatively low-cost delivery of associate and bachelor's degrees. CfA debuted in 2013 at a per student cost of USD $2,500 per year, and is currently billed in 2018 at USD $5,000 per year. Although this price point is still out of reach for the vast majority of refugees, it is more readily able to be covered by internal and external scholarships, grants, and fee waivers compared to average annual out-of-state tuition costs of USD $25,620 at public universities and USD $34,740 at private universities in the United States (College Board, 2018). In fact, cost has been one of the most significant barriers for western institutions seeking to provide higher education for refugees and other marginalized populations. The inability to cover the cost of a full undergraduate degree has led many universities and NGOs to offer smaller-scale packages such as a diploma or one-off courses, or even non-accredited certificates. The ultimate value of such certifications is questionable, given issues relating to recognition as well as a frequent lack of education or employment pathways that follow from such smaller-scale initiatives. Such advancements in online learning and the increasing number of universities seeking accreditation for competency-based learning degrees – although not driven with refugees, or even international learners, in mind – presents an important opportunity that can leverage newfound affordability of high-quality accredited degrees to dramatically expand access to higher education at a global level.

The accreditation of SNHU's project-based degree and the establishment of SNHU's partnership with Kepler in Rwanda, both in the same year, were fortuitous. The degree to which refugee and other vulnerable learners in Rwanda are able to excel in degree program originally designed for American learners has been impressive, and there is a compelling evidence to suggest that the inherent flexibility and adaptive structure – in addition to a low-price point – of SNHU's CfA degree is an indispensable factor in the successful delivery of a full university degree program for refugees and other marginalized learners. Of course, even if the mode of degree delivery proves to be a necessary element for success, it is not sufficient on its own; in Section 4, we turn our attention to the blended learning aspects of the GEM partnership model.

BLENDED LEARNING: A PARTNERSHIP MODEL

Having laid out the mode of delivery, in this section we turn our attention to the blended learning approach in GEM's partnership model. While GEM operates across all project sites to provide student and partner support services, in addition to the competency-based degree, the model relies extensively on the presence of a robust implementing partner who can provide continuous access to on-the-ground academic support for students. In this model, on-the-ground partners operate to provide assistance and services to support students while they are enrolled in and completing the CfA degree at SNHU.[9] Out of all of the elements identified for an effective higher education program, the most significant learning has occurred around the development and execution of a blended learning model to support marginalized students, including refugees. In Rwanda, the model relies on three central components: (1) online learning, (2) in-person facilitation, and (3) employment connections and workplace training. The nature of the Kepler and SNHU partnership lies at the intersection of these three components.

There are several models outlined in the literature of blended learning, ranging from almost completely in-person facilitation to completely online models with no in-person facilitation (Picciano, 2014). In the GEM model, there is no proscribed percentage of time spent in-person with a facilitator versus online. Rather, the amount of time spent online varies depending on the program, partner, and site context, as well as with the academic, life, and work circumstances of a student. In GEM's programs in Kenya and Malawi, the majority of student learning is expected to take place independently and online, while in South Africa the ratio of in-person to online learning is more balanced.

In the Rwanda program, Kepler relies heavily on in-person instruction at the beginning of a student cohort cycle, which gradually decreases over time as more independent online-learning is incorporated.[10] Kepler provides a robust support model for students on-the-ground, which includes: (1) an academic bridge program to prepare students with the skills needed to engage in university-level work; (2) development of foundational and modular courses delivered through course facilitators; (3) individualized academic and coaching support; (4) development and implementation of interventions targeting marginalized populations and women; (5) career guidance and support, including internship and work-study programs. In addition to academic and employment support, Kepler also provides laptop loans, monthly stipends, access to housing, access to internet, access to counseling services and school nurse, and regular social and extra-curricular activities.[11]

Following an intensive in-person bridging program, blended learning components begin to take on different percentages of online learning versus in-person learning based on the performance and needs of each student. Immediately following the bridge program, students are expected to engage in a series of foundational modules to prepare them to engage with the CfA degree platform. Benchmark assessments determine when students are ready to begin their CfA projects, engage in work-study or internship positions, and take other elective courses.[12] Even after a student begins on the CfA platform, they are still expected to interact with course facilitators through mandatory modules. In addition, student performance on the CfA platform also affects how much in-person support a student might receive. If a student is struggling to make progress on their CfA degree, they can choose – or be mandated – to meet with a coach who helps the student to understand and apply feedback received from CfA assessors.

Outside of academic performance, internship and work opportunities may also impact the amount of in-person engagement a student will experience. For example, a high-performing student who earns an internship opportunity that subsequently grows into full-time employment would meet with Kepler staff to build his or her schedule of online and in-person learning. The performance of the student is then tracked throughout the time of the student's employment and is cross-referenced with student progress and performance. The amount of in-person or online time is adjusted according to student performance. In many cases, students can determine schedule changes needed. In other cases, student performance – either with their employer or academically – may trigger more mandated in-person time on-campus.

In general, after the initial stages of the program, the amount of time spent with in-person facilitators and online is largely determined by the level of student performance and progress. Of course, creating systems that have the capacity and flexibility to respond to student needs and deliver individualized support is both resource- and time-intensive. It also requires a robust organizational approach to staffing and professional development.

Originally, Kepler envisaged a teaching staff model in which expatriate instructors – called Teaching Fellows – would enhance and guide students through MOOCs with the assistance of Rwandan Teaching Fellows-in-training. In 2013, Kepler's launch largely fulfilled this plan. However, it became apparent that a majority expatriate teaching model posed problems for cultural relevance, sustainability, and buy-in. Consequently, two months after the launch, —four to six Rwanda teachers were hired to join Kepler's team and a co-teaching model began. In the co-teaching model, local and expatriate teachers collaborated as equal partners to deliver, modify, and give feedback on lesson plans.

Over time, Kepler has continued to phase out expatriate teachers and invest more in local teachers, almost all Rwandan nationals or from neighboring countries such as Uganda and the DRC. The model has been extended to include high-performing students in their second and third years as teacher assistants, and subsequently many SNHU graduates in Rwanda have been hired as full-time instructional staff following graduation. Currently, there are 30 East African course facilitators employed by Kepler to ensure students can work through the cultural gaps of a Western-based degree, and to effectively apply the academic feedback they receive on projects from CfA.

For this kind of staffing model, capacity-building is key. The Kepler staffing model is supported by continuous professional development programming to train and equip course facilitators.[13] The curriculum for these professional development sessions are adapted from high-performing K-12 urban classrooms serving vulnerable youth in the United States, such as Teach Like a Champion to improve teaching techniques, and Rethinking Teacher Evaluation and Supervision by Kim Marshall, to give frequent, structured feedback to instructors. In an attempt to build capacity and foster leadership among national staff, Kepler's formalized professional development and feedback systems have focused on risk taking and higher-level managerial tasks, which can be challenging due to traditionally rooted hierarchies in Rwandan society. Kepler's approach to professional development has met with some success. Currently, the student bridge program is run entirely by Rwandan staff, and two of the original Rwandan course facilitators have been promoted to director roles for the Kigali campus, where they have been overseeing academic programs since 2016.

Of course, there are trade-offs to Kepler's robust in-person instruction and on-the-ground staffing approach. Blended learning models that lean heavily on in-person learning are usually resource-intensive, which can pose challenges for program scale and sustainability. For this reason, it would be useful to engage in longer-term comparative research across other GEM sites and partners to better understand the compromises available across a spectrum of blended learning models.

ADAPTIVE AND CONTEXT-SENSITIVE SUPPORT

This section will explore what we argue to be the third necessary component of an effective higher education delivery model for refugees and vulnerable learners, which is the availability of innovative interventions and resources to address context-specific needs. This can include but is not limited to: affirmative action admissions and financial aid policies; context-adapted curricula and academic resources; interventions that target and support the academic achievement of women; benefits and support services that meet the needs of students from impoverished populations; development of specific courses for skills-building and professional competence based on local labor and national market; context-specific services to support students to find work experience and employment pathways. Crucially, the GEM model's flexible degree program and blended learning partnership model creates space for the incorporation of these kinds of context-specific interventions and resources throughout the program.

From the outset of the program in Rwanda, there was a strong focus on enrolling young people with talent but without the financial means to access a high-quality university education on their own. This focus was compounded by the decision to expand access to refugee learners in Rwanda through the establishment of the second campus in Kiziba refugee camp as well as the active recruitment of refugee students to the urban Kigali campus. Equitable access goals such as these require robust support from organizational financial aid and admissions policies, which must help the university to engage in inclusive admissions practices for poor students and women with high academic potential. This was equally important when the program was extended to refugees in Rwanda, and in particular for the admission and support of female refugees. Given the significant gender gap in achievement between men and women in Rwanda and across sub-Saharan Africa, Kepler launched a number of interventions to support the enrolment and academic achievement of women, including gender-split reading groups, sexual and reproductive health classes, and women's activities.

Although the program was able to achieve 50:50 gender ratios for Kigali-based cohorts through an affirmative action admissions process, gender inequity was a significant issue for the program in Kiziba refugee camp. The first cohort selection in 2015 included only seven women out of 25 students, so a women-only "preparatory" program was introduced in the camp to help prospective students prepare for the Kepler admissions process. A second mixed gender preparatory program was also delivered at another refugee camp in Rwanda to increase the number of refugees who are competitive in the applications process for the Kigali-based campus, which serves both Rwandan nationals and refugees. The women-only program in Kiziba refugee camp was delivered for four months and had 26 participants coming to class Monday–Friday and was taught by two female Kepler second-year students hired through a work-study program. The second camp-based preparation program was a mixed-gender class with 19 regularly attending students, taught by a female third-year student and a male second-year student from Kepler. This was a smaller program that took place ran Friday–Sunday for three months. All participants in the preparation programs took the admissions examination and were eligible for entrance to the Kigali campus. Participants from the Kiziba camp were also eligible for admission into the Kiziba-based program. In the following year's admissions, 68% of students admitted to the Kiziba campus cohort were women, and the number of refugees admitted to the Kigali campus from across the two camps increased by a multiple of four (Kepler, 2016). This evidence suggests that such targeted interventions can be relatively high impact in supporting refugees and particularly women to at least enroll in higher education opportunities.[14]

GEM and Kepler have both also worked to create supplementary curricula and courses to address common professional and technical skills gaps for vulnerable student populations, including refugees. GEM has developed a student orientation that is geared toward inducting vulnerable students who may be underexposed to university standards and policies through sessions that focus on familiarizing students with academic honesty policies, informed consent practices around sharing of student information and data, and an adapted introduction to the technology and platform used for CfA. GEM also delivers a series of specialized workshops to help students in refugee contexts to learn and practice key networking skills and professional codes of conduct needed for employment in the formal sector. In Rwanda, Kepler has developed six-week modular courses that are shaped by direct feedback on student skill gaps from employers and as well as to supplement CfA degree content based on existing student knowledge gaps. Students can select from a variety of modular courses (electives) to build and improve their skill sets while maintaining flexibility to participate in jobs or internships and work on CfA projects for their degrees.

It is also critical that wraparound services for students coming from vulnerable background or refugee contexts be considered in overall program design. These include things such as housing and nutritional support, counseling services, and healthcare, as well as careful consideration of policies to support students who are working, have families, or need to take maternity or paternity leave. In Rwanda, Kepler provides additional student support services to both refugee and non-refugee students on the Kigali campus to ensure that basic living needs are covered. After the first year, in response to significant concerns about nutrition, physical, and mental health, Kepler introduced on-campus lunch and a clinical psychologist for counseling services, and these services remain intact in the current model. Initially, Kepler provided a modest living stipend of about $5 less than the average national salary for workers in Rwanda, as well as health services and housing.[15] Student housing at the Kigali campus location was originally mandatory and required all students in all levels of study must live in student housing.[16] Early evidence showed that this policy had the potential to positively impact female students in particular, since while living in student housing, women are freed from the household expectations and responsibilities typically required of young women in Rwanda – including fetching water, caring for sick family members, cooking, and cleaning the house. Mandatory student housing also indirectly discourages marriage until after a student has finished his or her degree.

At the refugee-based campus in Kiziba, new policies had to be developed after launch in 2015 that took into account the higher number of students with families and children, particularly for women in the program who traditionally tend to be primary caregivers. Since 2015, Kepler has developed and tweaked a series of new attendance and academic progress policies in Kiziba that allow more flexibility and support for students who need to go on maternity/paternity leave, students who experience family emergencies, students who are employed full-time, and students who are in the resettlement process – many of which were new or more significant challenges than previously experienced among students served at the Kigali-based campus.[17] New policies and protocols were developed in particular to support women with families, including a student-centered approach to academically support female students returning from maternity leave. In one case, discretionary funding was used to pay a female student's caregiving family member to bring the baby to campus each day at regular times for breastfeeding so that the student could resume her studies. In addition, remote-based internship and employment opportunities for both female and male students with families have become a more significant part of employment strategies for students living in the refugee camp, as compared to students who are based in Kigali.

Regardless of where they are based, higher education programs targeting vulnerable learners and refugees must ensure that students have the skills and experience needed to find access to and thrive in employment opportunities. For GEM and Kepler, internships have been a key part of this approach. Across GEM partners, internships are a mandatory component of an overall blended learning program; students are generally required by partners to complete three-month internships during their studies to gain work experience and develop professional skills. In addition, GEM has built and manages a "jobs portal" in which GEM students can directly apply for internship and employment opportunities made available across a variety of sectors and employers. These opportunities may be with physical, in-country companies or organizations, or they may be "remote-based" opportunities in which the intern or employee will complete work online for an international company. In particular, since expansion into countries where refugees do not have right to work or freedom of movement, GEM has been focusing the development of remote-based employment opportunities, in which graduates tend to have several comparative advantages including a high level of competence in professional English and technology and communications skills; in 2018, SNHU GEM became a member of the Global Impact Sourcing Coalition and actively engages with employers who have a need for remote- and online-based service work to open opportunities on behalf of students and graduates.

In Rwanda, Kepler has prioritized structured internships since the inception of the program. These were initially small-scale and began at the end of the institution's first year through connections that staff developed with local employers, and over time has grown into a cross-campus program that is supported by more formal organizational structures and full-time dedicated staff. Although Kepler staff do the networking to make the opportunities available, students must apply and interview for the placements.[18] Of course, prioritization of work experiences and employment can create tensions and challenges with academic progress in a blended learning program; students have expressed high levels of stress in navigating their jobs and studies, and in some cases have not been able to successfully transition their academic success into the workplace. Over time Kepler has adjusted policies around internships as well as placed academic requirements and thresholds that students must meet before taking on full-time work. These experiences and the lessons learned have also helped GEM partners in other sites to develop policies and provide guidance to build employment pathways for students and graduates throughout the program.

IMPLICATIONS

The preceding sections have offered an insight into some essential components for an efficacious higher education model for refugees and communities affected by displacement. However, these discussions also open up a number of implications and topics for further exploration.

Higher Education as an Alternative Displacement Solution

Over the past decades, there has been an increasing focus on the importance of re-imagining and designing possibilities for durable solutions to displacement. A central conversation has explored the role of livelihoods in humanitarian protection (see UNHCR, 2011, 2014), a discussion to which higher education programs should be closely linked.[19] It is well documented that refugees' access to livelihoods and income-generating opportunities can strengthen protection outcomes, including increased resilience, self-reliance, and better educational and health outcomes (Betts et al., 2017; De Vriese, 2006; Jacobsen, 2005). More recently, it has been suggested that livelihoods and employment could themselves serve as pathways to solutions for the challenges of displacement (UNHCR, 2016). Recognizing the increasingly limited availability of conventional "durable solutions," the Solutions Alliance formed in 2014 to explore the potential of alternative durable solutions to displacement, with a focus on livelihoods and economic solutions for refugee and local host populations (Solutions Alliance, 2015). Further commitments were made during the 2016 World Humanitarian Summit to support refugees' self-reliance and ensure their access to rights for employment and freedom of movement (WHS, 2016).

Advocates for the expansion of employment opportunities for refugees in the formal sector argue that it can support economic development for host countries. Recent studies by the World Bank and independent research institutions have highlighted the contributions that refugees can offer to local host communities and national economies, if allowed to pursue employment and microenterprise (Enghoff et al., 2010; Ruiz & Vargas-Silva, 2013). Jordan has recently made efforts to find work for refugees from Syria, and countries such as Uganda are supporting the entrepreneurial drive of their refugee populations by removing restrictions on employment and mobility (Betts & Collier, 2015). Education appears to have clear economic impacts on income for refugee populations, with research among refugee populations in Uganda revealing that that each additional year of primary and secondary education is associated with a 3.3% higher average income overall, and each additional year of tertiary education is associated with 27% higher earnings (Betts et al., 2017).

With robust employment rates for its graduates, blended higher education programs such as GEM can play an important role in providing pathways to livelihoods and employment – in particular, in host states in which refugees have right to work, and in the realm of digital and remote employment opportunities for countries with more restrictive employment policies. Degrees that are accredited and recognized internationally – such as US Bachelor degrees – can offer long-term mobility and further educational opportunities. In addition, high-quality degree programs also have the potential to fill high-skilled labor market gaps in emerging economies, including the technology sector. Companies such as Samasource and the Microsoft AppFactory, among others, have piloted programs to offer digital online employment, including coding and microwork, to refugees. These companies are early explorers in the under-developed realm of remotely-based employment, which – despite significant challenges including connectivity and legal barriers – has been hailed as a promising opportunity for the cross-border expansion of refugee livelihoods (Hegarty, 2011; Raja, Imaizumi, Kelly, Narimatsu, & Paradi-Guilford, 2013; Schwab, 2015).

As with all durable solutions, the solutions availed through higher education and employment pathways require concerted efforts for political and economic action. For instance, most refugee hosting countries place significant restrictions on refugees' rights to work and freedom of movement, which both prevent refugees from accessing employment opportunities and limit their economic contributions to the host state. Furthermore, even in the case of remote-based employment – in which a refugee in a hosting country completes work online for a company based in a different country – there are key political and legal barriers that need to be addressed, including policies around taxation, securing access to financial services including the ability to open a local bank account, as well as the fear of existing legal loopholes that enable remote-based employment being closed in the future.

Limitations of Online Learning and Technology

There has been significant excitement over the potential for technology and, in particular, MOOCs to expand and democratize access to higher education in developing countries (Wildavsky, 2015), and much of this enthusiasm has also been extended second-hand to refugee contexts. A key argument that this chapter seeks to forward is that while technology and open educational resources have an important role to play in improving access to higher education, online-only learning is not sufficient for the majority of displaced learners. Existing data reveals a significant "digital divide" across series of access, usage, and knowledge gaps for most MOOCs and MOOC-based programs, with extremely low completion rates and high inequality of access along gender, income, and educational levels in both developed and developing countries (Rohs & Ganz, 2015). In refugee and displacement contexts, these issues are exacerbated by issues of connectivity and access to technology. The few published research studies (Gladwell, et al., 2016a, 2016b; Moser-Mercer, 2014) exploring technology-supported higher education in forced displacement, identify language, information and digital literacy, connectivity, gender, sociocultural and religious background, disability, age, location, and documentation, as main impediments to access.

A recent report by Jigsaw Consult offers an overview of existing programs emerging in the field of refugee higher education, ranging from camp-based and host-community programs with a physical presence to remote learning initiatives that are completely online (Gladwell et al., 2016a, 2016b). Although opportunities for refugees to study through online universities have the potential to broaden access, there is currently a lack of data that demonstrates their ability to adequately support vulnerable and/or under-prepared refugee learners.

KIRON university program, a MOOC-based learning platform that targets refugees and seeks to provide future pathways to accredited degrees, has made strides toward adapting online content and offering more tailored online supports for refugee learners, and reports average course completion rate of 21% per course, as compared to 2–8% for the average MOOC user (KIRON, 2017).[20]

Alternatively, a number of emerging initiatives for refugee higher education have developed "connected learning," an approach that bends blended learning models to the goal of "supporting the collaborative construction and exchange of knowledge and ideas among learners and faculty through the use of information technology and specific technology-supported pedagogies" (Connected Learning in Crisis Consortium, 2017). Connected learning programs in refugee contexts have embraced blended learning, "where more than one delivery mode is used with the objective of optimizing the learning programme and cost of delivery" (Singh et al., 2001), to combine online content and e-learning programs (including MOOCs) with in-person academic support.

The GEM and Kepler partnership in Rwanda demonstrates the potential of connected learning programs to reach the most vulnerable learners, including refugees. In fact, when the SNHU and Kepler collaboration began in 2013, the initial vision was to integrate the CfA degree projects with a significant amount of learning time dedicated to externally developed MOOCs from institutions of higher education around the world. In the first cohort, students were enrolled in four MOOC-based classes. However, following the launch of the model and an attempt to implement the academic program, several challenges quickly became apparent.

The most urgent issue was low English competency, with particular challenges in writing; students had never composed essays independently given the rote copy-from-the-board pedagogy of their primary and secondary schools. Since the majority of MOOCs are developed by and for students coming from a Western cultural lens, the delivery of both written and spoken content was not designed for students speaking English as a second language, with no adaptations made for vocabulary or speech pace. As a result, the low English levels of the students in Rwanda meant that they were not able to adequately comprehend most of the content. These problems were compounded by the overall lack of engaging or innovative pedagogical methods found across most MOOCs. One underlying cause for this could be that most MOOCs are adapted from lectures at elite universities, where professors can rely on impressive student profiles rather than high-impact pedagogical techniques. Beyond language and writing skills, there are other areas for which students were significantly underprepared and required intensive support that could not be accessed through MOOC-based learning alone, such as cultural understandings about academic honesty, time management in a rigorous academic program with a high workload, and the building of a value-driven student learning community. As Saqib observed in a 2014 study, "facilitated face to face sessions were an integral part of the success" of the model in Rwanda, noting that an online-only model – even delivering the same academic content – is insufficient to support learners' academic and psychosocial support needs (Saqib, 2014).

While the Kepler board (and much of the world) was hopeful and buzzing about the potentially transformative impact of MOOCs for students lacking access to high-quality education, it became immediately clear on the ground that MOOCs would not be a silver bullet in transforming the educational experiences of bright and highly motivated but ill-prepared and impoverished first generation college-goers in Rwanda. Once it became clear that MOOCs could not be used as the backbone of the on-the-ground curriculum as originally intended, Kepler modified its MOOC use after the first term, relying instead on course facilitators to choose short segments that are engaging or explain content particularly well. Essentially, rather than MOOCs replacing the role of a professor, they became one of the main tools through which course facilitators help students understand content, much like a case study, film, or textbook.

Provision of Western Higher Education in Non-Western Contexts

There are a number of ethical implications and practical challenges surrounding the delivery of higher education degrees that have been designed for and produced by western institutions. Online-learning programs have been appropriately critiqued as "elitist instruments of Western academic dominance that are not appropriately tailored to non-Western cultures and risk undermining local institutions and academic traditions" (Wildavsky, 2015, p. 24). In addition, most online-learning programs struggle to some degree to appropriately contextualize their program delivery and learning content in order to address issues of technology access, language and contextually relevant content for learners, particularly those from underrepresented and/or vulnerable groups, such as refugees (Saqib, 2014). The majority of online educational content is developed for and by Western institutions, which means that assumptions made about the baseline knowledge of learners may be inappropriate and also that many of the cultural references integrated into curricula are unfamiliar to learners based in the Global South (Boga & McGreal, 2014).

In addition, it is important to consider language of instruction not simply as an issue of communication but also a mechanism of power (Bourdieu, 1992). Students that are ultimately able to master English through English-medium degree programs outperform their peers on language tests and report high levels of confidence due to their advantage in the job market. Since 2008, the national language in Rwanda has been English, empowering graduates from the CfA degree program to move to a higher economic class. While this benefits graduates, it also perpetuates inequality by further disempowering those who exclusively speak Kinyarwanda, the language spoken by over 95% of the country's population.

Some online-learning programs have sought to address these issues through multi-lingual instruction and translation of online content. While diversifying the language of instruction goes some way in overcoming the hegemony of monolingual teaching, the educational content remains problematic; Boga and McGreal (2014, p. 5) reflect that "even MOOCs that have been translated were originally created for a North American audience, so the content doesn't accurately reflect the reality of students in other countries." For example, SNHU students translated the MOOC "Beyond Silicon Valley: Growing Entrepreneurship in Transitioning Economies," originally delivered by Michael Goldberg from Case Western University, into Kinyarwanda. While this makes the content available to many Rwandans (including both those enrolled and not enrolled at SNHU), the content includes heavy use of examples, idioms, cultural references unfamiliar to many Rwandan viewers.[21] This means that learners engaging in such programs must be offered additional support such as coaching in order to make sense of and interpret the online content and to gain familiarity. Significant efforts need to be made in order to contextualize curriculum and academic content through in-person instructional delivery, with a focus on the "use of local instructors who can create their own content and conduct classes in local language [as] a potential solution" (Saqib, 2014, p. 29).

Beyond issues of language, it is also important to consider the ways in which educational institutions serve to replicate social classes and individual economic roles in society (Apple, 1990, Foster, [1965] 1998; Scudder & Colson, 1980). Engaging with Bowles and Gintis's (1976) "correspondence theory," it is critical to examine the ways that higher education institutions operating in the Global South function under a hierarchy in which "workers" are being prepared according to rules of the Western, largely White, middle class. In the context of pursuing an enrolling in an American degree program in Rwanda, students must navigate a Western, American university program in their home country.[22]

Some argue that Western-produced and anglophone programs may expose learners to information that empowers them to draw upon hegemonic structures and practices for their own use. For instance, it may allow students to deploy techniques such as code-switching to access and navigate within institutions of power (Wheeler & Swords, 2006). On the one hand, Western higher education programs can teach the social skills, habits, academic content, and builds the social networks needed for social mobility within existing economic and social hierarchies. On the other hand, the very program that elevates the students may also make them dependent on the status quo of existing power imbalances.[23] To gain the academic skills that previous graduates have shown lead to employment, he or she is forced to choose between participating in a post-colonialist academic endeavor via a Western institution, or refusing the program and accepting relegation to limited to fewer academic or future economic opportunities. The prospective SNHU student, then, faces a conundrum when considering becoming an American degree student.

CONCLUSION

Our participation in implementing the GEM programs suggests the potential efficacy of a model that combines a flexible, project-based degree with on-the-ground academic and non-academic support as a way to overcome challenges in delivering higher education to refugee populations. Blended learning programs bring together online learning and in-person facilitation in a combination tailored to the disadvantages faced by refugee learners in restricted environments such as refugee camps and informal settlements. This offers an opportunity to develop models that include adequate course preparation and remedial skill development, focusing on skills that many refugee learners lack, as well as on-the-ground instruction to facilitate the consumption of course materials, including those provided through MOOCs.

The case study explored in this chapter is notable because of its successes in navigating a number of issues that face refugee students and other vulnerable learners who want to access higher education, with a strong focus on supporting students through to successful degree completion and acquiring employment opportunities. However, the shortcomings of this project-based, blended learning degree model should not be overlooked. Although the employment imperative is generally supported by refugee learners, who are motivated by personal ambitions and family pressure to generate income, the risk of such a program is it inculcates students to a different educational ethos than learners in traditional university settings. As such, learners may not be as well prepared for academic careers as students enrolled in more conventional programs.

Moreover, universities and educators must understand that a successful degree program can only go so far in addressing problems confronting refugees and those affected by forced displacement. Those displaced from their home countries continue to face global discrimination under national laws limiting employment and freedom of movement for refugees. In addition, asylum-seekers and refugees who lack legal and educational documents face particular challenges accessing opportunities for employment and further education. The cumulative impact of these denied rights and opportunities is far-reaching; for universities, expanding access to educational opportunities for those whom it is currently out of reach can be a first step.

NOTES

1. UNHCR notes that "access to accredited quality higher education for refugees is an integral part of UNHCR's protection mandate and included in our strategic directions for 2017–2021." http://www.unhcr.org/tertiary-education.html.

2. In Rwanda, refugees are granted the right to work and relative freedom of movement, which is unusual among refugee-hosting countries in the region.

3. Research findings based on SNHU's 2013 and 2014 Rwanda cohorts include all results statistically significant at the 5% significance level unless otherwise noted. All test scores were analyzed as percentage of total possible score, and results are presented in terms of percentage point (pp) gain of SNHU students over the comparison group. As indicated by the standard effect sizes below, all of the statistically significant results above are particularly large in magnitude; in education studies, effect sizes larger than 0.3 SD are considered large, while effect sizes larger than 0.5 SD are considered very large. Results are also expressed as standard effect sizes in terms of SD of comparison students' test scores at the Year 2 endline:

1. Critical thinking: 4.9 pp (0.53 SD), as measured by the Watson-Glaser critical thinking test.
2. Cognitive skills: English: 9.0 pp (0.45 SD), math: 2.5 pp (0.14 SD, not statistically significant), logic: 7.0 pp (0.41 SD).
3. English: Reading: 5.8 pp (0.39 SD), writing: 2.8 pp (0.60 SD), as measured by the International English Language Testing System (IELTS) reading and writing tests).

4. Computer literacy: 25.0 pp (2.22 SD), as measured by a test that included typing speed, web research, assessing website credibility, Microsoft Word, Microsoft Excel, and email.

4. In the CfA model of direct assessment, a competency is defined as the capacity to apply skills, knowledge, or abilities to a real-world situation. It is more than theoretical knowledge, a learning outcome, or a skill by itself. When a competency is mastered, it means the student has a knowledge or skill that they have demonstrated through application that they have demonstrated they know to use it – often in a real-world context. Projects for the degree are based on market-level research, preferences from industry leaders, and guidance from academic experts. Graduates engage in real-world tasks and can demonstrate the competencies demanded by employers in today's complex workplaces. Theoretically, there are no limitations on the number of times a student can resubmit before achieving mastery.

5. Competency-based education is not synonymous with direct assessment; other competency-based programs still track learning back to seat time under the credit hour, which assumes one hour of instruction and three hours of coursework per week. Data from CfA show that, on average, it takes students about two-and-a-half submissions before reaching mastery.

6. An initial evaluation by an outside firm showed that CfA students in the US outperformed peers in traditional institutions for a majority of measured categories. An external evaluation that tracked the performance of students enrolled in the CfA degree program in the US in comparison to students at traditional community college programs. Findings showed comparable or higher learning outcomes for CfA over community college students; in an independently administered assessment of 7,000 students attending community colleges, CfA students performed as well or better on ETS's examination. https://www.insidehighered.com/news/2015/11/25/early-glimpse-student-achievement-college-america-competency-based-degree-provider

7. Compare to the official unemployment rate for university graduates in Rwanda of 17.2% in 2016 and 15.9% in 2017 (NISR, 2017). However, there is reason to believe that these figures may be misleadingly low due to wide survey parameters used in official definitions of employment and a widespread crisis of "underemployment" in Rwanda (Laterite, 2015).

8. There are several exceptions to this, such as projects that require students to search for external resources online or projects that require students to work in groups digitally.

9. GEM students enrolled in the CfA degree program choose among the following majors/concentrations for study:

- Associate of General Studies concentration options are: Business or Transforming the Customer Experience.
- Associate of Healthcare Management concentration option is: Business.
- Bachelor of Healthcare Management concentration options are: Communications or Global Perspectives.
- Bachelor of Communication concentration options are: Business or Healthcare Management.
- Bachelor of Business/Management concentration options are: Insurance Services, Logistics and Operations, or Public Administration.

10. It should be noted that Kepler's model has changed significantly since the program's inception, as outlined in subsequent sections. Relatedly, the academic model used at the Kiziba refugee camp campus has gone through multiple iterations and currently employs a multiphase and multischedule approach that includes a pre-program bridge phase, a pre-CfA on-boarding phase, and a mandatory internship phase, as well as separate schedule for students who are employed as primary or secondary school teachers in the camp.

11. Stipend and housing access are not provided to students studying at the Kiziba refugee camp campus.

12. The original foundational year courses were called Technology Skills, Methods of Thinking for Business, Professional Competencies, and Communications. In the original formulation of these courses, students took benchmark assessments every six weeks to track their progress and determine their readiness to begin the SNHU degree.

13. In addition to the regular professional development schedule, each academic year begins with two weeks of full-time professional development, as well as a full staff retreat. Staff evaluations for teachers follow a model where routine observations and frequent, real-time feedback is offered rather than annual performance evaluations.

14. In subsequent years, the "preparatory" program has expanded into a broader program called "Iteme" focused on refugees and local hosting communities in Rwandan: https://www.kepler.org/iteme-program/.

15. Students at the campus in Kiziba refugee camp do not receive housing or stipendiary support but do have access to health services, psychologist and counselling services, and an on-campus lunch program.

16. As Kepler has grown and sought opportunities to reduce cost, student housing has become optional. It is too early on in this policy shift to know if the change will impact academic outcomes for female, male, or both groups of students.

17. There are a number of reasons for this. Although the Kigali-based campus also serves refugee students – in addition to vulnerable Rwandan and migrant students – in general the age of students served at the Kigali campus has tended in the past to be closer to traditional university student age, when students are less likely to have families – and, as discussed, the nature campus-based policies tend to indirectly act as a deterrent for students to get married or have families during their studies. It is not possible to determine if the fact that family-based considerations are more prevalent in the camp-based program is in fact an outcome of not having housing or stipends provided for students who are based in the refugee camp, since students do not have the deterrent effect of student housing policies and must usually keep their "incentive-based" work within the camp if already employed when they join the degree program (refugees are considered to be "volunteer" workers when they are working with camp-based agencies and partners and receive a small monthly stipend to do this work, which is nonetheless still critical to the economic survival of their families). On the other hand, it's apparent that a refugee camp-based campus does open up more opportunities for non-traditional students who may be older, have families, and/or be working full time, since they are able to continue to live in the camp during their studies.

18. For students who are based in the refugee camp, they may choose to apply for internships that are based outside of the camp or remote-based internship opportunities if they are unwilling to leave their families or incentive work.

19. UNHCR's core mandate is to ensure the international protection of refugees worldwide and seek permanent solutions for their displacement. This mandate is derived from international law and is primarily defined by the 1951 Convention relating to the Status of Refugees and the 1967 Protocol relating to the Status of Refugees, as well as other core international and regional legal instruments (UNHCR, 2013).

20. This is a per-course completion rate; there is no available data from KIRON on completion rates for the full bachelor's degree program.

21. One solution is to support the development of locally or regionally produced MOOC content and open educational resources for learners. For instance, Edraak, a MOOC platform based in Jordan, has been a pioneer in offering original Arabic MOOCs developed by regional professors, alongside more traditional online courses from edX, translated into Arabic.

22. The high-level of value placed on American accredited programs in Rwanda could be considered indicative of the processes of normalization and debasement towards White thinking that Fanon (1986) discusses; it also simultaneously creates institutional structures in which Black students in such a program must consistently encounter and endure trauma due to the categorization of their selves as inferior "others" in a system that privileges White systems of power (Fanon, 1986).

23. In post-colonial contexts in particular, the works of Fanon (1965, 1967, 1986) offer a critical perspective on the connection between university education and colonialism in Africa. See also broader discussions on education and power (Carnoy, 1974); colonial "knowledge hierarchies" (Singh, 2012); and decolonizing university education (Alvares & Faruqi, 2012).

REFERENCES

Alvares, C., & Faruqi, S. (Eds.). (2012) *Decolonising the university: The emerging quest for non-Eurocentric paradigms*. Pulau Pinang, Malaysia: Penerbit Universiti Sains Malaysia.

Apple, M. W. (1990). *Ideology and curriculum* (2nd ed.). New York, NY: Routledge.

Betts, A., Bloom, L., Kaplan, J. D., & Omata, N. (2017). *Refugee economies: Forced displacement and development*. Oxford: Oxford University Press.

Betts, A., & Collier, P. (2015). Help refugees help themselves: Let displaced Syrians join the labor market. *Foreign Affairs, 94*, 84.

Boga, S., & McGreal, R. (2014). Introducing MOOCs to Africa: New economy skills for Africa program. *Commonwealth of Learning, 2014*, 01.

Bourdieu, P. (1992). In G. Raymond & M. Adamson (Trans.), *Language and symbolic power*. Cambridge: Polity Press.

Bourdieu, P. (2011). The forms of capital. In I. Szeman, & T. Kaposy, (Eds.), *Cultural theory: An anthology* (pp. 81–93). Malden, MA: John Wiley & Sons.

Bowles, S., & Gintis, H. (1976). *Schooling in capitalist America: Educational reform and the contradictions of economic life*. New York, NY: Basic Books.

Carnoy, M. (1974). *Education as cultural imperialism*. Philadelphia, PA: D. McKay Company.

Christensen, G., Steinmetz, A., Alcorn, B., Bennett, A., Woods, D., & Emanuel, E. J. (2013). *The MOOC phenomenon: Who takes massive open online courses and why?* Philadelphia, PA: University of Pennsylvania.

Connected Learning in Crisis Consortium. (2017). Website. http://www.connectedlearning4refugees.org/

Crea, T. M. (2016). Refugee higher education: Contextual challenges and implications for program design, delivery, and accompaniment. *International Journal of Educational Development, 46*, 12–22.

Crondahl, K., & Eklund, L. (2012). Perceptions on health, well-being, and quality of life of Balkan Roma adolescents in West Sweden. *Romani Studies, 22*(2), 153–173.

Dankova, P., & Giner, C. (2011) Technology in aid of learning for isolated refugees. *Forced Migration Review, 38*, 11–12.

De Vriese, M. (2006). *Refugee livelihoods: A review of the evidence*. Geneva, Switzerland: UNHCR.

Dryden-Peterson, S., & Giles, W. (2010). Introduction: Higher education for refugees. *Refuge: Canada's Journal on Refugees, 27*(2), 3–9.

Enghoff, M., Hansen, B., Umar, A., Gildestad, B., Owen, M., & Obara, A. (2010). *In search of protection and livelihoods: Socio-economic and environmental impacts of Dadaab refugee camps on host communities*. Nairobi, Kenya: Royal Danish Embassy.

Fanon, F. (1967). *A dying colonialism*. New York, NY: Grove Press.

Fanon, F. (1986). *Black skin, white masks*. London: Pluto Press.

Fanon, F., Sartre, J., & Farrington, C. (1965). *The wretched of the earth*. New York, NY: Grove Press, Inc.

Fiddian-Qasmiyeh, E., Ruiz, I., Vargas-Silva, C., Zetter, R. (2012). *Assessing the impacts and costs of forced displacement* (Vol. 1). A Mixed Methods Approach. Washington, DC Retrieved from https://openknowledge.worldbank.org/handle/10986/16096 License: CC BY 3.0 IGO

Foster, P. ([1965] 1998). *Education and social change in Ghana*. London: Routledge.

Gladwell, C., Hollow, D., Robinson, A., Norman, B., Bowerman, E., Mitchell, J., ..., Hutchinson, P. (2016a). *Higher education for refugees in low-resource environments: Research study*. London: Jigsaw Consult.

Gladwell, C., Hollow, D., Robinson, A., Norman, B., Bowerman, E., Mitchell, J., ..., Hutchinson, P. (2016b). *Higher education for refugees in low-resource environments: Landscape review*. London: Jigsaw Consult.

Hegarty, S. (2011) How Silicon Valley outsources work to African refugees. *BBC World Service*. Retrieved from http://www.bbc.com/news/world-africa-13784487

IDinsight. (2015). Kepler Cohort 2014 Evaluation Endline Report. Internal report, August 2015.

IDRC. (2015). Youth employment in Rwanda: A scoping paper. *Laterite*. Retrieved from https://www.idrc.ca/sites/default/files/sp/Documents%20EN/Youth_Employment_RWANDA_REPORT_WEB-FINAL.pdf

International Labour Office. (2016a). The Future of Work Centenary Initiative: Technological changes and the future of work: Making technology work for all. Geneva, Switzerland: ILO. Retrieved from http://www.ilo.org/wcmsp5/groups/public/—dgreports/—dcomm/documents/publication/wcms_534201.pdf. Accessed on January 31, 2017.

International Labour Office. (2016b). The Future of Work Centenary Initiative: The Future of Labour Supply: Demographics, Migration, Unpaid Work. Geneva, Switzerland: ILO. Retrieved from http://www.ilo.org/wcmsp5/groups/public/—dgreports/—dcomm/documents/publication/wcms_534204.pdf. Accessed on January 31th, 2017.

Jacobsen, K. (2005). *The economic life of refugees*. Sterling, VA: Kumarian Press.

Khoudour, D., & Andersson, L. (2017). Assessing the contribution of refugees to the development of their host countries. Organisation for Economic Co-operation and Development. Retrieved from http://www.oecd.org/officialdocuments/publicdisplaydocumentpdf/?cote=DEV/DOC(2017)1&docLanguage=En

KIRON. (2017). Presentation: EU Conference on Higher Education and Refugees in the Mediterranean Region. Retrieved from https://ec.europa.eu/education/sites/education/files/eac-hopes-grace-atkinson.pdf

MacLaren, D. (2012). Tertiary education for refugees: A case study from the Thai–Burma border. *Refuge: Canada's Journal on Refugees, 27*(2), 103–110.

Mitschke, D. B., Aguirre, R. T., & Sharma, B. (2013). Common threads: Improving the mental health of Bhutanese refugee women through shared learning. *Social Work in Mental Health, 11*(3), 249–266.

National Institute of Statistics of Rwanda. (2017). Labour Force Survey. The Republic of Rwanda. Retrieved from http://www.miniyouth.gov.rw/fileadmin/MINIYOUTH_Policies__Laws_and_Regulations/LEBOUR_FORCE_SURVEY_REPORT_FEB_2017.pdf

Palin, A. (2014). Moocs: Young students from developing countries are still in the minority. *Financial Times*. Retrieved from https://www.ft.com/content/8a81f66e-9979-11e3-b3a2-00144feab7de

Picciano, A. G. (2014). A critical reflection of the current research in online and blended learning. *Lifelong Learning in Europe (LLinE), 4*.

Raja, S., Imaizumi, S., Kelly, T., Narimatsu, J., & Paradi-Guilford, C. (2013). *Connecting to work: How information and communication technologies could help expand employment opportunities*. Washington, DC: World Bank.

Rohs, M., & Ganz, M. (2015). MOOCs and the claim of education for all: A disillusion by empirical data. *The International Review of Research in Open and Distributed Learning, 16*(6).

Ruiz, I., & Vargas-Silva, C. (2013). The economics of forced migration. *The Journal of Development Studies, 49*(6), 772–784.

Sanghi, A., Onder, H., & Vemuru, V. (2016). '"Yes" in my backyard? The economics of refugees and their social dynamics in Kakuma, Kenya.' Washington, DC: World Bank.

Saqib, A. (2014). *The use of Massive Open Online Courses (MOOCs) to deliver higher education – A case study of Kepler, Rwanda*. Ph.D. thesis.

Schwab, K. (2015). The Fourth Industrial Revolution. *Foreign Affairs*. Retrieved from https://www.foreignaffairs.com/articles/2015-12-12/fourth-industrial-revolution. Accessed on January 31, 2017.

Scudder, T., & Colson, E. (1980) *Secondary education and the formation of an elite: The impact of education on Gwembe District, Zambia*. London: Academic Press.

Singh, S. (2012). World Social Science Report 2010: Whither India and South Asia? In C. Alvares & S. S. Faruqi (Eds.), *Decolonising the university: The emerging quest for non-Eurocentric paradigms* (pp. 118–125). Pulau Pinang, Malaysia: Penerbit Universiti Sains Malaysia.

Solutions Alliance. (2015). 2015 Solutions Alliance Annual Report. Retrieved from http://www.europe.undp.org/content/dam/geneva/docs/Sollutions%20Alliance%20Annual%20Report%202015.pdf

Taylor, S., & Sidhu, R. K. (2012). Supporting refugee students in schools: What constitutes inclusive education? *International Journal of Inclusive Education, 16*(1), 39–56.

UNHCR. (2011). Promoting livelihoods and self-reliance operational guidance on refugee protection and solutions in urban areas. Division of Programme Support and Management. Retrived from http://www.unhcr.org/4eeb19f49.pdf

UNHCR. (2013). Note on the mandate of the high commissioner for refugees and his office. Division of International Protection. Retrieved from http://www.unhcr.org/protection/basic/526a22cb6/mandate-high-commissioner-refugees-office.html

UNHCR. (2014). global strategy for livelihoods: A UNHCR strategy 2014–2018. Division of Programme Support and Management. Retrieved from http://www.unhcr.org/530f107b6.pdf

UNHCR. (2016). New approaches to solutions. Executive Committee of the High Commissioner's Programme. Standing Committee 66th Meeting. Retrieved from http://www.unhcr.org/575a74597.pdf. Accessed on June 7, 2016.

UNHCR. (2017). Left behind: Education in crisis." Report. Retrieved from http://www.unhcr.org/59b696f44.pdf

Valerio, A. (2015). MOOCs to the rescue? Devex. Retrieved from https://www.devex.com/news/moocs-to-the-rescue-85589

Wildavsky, B. (2015). MOOCs in the developing world: Hope or hype? *International Higher Education*, (80), 23–25.

Wheeler, R. S., & Swords, R. (2006). *Code-switching: Teaching standard English in urban classrooms*. Urbana, IL: National Council of Teachers of English.

Wright, L-A., & Plasterer, R. (2012). Beyond basic education: Exploring opportunities for higher learning in Kenyan refugee camps. *Refuge: Canada's Journal on Refugees*, *27*(2), 42–56.

Zeus, B. (2011). Exploring barriers to higher education in protracted refugee situations: The case of Burmese Refugees in Thailand. *Journal of Refugee Studies*, *24*(2), 272.

CHAPTER 11

CREATING A BORDERLESS WORLD OF EDUCATION FOR REFUGEES

Enakshi Sengupta, Shai Reshef and Patrick Blessinger

ABSTRACT

Today, there are 16.1 million refugees worldwide under the United Nations High Commissioner for Refugees' mandate. Among the refugee population, half of them are children and six million are of primary and secondary school-going age. The number of displaced people around the world has reached unprecedented levels in the recent years since the Syrian crisis escalated. Refugees, because of language and other barriers, face a particularly difficult challenge in attaining even a basic education. Keeping the barriers and challenges in mind, education is now seeking the help of technology to create new and sometimes unexpected opportunities for pathways to education for refugees. This chapter will highlight the contribution of University of the People, a tuition-free, non-profit, American accredited, online university that has been working with refugees to enable access to higher education for those living in refugee camps and other displaced people around the world.

Keywords: Displaced; asylum; short-term need; long-term need; social inclusion; integration; technology; ICT; online education; distance education; scholarship; meritocratic model

Language, Teaching and Pedagogy for Refugee Education
Innovations in Higher Education Teaching and Learning, Volume 15, 181–191
Copyright © 2019 by Emerald Publishing Limited
All rights of reproduction in any form reserved
ISSN: 2055-3641/doi:10.1108/S2055-364120180000015013

INTRODUCTION

Just after the devastation of the Second World War when the Office of the United Nations High Commissioner for Refugees (UNHCR) began work on January 1, 1951, it was given three years to complete its task of helping millions of European refugees who were left homeless or in exile after the war. The visionaries and policy makers at that time thought three years was deemed long enough to resolve the refugee problem once and for all, and then it was expected that UNHCR's task would be complete and perhaps such a United Nations body might not have much work to do. Unfortunately, the refugee crisis over the years never got resolved and has increased. Today, there are 16.1 million refugees worldwide under UNHCR's mandate. Among the refugee population, half of them are children and six million are of primary and secondary school-going age. The number of displaced people around the world has reached unprecedented levels in recent years since the Syrian crisis escalated. The UNHCR estimates that more than 65 million people worldwide have been forcibly displaced from their homes due to extreme violence, war, persecution, and similar factors; in addition, the numbers are growing at an alarming rate. Currently, people are being displaced at a rate of about 20 people per minute.

Particularly disturbing is that most of the growth in displaced people has occurred over the past five years. About one-third of the 65 million displaced people are classified as refugees. The UNHCR defines a refugee as a person who is forced to leave their home country to escape extreme violence, war, persecution, and man-made disasters and is granted asylum in another country (Blessinger & Sengupta, 2017). Apart from refugees, there are asylum seekers, migrants, and internally displaced people. The name and label given to their status may vary but they are the vulnerable population of the world, who are in desperate need of assistance.

Once a refugee, one continues to be a refugee for a very long part of their life. It has been estimated that the average length of time a refugee spends in exile is about 20 years. Twenty years means an entire childhood and youth and comprises a significant portion of a person's productive working years. Given this sobering picture, it is critical that we think beyond a refugee's basic survival of food shelter and medicine. Refugees have skills, ideas, hopes, and dreams and they have a right to express them in a constructive manner. Being vulnerable with nowhere to go, they face huge risks and challenges and may fall victim to human traffickers. As the number of people forcibly displaced by conflict and violence rises, demand for education grows exponentially and the resources in the countries that shelter them are stretched thinner (UNHCR, 2016).

Refugees, because of language and other barriers, face a particularly difficult challenge in attaining even a basic education. According to the UNHCR statistics, only about half of all refugee children attend a primary school, just a quarter attend a secondary school, and only about 1% access higher education (Blessinger & Sengupta, 2017). The European governments have taken commendable steps toward improving the access to education for refugee and migrant children in order to minimize the legal and practical barriers and protocols. A notable progress can be measured in enrolment of refugee and migrant children into formal education – reaching up to 40% of stranded refugee and migrant children in Greece and the Balkans, but the daily surge of migrants makes this relief effort look insignificant (Sengupta & Blessinger, 2018).

For refugees education may be the only key for socioeconomic success and overcoming disadvantages in societies. Proper education results in social inclusion, socioeconomic mobility, and development of the individual. While the education of migrants may have higher costs for a country hosting the refugee population than for non-migrants in a short-term perspective, it is a social investment in the long term (Bonin, 2017). This is true from the perspectives of receiving societies of the European Union (EU) and building peace and stability in the countries of origin of refugees, where they are ultimately expected to return back after their prolonged stay in the host countries. When they eventually return to their country of origin, the education and skills they acquire in other countries will be used by them toward the transformation of their own country, where civilization has hitherto suffered a setback. Enhancing education for migrants can be a daunting task and requires coordination of different policy areas and multi-stakeholder involvement (Bonin, 2017). In the recent past, the media has been highlighting how the EU members have been facing challenges in shouldering the burden of the refugees. Faced with severe constraints, they are struggling to provide decent opportunities in education for newly arriving refugees and integrating them into mainstream education and society. These challenges have deepened since 2015 with the arrival of larger numbers of refugees and asylum seekers (Koehler, 2017).

The refugee crisis involves many overlapping issues dealing with justice, equity, rights, power, identity and pluralism, among others. Within the context of these intertwined complex issues, the UN has reached an agreement (The New York Declaration for Refugees and Migrants) on several commitments that member states should pledge to adhere. Given the centrality of teaching and learning to all educational institutions worldwide, the effort to make educational environments increasingly inclusive to all is one of the top human rights issues of our time (Blessinger & Sengupta, 2017).

Considered a universal empowering right and a common good, education is the only path through which economically and socially marginalized adults and children can rise above poverty, become self-sufficient, and obtain the means to participate fully in their societies. All individuals, refugees, migrants, and forcibly displaced people have the right to education, which is an indispensable means for the full realization of their human rights. (UNESCO, 2017).

THE CHALLENGES

Access to education is not universally guaranteed, especially for children having irregular or undefined status. Such children are denied access to schools or charged fees beyond their means (Sengupta & Blessinger, 2018). In addition to formal restrictions, migrants with an irregular status on their own avoid formal enrolment in schools for fear of revealing their identity, which might result in detention or deportation. Children who migrate unaccompanied by adults are especially vulnerable, as work requirements to survive, poverty, poor health, and language barriers can easily exclude them from schools (United Nations Development Programme [UNDP], 2009). Deportation policies have been found to have detrimental effects on migrant children and their education. Parental detention and deportation result in the disruption of education, which causes economic strain and housing instability, and even adversely affects the health of children, through lack of food and increased cases of depression (Chaudry et al., 2010; Suárez-Orozco, Todorova, & Louie, 2002). Studies conducted in the United States show that such segregation during the period of detention results in diminished academic achievement and learning outcomes, increased drop-out rates, and impaired intergroup dynamics and life-course outcomes (Mickelson, 2014; Mickelson & Nkomo, 2012).

Support for language learning is an essential component for refugee children's education. Learning the language of the host country is necessary for integration with the host community and other fellow students. Learning a language that was hitherto unheard of can be a very daunting and challenging exercise unless accompanied by some positive learning experience and gaining slow confidence in their efforts (Sengupta & Blessinger, 2018). Methodical and continuous language support is necessary at all levels of education especially for the refugees (Cummins, 1979). There are significant debates whether to provide second language education through immersion, transitional bilingual education, or true bilingual education (Organisation for Economic Co-operation and Development [OECD], 2006; Slavin & Cheung, 2005). Teaching quality has a tremendous influence on student outcomes, regardless of student socioeconomic and demographic background factors, and yet migrant children are often least likely to experience that support (Field et al., 2007; OECD, 2005).

Current UNHCR policies lay stress to pursue "alternatives to camps" in order to remove the "limitation on the rights and freedoms of refugees" inherent in a camp structure (UNHCR, 2014, p. 4). However, taking students out of refugee camps and placing them in the host community is an uphill task. Forty percent of refugees globally continue to live in refugee camps, and the camps still remain an important site of access to education for refugees globally. When the refugee population can be settled in the host community, "integration of refugee learners within national systems" will need adequate attention from the school teachers (UNHCR, 2012, p. 8).

AN ALTERNATIVE ROUTE

Keeping the obstacles and challenges in mind that refugee education faces, it is now using technology to create new opportunities for pathways to education for refugees. Technology is not a panacea, but extensive research in this field has shown that information and communication technology (ICT) for refugees, ICT for development, and ICT for education support the possibility of using

ICT to enhance and enable education for refugees (Annan, Traxler, & Ofori-Dwumfou, 2014; Dahya, 2016; Kleine, 2013; Raftree, 2013; Wagner, 2014). The role of technology in education is increasingly important in this landscape, where online education and mobile technologies are rapidly growing in the developing world and among refugee communities (Ally & Mohammed, 2013; Dahya, 2016). Sociotechnical theory emphasizes the mutually shaping powers of technology and society, mapping the shifting values and practices that change and connect local and global communities (Latour, 2005; Sawyer & Jarrahi, 2014) and that impact transnational structures related to accessing higher education for refugees (Dahya & Dryden-Peterson, 2016).

When we explore in a historical context, we witness that global communication networks have been the privilege of the elite. Research in the past on start-ups has shown that access to the internet has shifted opportunities for youth and less-educated people and resulted in flourishing business opportunities and growth. In Ghana, Burrell (2012) documented how spaces like internet cafés resulted in seeking foreign contacts, a rise in travel experiences, and a desire to enhance global contacts for growth. Kekwaletswe (2007) posits that the role of social network and online communities through usage of mobile devices in higher education in South Africa has resulted in an enhanced knowledge-sharing space among the learners.

In a refugee camp most of the inhabitants, if not all, are economically poor and access to a mobile phone is considered to be an vital asset to help them connect to the outside world as well as become a key component to the knowledge sharing and creating higher education pathways (Dahya & Dryden-Peterson, 2016). Mobile phone-based access to internet communication opens up a new world for them in different realities of time, space, and possibilities. Such a world is free of geographical and political manipulations and boundaries. Barriers to space, time, and mobility disappear, thus empowering the refugees with handheld devices to access the vast pool of knowledge lying outside the walls of the refugee camps. Social realities related to gender and education also change through the usage of information and technology with regard to accessing higher education. Educationists around the world are now actively using technology and online education is no longer a fad but a necessity.

DISTANCE EDUCATION

Distance education may be defined as a method of teaching where the student and teacher are not found in the same geographical space as in a classroom, but are physically separated. Distance education, in most cases, is technology driven and dependent on correspondence, audio, video, computer, and the internet (Roffe, 2004). Today's version of distance education is online education, which uses computers and the internet as the delivery mechanism with at least 80% of the course content delivered online (Allen & Seaman, 2011; Shelton & Saltsman, 2005).

Online education differs from correspondence education, which is generally known as a parcel-based education and considered a means to provide education to non-residents and adults, who learn at a distance via mail or other means and then submit their completed work for grading (Encyclopaedia Britannica, 2012). The primary objective of distance education is to create educational opportunities for the under-represented and those without access to a traditional educational institution (Jonasson, 2001).

Universities and colleges began experimenting in online courses in the early to mid-1990s with the growth of the World Wide Web. However, the rapid growth of online education in traditional non-profit institutions did not start until 1998 (Arenson, 1998). In October of 1998, New York University (NYU), with its largest continuing education schools in the country, was a pioneer as a non-profit university to create a for-profit online education subsidiary, NYU Online (Kentnor, 2015). Many fledgling online educational programs started during this time but failed to survive. Numerous factors led to the demise of these online institutions, but perhaps the most significant were the lack of understanding of effective online teaching and learning practices, as well as the lack of faculty buy-in for online education (Marcus, 2004). Online education is a different medium for teaching and learning and therefore requires a different approach (Bernard et al., 2004).

Mark West, a specialist in ICT for education at UNESCO, said that the potential of mobile technology can be used to facilitate learning in emergencies and crises but such potential has vastly remained unexploited and we are learning how to best leverage it. (Mobile Learning Week, 2017). There has been a large and growing number of initiatives and projects in the field of online education, including work conducted by University of the People to impart education to a vast number of refugees.

UNIVERSITY OF THE PEOPLE

University of the People (UoPeople) was founded in 2009. It is a tuition-free, non-profit, American accredited, online university. UoPeople has rapidly gained a foothold in the international arena of online higher education. With a collaborative online learning model and volunteer instructors from top-ranked universities, UoPeople offers the opportunity to pursue a high-quality American degree to any student desiring a university degree. UoPeople's students come from more than 200 countries and territories. Among their students are refugees in camps, survivors of the earthquake in Haiti and other disasters, survivors of the Rwandan genocide, and individuals living in extreme poverty – as well as those simply seeking a high-quality affordable education (UoPeople Annual Report, 2017).

UoPeople creates a learning community built around a democratic, meritocratic model that encourages the best result for every student. By opening the gates to higher education for every qualified person, regardless of racial, geographic, political, cultural, or personal constraints, UoPeople provides an opportunity for a better future for individuals and communities (UoPeople Annual Report, 2017). UoPeople remains tuition-free because of its use of volunteers, open educational resources, open-source technology, and peer-to-peer learning. More than 6,000 professionals have volunteered for the university, filling key UoPeople leadership positions including University President, Provost, Academic Deans, Course Developers, Academic Advisers, and Course Instructors. UoPeople is building a sustainable new model for higher education in which students are asked to pay a small assessment fee at the end of each course; for students who might find even these fees prohibitive, the university offers a variety of scholarships.

OPPORTUNITIES FOR REFUGEES

UoPeople provides tuition-free degree programs to all qualified students. This accessibility makes UoPeople particularly attractive to the one-third of its US student body that is foreign-born. UoPeople allows students of all backgrounds and statuses to pursue their educational goals. UoPeople works with refugees to enable access to quality education for those living in camps and most of the time as non-entities in host countries. With the assistance from the donors, the university has set up the Emergency Refugee Scholarship fund, the Small Giants Scholarship Fund, and the Myanmar Scholarship Fund. These resources provide access to education to hundreds of refugees and asylum seekers from Syria, Myanmar, Somalia, Democratic Republic of Congo, Afghanistan, Iraq, Nigeria, and many other countries (UoPeople Website, 2018).

UoPeople has offered 600 Syrian refugees the opportunity to study in their degree programs. Empowering these students has meant providing educational access to half of whom are still in Syria and half of whom have fled abroad. Educating these refugees not only enables them to pursue careers and be self-sufficient wherever they have migrated, but has also given them the tools they need to rebuild their homeland and forge a brighter future for Syria. This initiative was made possible by the support of the Ford, Hoffmann, Oak, and Frankel Foundations, as well as Steve and Roberta Denning. This scholarship is available to all students around the world who identify as a refugee or asylum seeker. Recipients of this scholarship will have up to 10 assessment fees funded. Upon completion of the funds awarded, students may apply for another scholarship, and thus potentially cover the entire cost of a two-year Associate or four-year Bachelor's degree.

Apart from Syrian students, UoPeople has initiated a scholarship program dedicated to students from Myanmar. This scholarship is generously funded by Fondation Hoffmann and the Frankel Family Foundation and available to students from Myanmar. It is awarded toward associate degree programs and will fund up to 10 assessment fees per award with potential renewal. This scholarship is intended to enable motivated students from Myanmar to have the opportunity to earn an accredited, academic degree. Sarah Vanunu, the director of public relations of UoPeople, says there has been a growing interest from applicants from Myanmar (Irrawaddy, 2016). The scholarship is especially aimed at students born in Myanmar, to facilitate tuition-free study toward American accredited degrees at the university's virtual campus, according to a statement released by the school.

By earning such a degree, students will be better able to contribute to their families, societies and their countries. Obtaining a university education provides students the knowledge and skills they need to start and run their own business or be hired by a company (Irrawaddy, 2016). UoPeople accepts applicants to study despite transitory circumstances, such as those experienced by many along the Thai–Myanmar border. The university's vision includes offering opportunities of higher education to migrants, refugees, asylum seekers, and displaced people. It has enrolled 1,000 refugee students from among its 15,000 student body from more than 200 countries and territories so far. By holding an accredited American degree, the impact would extend to the social development of the graduates' host countries as well (Irrawaddy, 2016).

University of Edinburgh and UoPeople have entered into an alliance to support those uprooted by war, famine, and natural disasters. Health Science graduates from UoPeople will be eligible to apply to Edinburgh to complete a bachelor's degree in health, science, and society. The initiative will later be expanded to include other subjects. Refugees living in Scotland who begin learning online with UoPeople, once they have achieved their qualifications, may have the opportunity to apply to transfer to the University of Edinburgh. The program is open to students with permission to stay in the UK as a refugee and domiciled in Scotland, and Syrian nationals domiciled in Scotland with humanitarian protection in the UK. Students worldwide, who have completed UoPeople undergraduate programs, may also be able to enter Edinburgh postgraduate programs via online distance learning. The partnership reflects the University of Edinburgh's commitment to provide educational opportunities for disadvantaged people around the world.

UoPeople aims to provide higher education to students worldwide, despite various constraints, by offering accessible and affordable online degree programs. Obtaining a university degree allows refugee and migrant and displaced students to operate on a more level playing field, thereby mitigating some of the disadvantages they might otherwise encounter. Vice-Chancellor Emeritus of Oxford University Professor Sir Colin Lucas, UoPeople President's Council member, and head of UoPeople Emergency Refugees Initiative noted that the UoPeople's collaboration with the University of Edinburgh to support displaced people in Scotland fits well with their mission to provide higher education opportunities for students around the world, especially those affected by conflict (UoPeople Website, 2018).

CONCLUSION

Open educational resources have been the growing trend of delivering education all over the world in an affordable way and can be a useful tool to help refugees, for whom physical access to education is often difficult. Mobile learning is a preferred method that helps to maximize access to these resources in a flexible way and can be used in various circumstances, including those of refugees and internally displaced persons. When used efficiently, technology can help and improve education stakeholders' activities in emergency contexts (Barry & Newby, 2012).

The refugee crisis has disproportionately affected some specific countries who were left with no alternative but to serve as the host country on the basis of their proximity to countries ridden with conflict, thus becoming a transnational issue. Receiving States cannot meet refugees' short-term and long-term needs alone; they are counting on international support to establish sustainable responses. This context calls for comprehensive, global action based on responsibility and sharing of burden. Overall, "among both internally displaced and refugee populations, there are large numbers of over-age learners who have missed significant periods of schooling" (Global Education Monitoring Report/UNHCR, 2016, p. 9). Carefully designed online educational programs could prove to be a solution to young adults to access education appropriate for their age and learning abilities. Online education is the only medium to provide youth with skills that they would otherwise lack due to their circumstances. Such education helps resolve unemployment in camps (UNHCR, 2016).

An increased collective effort by governments, communities, and the private sector is needed to provide education. In relation to refugees, as we have seen in the chapter, the private actors have played an important role and successful in their effort of imparting education. Definitely more volunteers are needed as well as more coordination and better understanding of the context by private actors. There is evidence that quality education gives refugees a place of safety and reduces exploitative work and human trafficking. In a free environment of knowledge sharing and education, refugees can find the opportunity to make friends and find mentors and thus become self-reliant with an ability to solve problems, think critically, and be ready to face the global world of employability and self-sustainability (UNESCO, 2017).

REFERENCES

Allen, I. E., & Seaman, J. (2011). *Going the distance: Online education in the United States.* The Online Learning Consortium. Retrieved from http://sloanconsortium.org/publications/survey/going_distance_2011

Ally, M., & Mohammed, S. (2013). Open education resources and mobile technology to narrow the learning divide. *The International Review of Research in Open and Distance Learning, 14*(2).

Ally, M., & Samaka, M. (2013). Open Educational Resources and Mobile Technology to Narrow the Learning Divide. *The International Review of Research in Opening and Distributed Learning, 4*(2). Retrieved from http://www.irrodl.org/index.php/irrodl/article/view/1530/2479.

Annan, N. K., Traxler, J., & Ofori-Dwumfou, G. (2015). Mobile communication for the development of education: A developing country's perspective. In I. N. C. Scharff and C. Wamala (Eds.), *Proceedings of 4th international conference on M4D mobile communication for development.* Retrieved from http://www.divaportal.org/smash/get/diva2:709233/FULLTEXT03.pdf#page=146

Arenson, K. (1998). More colleges plunging into uncharted waters of on-line courses. *The New York Times,* Sec. A, *16*(1).

Barry, B., & Newby, L. (2012). *Use of technology in emergency and post crisis situations.* Global Education Cluster Working Group and IIEP-UNESCO, (p. 1). Retrieved from http://educationcluster.net/?get=000388%7C2013/12/Technology-in-Emergencies-Post-Crises.pdf

Bernard, R. M., Abrami, P. C., Lou, Y., Borokovski, E., Wade, A., Wozney, L., & Huang, B. (2004). How does distance education compare with classroom instruction? A meta-analysis of the empirical literature. *Review of Educational Research, 74*(3), 379–439.

Blessinger, P., & Sengupta, E. (2017). Inclusive higher education must cater for refugees. *University World News, 471,* pp. 1–2.

Bonin, H. (2017). *Education of migrants: A social investment*. European Expert Network on Economics of Education (EENEE) Policy Brief 3/2017. Retrieved from http://www.eenee.de/eeneeHome/EENEE/Policy-Briefs.html. Accessed on October 5, 2018.

Burrell, J. (2012). *Invisible users: Youth in the internet cafés of urban Ghana*. Cambridge, MA: MIT Press.

Chaudry, A., Capps, R., Pedroza, J., Castaneda, R. M., Santos, R., & Scott, M. (2010). *Facing our future: Children in the aftermath of immigration enforcement*. Washington, DC: Urban Institute.

Cummins, J. (1979). Linguistic interdependence and the educational development of bilingual. *Review of Educational Research, 49*(2), 222–251. doi: 10.2307/1169960.

Dahya, N. (2016). *Education in conflict and crisis: How can technology make a difference? A landscape review*. Germany: GIZ, USAID, WVI. Retrieved from http://www.ineesite.org/en/resources/landscape-review-education-in-conflict-and-crisis-how-can-technology-make-a

Dahya, N., & Dryden-Peterson, S. (2016). Tracing pathways to higher education for refugees: The role of virtual support networks and mobile phones for women in refugee camps. *Comparative Education* (December), 1–18. doi:10.1080/03050068.2016.1259877

Encyclopaedia Britannica. (2012). *Correspondence education*. Retrieved from http://www.britannica.com/EBchecked/topic/138674/correspondence-education.

Field, S., Kuczera, M., & Pont, B. (2007), *No More Failures: Ten Steps to Equity in Education*. Paris: OECD

Global Education Monitoring Report/UNHCR. (2016). *No more excuses: Provide education to all forcibly displaced people*. Policy Paper 26.

Irrawaddy. (2016). *US Online University Offers 50 Scholarships to Burmese Refugees*. Retrieved from https://www.irrawaddy.com/news/burma/us-online-university-offers-50-scholarships-to-burmese-refugees.html

Jonasson, J. (2001). *On-line distance education a feasible choice in teacher education in Iceland?* Unpublished Master's thesis, University Strathclyde, Glasgow. Retrieved from https://notendur.hi.is/jonjonas/skrif/mphil/thesis.pdf

Kekwaletswe, R. M. (2007). Social presence awareness for knowledge transformation in a mobile learning environment. *International Journal of Education and Development Using Information and Communication Technology, 3*(4), 102–109.

Kentnor, H. E. (2015). Distance education and the evolution of online learning in the United States. *Curriculum and Teaching Dialogue, 17*(1 & 2).

Kleine, D. (2013). *Technologies of choice? ICTs, development and the capabilities approach*. Cambridge, MA: MIT Press.

Koehler, C. (2017). *Continuity of learning for newly arrived refugee children in Europe*. Network of Experts working on the Social Dimension of Education and Training, funded by the European Commission, DG Education and Culture.

Latour, B. (2005). *Reassembling the social: An introduction to actor-network-theory*. Oxford: Oxford University Press.

Marcus, S. (2004). Leadership in distance education: Is it a unique type of leadership? A literature review. *online Journal of Distance learning Administration*. Retrieved from http://www.westga.edu/~distance/ojdla/spring71/marcus71.html

Mickelson, R. A. (2014). The problem of the color lines in twenty-first-century sociology of education: Researching and theorizing demographic change, segregation, and school outcomes. *Social Currents, 1*(2), 157–165.

Mickelson, R. A., & Nkomo, M. (2012). Integrated schooling, life-course outcomes, and social cohesion in multi-ethnic democratic societies. *Review of Research in Education, 36*, 197–238.

Mobile Learning Week. (2017). https://en.unesco.org/events/mobile-learning-week-2017. Paris.

OECD. (2005). *Formative assessment: Improving learning in secondary classrooms*. Centre for Educational Research and Innovation (CERI). Paris: OECD.

OECD. (2006). *Starting strong II: Early childhood education and care*. Paris: OECD.

Raftree, L. (2013). *Landscape review: Mobiles for youth workforce development*. Washington, D.C.: Aguirre Division of JBS International for the MasterCard Foundation. Retrieved from http://www.youtheconomicopportunities.org/sites/default/files/uploads/resource/mywd_landscape_review_final2013_0.pdf

Roffe, I. (2004). *Innovation and e-learning: E-business for an educational enterprise*. Cardiff: University of Wales Press.

Sawyer, S., & Mohammad, J. (2014). The sociotechnical perspective. In A. Tucker & H. Topi (Eds.), *CRC handbook of computing* (Vol. 5(1), pp. 5–27). New York, NY: Chapman and Hall.

Sengupta, E., & Blessinger, P. (2018). *Introduction to refugee education: Strategies, policies and directions* (Vol. 13). Innovations in Higher Education Teaching and Learning. London: Emerald Publishing.

Shelton, K., & Saltsman, G. (2005). *An administrator's guide to online education*. Greenwich, CT: Information Age Publishing.

Slavin, R. E., & Cheung, A. (2005). Synthesis of research on language of reading instruction for English language learners. In J. Söhn (Ed.), *The effectiveness of bilingual school programs for immigrant children, programme on intercultural conflicts and societal integration (AKI)*. Berlin: Social Science Research Center Berlin (WZB).

Suárez-Orozco, C., Todorova, I., & Louie, J. (2002). Making up for lost time: The experience of separation and reunification among immigrant families. *Family Process 41*(4), 625–643.

UNDP. (2009). *Human development report: Overcoming barriers – Human mobility and development*. New York, NY: UNDP.

UNESCO. (2017). *Protecting the right to education for refugees*. Working Papers on Educational Policy 04.

UNHCR. (2012). *Education strategy, 2012–2016*. Geneva, Switzerland: UNHCR.

UNHCR. (2014). *Suriyeli multicolour*. [Syrian refugees]. Retrieved from http://data.unhcr.org/syrian-refugees/country.php?id=22. Accessed on April 21, 2014.

UNHCR. (2016). *Missing out: Refugee education in crisis*. Retrieved from http://www.unhcr.org/missing-out-state-of-education-for-the-worlds-refugees.html

University of the People Annual Report. (2017). Retrieved from https://3w1fdw3g237j15p5421zov1f-wpengine.netdna-ssl.com/wp-content/uploads/2017/10/AnnualReport2017.pdf. Accessed on July 10, 2018.

University of the People Website. (2018). Retrieved from https://www.uopeople.edu/tuition-free/our-scholarships/syrian-refugee-scholarship/. Accessed on July 10, 2018.

Wagner, D. A. (2014). *Mobiles for reading: A landscape research review.* Washington, DC: USAID and mEducation Alliance. Retrieved from http://literacy.org/sites/literacy.org/files/publications/wagner_mobiles4reading_usaid_june_14.pdf

ABOUT THE AUTHORS

Dr Carine Allaf has 15 years of experience in education and the Arab world, working as a Teacher, Scholar, and Practitioner in the United States and in multiple countries across the Arab world. Currently, she is the Senior Programs Advisor at Qatar Foundation International whose mission is dedicated to connecting cultures and advancing global citizenship through education. Previously, Dr Allaf was a full time lecturer in Teacher College, Columbia University's International Education Development program from 2010 to 2013. Her courses centered on women in the Arab world, education in conflict and emergency settings, strategic planning in international settings, and international development. These courses are an outgrowth of her research agenda that looks at women's positioning in development specifically in the Arab world and on education in conflict and post-conflict situations. Dr Allaf was an elementary school teacher at the American Community School in Beirut, Lebanon, and domestically in the Philadelphia and New York City public school systems from 2001 to 2006. As a Practitioner, Carine has assisted organizations in implementing and evaluating education programs in addition to conducting trainings. Carine has worked for the Center for International Development and Education at UCLA; Save the Children in Iraq; and UNICEF in Jordan, Sudan, and Palestine. She has also served as a consultant for the Inter-Agency Network for Education in Emergencies on a variety of projects. Dr Allaf obtained her Ph.D. in Comparative and International Education from the University of California, Los Angeles and her Master's degree in Elementary Education from the Department of Curriculum and Teaching at Teachers College, Columbia University.

David Banes is Director at David Banes Access and Inclusion Services and was formerly CEO, at Mada the Qatar Assistive Technology and Accessibility Centre based in Doha where he worked for six years. Throughout his career, he has been responsible for developing services to ensure that people with a disability are digitally included, and in shaping the broad policy framework required to ensure and sustain this. As a Consultant addressing all aspects of access and inclusion through disability, he is currently working a range of issues the Middle East and Europe and has a special interest in how access will be ensured as technology and our understanding of disability shifts. Much of his work is designed to build capacity in emerging access ecosystems, supporting an end to end approach from awareness to policy, and from production of assistive technologies to approaches to training and development.

Prior to taking up his post in Qatar, he worked as a teacher of children with special needs and principal of a major special school before working in the realm of digital

Inclusion in the UK and Europe as Director of Operations and Development for a UK NGO. He now seeks to support the emerging Access ecosystem in the region promoting cooperation between states and supports the development of assistive technology solutions and digital content that meet the needs of Arabic speaking people with a disability. His recent work has focused on the development of a framework for responding to disruptive innovation in the AT Industry, identifying solutions to meet the needs of refugees with a disability, consulting on the creation of a business case for public investment in assistive technology, and supporting innovation and research to bring products and services to market.

Patrick Blessinger is an Adjunct Professor of Education at St. John's University, a Math and Science Teacher with the New York State Education Department, and Founder and Chief Research Scientist of the International Higher Education Teaching and Learning Association (in consultative status with the United Nations). Dr Blessinger is the Editor and Author of many books and articles and he is an Educational Policy Analyst and Contributing Writer with UNESCO's Inclusive Policy Lab, University World News, The Hechinger Report, and Higher Education Tomorrow, etc. Dr Blessinger teaches courses in education, leadership, and research methods. Dr Blessinger has received several educational awards, such as Fulbright Senior Scholar to Denmark (Department of State, USA), Governor's Teaching Fellow (Institute of Higher Education, University of Georgia, USA), and Certified Educator (National Geographic Society, USA).

Marika Gereke is a Research Associate in the Institute of Political Science at Goethe-University Frankfurt. In her research and teaching, she focuses on transnational civil society networks and issues of global justice. She acts as a supervisor in the program *Start ins Deutsche.*

Haydeé Ramírez Lozada is a Ph.D. in Pedagogical Sciences and Bachelor of Education, English Specialty, with 37 years of experience as a teacher–researcher. She studied advanced courses on English for Medical Purposes and Grammar and Communicative Teaching in the Institute for Applied Language Studies in the University of Edinburgh. She has received some graduate courses on Advanced Research, Academic Writing, Pedagogical Culture, Systems Dynamics, University Formative Processes, etc. She works as a teacher–researcher in the Applied Linguistics School from the Pontifical Catholic University of Ecuador in Esmeraldas, where she has carried out a project of investigation entitled The Teaching of English to Refugees, in the Line of Investigation the Didactics of English. She has leaded a project of university connection with the community in relation to a Literacy Program to Refugees in the English Language. She has several articles published in scientific journals and is the author of a communicative course on Medical English entitled Bedside English, with two books, one for students and one for teachers. She has directed some graduate and Master's thesis.

Wadzanai F Mkwananzi is a Post-Doctoral Researcher under the SARCHi Chair in Higher Education and Human Development at the University of the Free State, South Africa.

Subin Nijhawan is a Research Associate in the Department of English and American Studies and an Associated Member in the Institute of Political Science at Goethe-University Frankfurt. His research interests include education for global justice, foreign language and bilingual learning, and international economics and globalization. He acts as a supervisor in the program *Start ins Deutsche*.

Kathy O'Hare has an undergraduate degree in Youth & Community Work, a H.Dip in Politics, a Master's in Digital Cultures, and is currently studying a Ph.D. in Digital Arts and Humanities all in University College Cork, Ireland. Her pedagogical interests include community education, community development, multimedia, and how technology can empower minority communities. Kathy has worked as a community radio documentary producer for over 10 years.

Kathy works as a Research Assistant in the University College Cork on a project funded by the National Forum for Teaching and Learning in Higher Education. Social Policy Education: Enhancing Digital Skills aims to expand social policy educators' digital capacities and improve their confidence in integrating digital skills into curricula in Higher Educational Institutes in Ireland.

Donald Reddick is the Economics Department Chair at Kwantlen Polytechnic University [KPU], a British Columbia Special Purpose Teaching University. In addition to administrative and teaching duties, Don gives leadership to a number of broader, university and community-based initiatives. Between 2010 and 2015, Don hosted KPU's Economics Café, a popular speaker series introducing university audiences to the power of economic thinking. In 2013, Don completed a community-based study with several co-authors that identified post-secondary access barriers faced by government-assisted refugees living in the BC's South Fraser region. More recently, Don's concern for continuous improvement in the quality of post-secondary education led to his 2016–2017 appointment as School of Business faculty champion for learning outcome assessment.

Shai Reshef is an Educational Entrepreneur, Founder and President of University of the People, the world's first non-profit, tuition-free, accredited online university. He earned his M.A. in Chinese Politics from the University of Michigan. He served as Chief Executive Officer and then Chairman of the Kidum Group, a for-profit educational services and test preparation company. He also chaired KIT eLearning, a subsidiary of Kidum. KIT became the eLearning partner of the University of Liverpool in 1999, and was the first online university outside of the United States, providing MBA and M.Sc. degrees in Information Technology. In January 2009, he founded University of the People, a non-profit, accredited online academic institution that seeks to increase the availability of higher education by offering tuition-free degrees. In 2009, he was named one of Fast Company magazine's "100 Most Creative People in Business" and was selected by One World as one of its "People of 2009." In 2010, he was awarded a Fellowship by Ashoka, and in the same year became a high-level Adviser to the United Nations Global Alliance for Information and Communication Technologies and Development (GAID). He has been named as a "Top Global Thinker" by Foreign Policy Magazine's Top 100 Global Thinkers 2012 and as one of the "50 People Changing the World" by Wired Magazine's Smart List 2012. In 2016, he was awarded the Prince's Prize for Innovative Philanthropy by the Prince Albert II of Monaco Foundation. Reshef is married and has four children and lives in Pasadena, California.

Chrystina Russell, Ph.D., spearheads the GEM at Southern New Hampshire University, an innovative initiative to bring tertiary education and employment pathways to refugees and traditionally underserved learners. She's most passionate about building university programs in refugee camps and urban areas where students who normally would not access higher education use online and in-person learning to earn a Bachelor's degree from Southern New Hampshire University. Currently, Chrystina is leading an expansion of the program into four new countries in 2018 (Kenya, Malawi, South Africa, & Lebanon) as well as the launch of an assessment center in Rwanda to pilot lowering the delivery cost of Bachelor's degrees through a combination of training local talent and artificial intelligence. Previously, she was the Chief Academic Officer of Kepler, a blended learning university program based in Rwanda. The organization has two campuses opened and lead by Chrystina – one in the capital city of Kigali and the other in Kiziba refugee camp. Prior, she was the Founding Principal of Global Tech Prep, a high-performing public school in East Harlem, New York and was faculty at the City College of New York. Chrystina began her career as a bilingual special education teacher in the Bronx, where she became addicted to understanding educational challenges and using innovation and technology to find creative solutions in vulnerable communities. Chrystina graduated Phi Beta Kappa from the University of Michigan with a Bachelor's degree in Social Organization & Minority Communities, has Master's in Bilingual Special Education, and holds a Ph.D. in Urban Education Policy from the City University of New York Graduate Center.

Elizabeth Rutten-Turner, LCSW, is a Social Worker and Counselor at Saint Alphonsus Center for Global Health and Healing in Boise, Idaho USA. She provides individual and family healing opportunities for survivors of war trauma and torture in an integrated medical setting that includes primary care providers, midwives, cultural liaisons, and social workers. Since earning her MSW from Boise State University in 2014, she has sought trainings to assist her cross-cultural work such as Bringing the Body into Therapy, The Neurobiological Effects of Trauma, and the Harvard's Global Mental Health: Trauma and Recovery Master Class. She is also a trained birth and post-partum doula, a childbirth educator, a yoga instructor and is an adjunct professor at BSU teaching Principles of USA Refugee Resettlement. Prior to becoming a social worker, Elizabeth earned her Bachelors in Education from Minnesota State University, Mankato specializing in teaching English to Speakers of Other Languages (ESOL). She then worked in Minnesota, Nebraska, and Georgia to support families affected by the immigration/refugee resettlement systems in various settings. She has also worked with community-based NGOs in Kenya, Uganda, and Nepal and attended cultural and linguistic immersion classes in Argentina, Chile, and Mexico.

Lisa Sadler is currently the Manager of the Settlement Workers in Schools program for the Langley School District, where she's been working with refugee and immigrant families since 2008. Lisa also volunteers in the community, privately sponsoring refugees and helping churches and groups through the sponsorship and settlement process. Lisa began working with refugees as a volunteer in 2007, when a large group of Government-assisted Karen refugees were resettled in the Lower Mainland. Together with a group of volunteers, Lisa was involved in starting the Karen Initiative, a non-profit organization whose purpose was to advocate for refugees and fill gaps in service through volunteer initiatives. The Karen Initiative was later recognized by the province of British Columbia with the 2009 Nesika Award for Excellence in Multiculturalism.

Lisa completed her Master of Arts in Community Development at the University of Victoria in 2013. Her thesis research focused on the barriers that refugee students face in accessing post-secondary education, which was a collaborative project with Kwantlen Polytechnic University to increase access to KPU programs for refugee students. Lisa's research won the award from the University of Victoria for Best Masters' Project in Community Development.

Maggie Mitchell Salem is the Founding Executive Director of Qatar Foundation International, a not-for-profit organization based in Washington, DC, which champions student-centered K-12 Arabic language & Arab culture education in the America, Europe, and the Middle East. Previously, Maggie was Regional Director for the Middle East and North Africa region at the International Foundation for Electoral Systems (IFES), a leading democracy and governance NGO, where she implemented innovative programs in Egypt, Iraq, Iran, Jordan, Lebanon, Palestine, and Yemen. Prior to IFES, Maggie worked as an independent communications consultant to leading US, Europe, and Middle Eastern companies, NGOs, and academic groups. From 2001 to 2004, she was the Director of Communications and External Relations at the Middle East Institute. Maggie's career began as a Foreign Service Officer at the US State Department where she served as a Special Assistant to Secretary of State Madeleine Albright and as a Special Assistant to Ambassador Martin S. Indyk at the US Embassy in Tel Aviv, Israel. She also served at the US Consulate in Mumbai, India. Maggie completed coursework for a Master's degree in contemporary Arab studies at Georgetown University and was a Fulbright scholar in Syria. She holds Bachelor's degrees from The Johns Hopkins University in political science and psychology.

Enakshi Sengupta is working as the Dean, College of Business in the American University of Kurdistan. Enakshi is the Associate Series Editor of Innovations in Higher Education Teaching and Learning, Emerald Group Publishing Book Series. She is also the senior editor: Journal of Applied Research in Higher Education, Emerald Publishing, and serves as the Vice Chair of the Editorial Advisory Board of the Innovation in Higher Education Teaching and Learning, Emerald Publishing. Enakshi is a Ph.D. holder from the University of Nottingham in research in higher education, prior to which she completed her MBA with merit from the University of Nottingham and Master's degree in English Literature from the Calcutta University, India. Her research interest includes integration of racially diverse student communities, curricular changes to incorporate integration in a class room situation, strategizing and creating scorecards to measure levels of integration, refugee education, and in group and out group integration in higher education as an aftermath of racial hatred and genocide.

Heather Smyser received her Ph.D. in Second Language Acquisition and Teaching from the University of Arizona in 2016. She currently works as a curriculum developer and English as a second language instructor. Her research concentrates on the emergence of alphabetic print literacy among those developing print literacy in a second language and often adopts a developmental view of reading. Her goal is to better understand efficient ways of fostering alphabetic print literacy development while working within the current constraints of refugee resettlement, particularly within the US context wherein those resettled are expected to receive employment within six months or risk losing funding. Her research is informed by her years working as a job skills and English instructor of refugees at a local non-profit and community education center. She continues to volunteer with and research the needs of her local refugee population as an independent researcher.

Damian Spiteri, Ph.D., is a published author in the field of multicultural education. He has recently published a book *Multiculturalism, Higher Education and Intercultural Communication* with Palgrave Macmillan Publishers; and is also the author of several peer-reviewed publications and chapters in edited books on different facets of education. He is currently working on a second book on the education of students who are displaced from their countries-of-origin. He is a reputed Keynote Speaker at an international conferences and seminars, and has lectured at universities in Malta, England, and Scotland. He is currently in Malta and is a Senior Lecturer at The Malta College of Arts, Science and Technology, Malta. Dr Spiteri has also an artistic side; and is a song-writer and singer. Mainly, his songs are aimed at raising consciousness about social issues. His most recent release Shine at Christmas can be seen on YouTube.

Matt Thomas, Ph.D., is a Professor of Reading and Literacy Program Coordinator at the University of Central Missouri. His past professional experience includes teaching English/Language Arts and K-12 school administration. He has also worked as a university research fellow and in helping develop school-wide content area literacy programs. His research interests include content area literacy, "reading maturity," and "transformational literacy" or reading, writing, and thinking that not only informs, but also transforms learners toward whole-person growth. In addition to these research interests, he has helped author a textbook, has served in the past as the Co-Editor of the *Journal of Content Area Reading*, and is working on some additional reading maturity and content area literacy projects. He earned his Ph.D. from the University of Missouri–Kansas City.

Nina Weaver is the Director of Partnerships and Research at the Southern New Hampshire University's Global Education Movement (GEM), an innovative initiative to bring higher education and employment pathways to refugees and traditionally underserved learners worldwide. Her role focuses on developing strategic partnerships across local, regional, and global levels and leading monitoring, evaluation, and research for GEM's refugee partnership programs in Kenya, Lebanon, Malawi, Rwanda, and South Africa. Previously, Nina was the Director of Refugee Education Programs with Kepler, a university program in Rwanda, and worked with refugee students in Kiziba refugee camp. Prior to joining Southern New Hampshire University, Nina worked with the Humanitarian Innovation Project, a research group based in the Refugee Studies Centre at the University of Oxford conducting research on bottom-up innovation, refugee livelihoods, and the economics of forced displacement. Nina holds an M.Sc. in Refugee & Forced Migration Studies from the University of Oxford.

Merridy Wilson-Strydom is Associate Professor under the SARCHi Chair in Higher Education and Human Development at the University of the Free State, South Africa.

Katherine L. Wright is an Assistant Professor in Literacy, Language, and Culture in the College of Education at Boise State University and Director of the Boise State University Literacy Lab. She earned her Ph.D. in Curriculum and Instruction from Texas A&M University, focused in Reading and Language Arts Education and she earned an additional Advanced Research Methods certification. Her dissertation research, funded by the International Literacy Association's Steven A. Stahl Research Grant, developed writing-to-learn practices for middle and high school science classes. At Texas A&M, she worked on a grant funded by the Qatar National Research Foundation investigating methods for supporting Qatari students' scientific content-knowledge and English language acquisition. Prior to entering academia, she was a middle school English and Social Studies teacher. Her experiences working with both native speaking and language-learning students in the classroom motivate her research focused on developing strategies for engaging and supporting middle and high school readers and writers.

Yuankun Yao, Ph.D., is a Professor of Education at the University of Central Missouri. He teaches educational assessment and introduction to research courses. His previous professional experience includes teaching English at a university in Shanghai, China, and working as a coordinator of research and program evaluation at a school district in South Carolina. His research interests include educational assessment, literacy education, and multicultural competencies. He earned his Ph.D. from the University of Nebraska–Lincoln.

NAME INDEX

SUBJECT INDEX

Note: Page numbers followed by "*n*" with numbers indicate notes.

Printed in the United States
By Bookmasters